web
developer's
guide to

javabeans

web
developer's
guide to
javabeans

Jalal Feghhi

 **CORIOLIS GROUP BOOKS**

an International Thomson Publishing company I(T)P®

Albany, NY ▪ Belmont, CA ▪ Bonn ▪ Boston ▪ Cincinnati ▪ Detroit ▪ Johannesburg ▪ London ▪ Madrid
Melbourne ▪ Mexico City ▪ New York ▪ Paris ▪ Singapore ▪ Tokyo ▪ Toronto ▪ Washington

PUBLISHER	**KEITH WEISKAMP**
PROJECT EDITOR	**MICHELLE STROUP**
COVER ARTIST	**GARY SMITH**
COVER DESIGN	**ANTHONY STOCK**
INTERIOR DESIGN	**NICOLE COLÓN**
LAYOUT PRODUCTION	**ROB MAUHAR**
COPYEDITOR	**CHRIS KELLY**
PROOFREADER	**KATHY DERMER**
INDEXER	**LENITY MAUHAR**

Web Developer's Guide to Java Beans
Copyright © 1997 by The Coriolis Group, Inc.

Limits of Liability and Disclaimer of Warranty

The author and publisher of this book have used their best efforts in preparing the book and the programs contained in it. These efforts include the development, research, and testing of the theories and programs to determine their effectiveness. The author and publisher make no warranty of any kind, expressed or implied, with regard to these programs or the documentation contained in this book.

The author and publisher shall not be liable in the event of incidental or consequential damages in connection with, or arising out of, the furnishing, performance, or use of the programs, associated instructions, and/ or claims of productivity gains.

Trademarks

Trademarked names appear throughout this book. Rather than list the names and entities that own the trademarks or insert a trademark symbol with each mention of the trademarked name, the publisher states that it is using the names for editorial purposes only and to the benefit of the trademark owner, with no intention of infringing upon that trademark.

The Coriolis Group, Inc.
an International Thomson Publishing Company
14455 N. Hayden Road, Suite 220
Scottsdale, Arizona 85260

602/483-0192
FAX 602/483-0193
http://www.coriolis.com

Printed in the United States of America

10 9 8 7 6 5 4 3 2 1

*My family, Adna, Abbas, Saeed, Farzaneh, Khalil, Jalil, Jamal,
Ghazaleh, and Afsaneh, for their encouragement;*

To the memory of my father, Hassan;

To my wife, Paula, for her support while writing this book;

To Steve Baunach, for introducing me to the world of components.

Acknowledgments

There are many people who have contributed to this book. Special thanks to my two reviewers, Payam Shahidi and Jalil Feghhi, who read all the chapters and pointed out the areas that required further explanation. Jalil also wrote the last three chapters of this book.

The project team at Coriolis provided exceptional support. In particular, I would like to thank Michelle Stroup, the Project Editor, who managed this project and resolved all the issues that came up when writing this book. I would also like to thank Chris Kelly for doing an excellent job of copyediting the chapters.

Contents

Chapter 14   Automatic Software Update 337

Chapter 15   The ActiveX Bridge   369

References   387

Index   389

Foreword

There are many ways to read this book. If you are already familiar with Java Beans, you can start with Part III and use our sample Java Bean applications as a basis to develop your own applications, referring back to Part II if you encounter a topic that you are not familiar with. You may want to read Part I to understand more about the reusable software component technology, and gain an understanding of ActiveX, COM, CORBA, and OpenDoc.

If you are new to Java Beans, you can start with Part II to learn about the fundamentals of Java Beans. You can proceed to Part III and see some rather complex Java Beans applications, and then read Part I for a general review.

Finally, you may want to read Part I, Part II, and Part III in the order that they were written. This approach provides a more systematic learning of the reusable software technology in general and Java Beans in particular.

Jalal Feghhi
March 17, 1997

PART

1

The Big Picture

Java Beans is an infrastructure for developing *component-based software*. There are three underlying concepts in a *Software Component Infrastructure* (SCI): *framework*, *component*, and *object bus*. A framework represents a partial solution to a problem. It is an architecture that allows a user to assemble components. The assembly of components forms a software application, usually targeted to a particular problem. A component is the quantum (or unit) of software. A component is small enough so that it can be maintained, but large enough so that it is functional and can be packaged and deployed. An object bus is the mechanism that allows a component or a framework to invoke the services of another component or framework in a distributed environment.

The above characterization of an application based on SCI might sound quite revolutionary. It is actually *evolutionary* and represents the next natural step in the evolution of software from mainframe-based homogenous environments to object-oriented, distributed heterogeneous environments.

The first part of this book is dedicated to establishing a frame of reference for Java Beans. The first chapter covers SCI. Java Beans, although a new addition to the Java programming environment, is not a new concept in reusable software components. There are other architectures for component-based software development, most notably OpenDoc/ CORBA and ActiveX (OLE) /DCOM. An understanding of these environments sheds light on the underlying concepts in Java Beans. Chapters 2 and 3 provide an overview of these technologies. The last chapter of Part 1 (chapter 4) presents the architecture of Java Beans.

Chapter 1

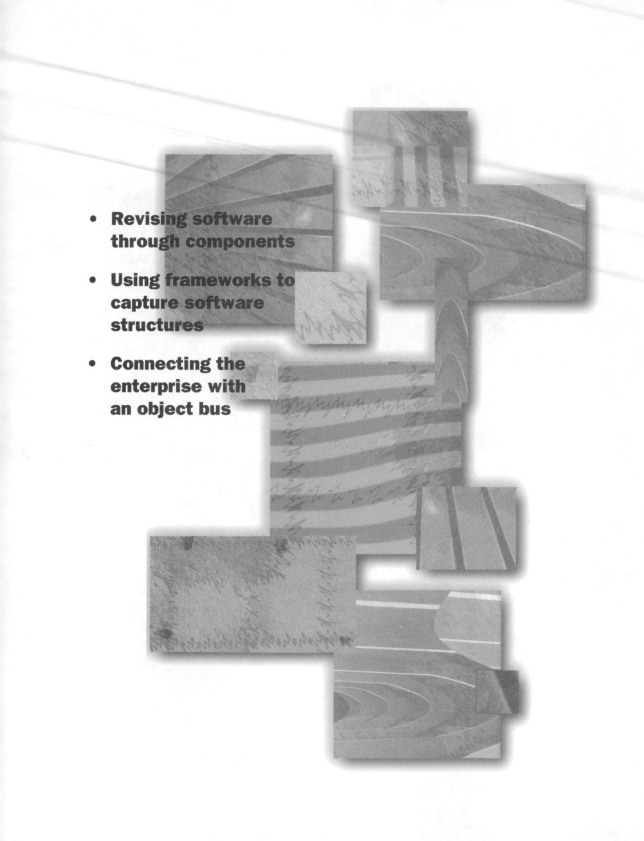

- **Revising software through components**

- **Using frameworks to capture software structures**

- **Connecting the enterprise with an object bus**

Software Component Infrastructure

Software Component Infrastructure (SCI) is the next logical model for software engineering after procedural and object-oriented paradigms. After thirty years from its conception, object technology has proved to be useful in solving read-world problems. Fortune 500 companies have even reported success stories in applying principals of object orientation to mission-critical applications.

However, as more object-oriented solutions are developed and deployed, it is becoming evident that object orientation alone cannot cope with the increasing complexity of today's software applications. Object-oriented methodology provides valuable methods to create self-managed entities through information hiding and object abstraction. The promise of object technology is code reuse by reusing objects in class libraries. It is true that class libraries can indeed increase a programmer's productivity through the reuse of existing classes. However, objects form only a part of an application: they totally fail to capture the structure (flow of control) of the application. It turns out that many applications, especially in the same domain, share similar structures. Different programmers use different techniques to capture and implement these structures. As a result, such structures are not reused through usual object-oriented techniques.

This chapter provides an in-depth overview of SCI. It defines components and frameworks, and it provides a different view of software applications based on frameworks, components, and an object bus. Finally, it explores object buses and explains their usage in distributed environments.

Object-oriented techniques, objects, classes, and class libraries are inherently incapable of providing a high degree of code reuse since they totally fail to capture the structures of applications. SCIs provide the highest level of code reuse.

The Paradigm

Software Component Infrastructure is the latest paradigm in software development. Through an object bus, this paradigm enables application development in heterogeneous environments that span different operating systems, hardware architectures, programming languages, and compilers. It also takes the evolution of software engineering from procedural programming to class libraries one step further by introducing frameworks. Frameworks carry the concept of code reuse one step forward by providing a structure for components. Components are reusable, off-the-shelf software units that can be purchased from component vendors. The components plug into frameworks; frameworks and components connect to other frameworks and components through the object bus. The components, frameworks, and the object bus form a software application.

Different components of the application can reside in different operating systems and can be implemented in different languages. Legacy code can be wrapped within components and be used with the rest of the system. New technologies in hardware and software can be immediately leveraged on by implementing new components in the new environments. The new components interoperate with the existing components through the object bus.

A component of the application can be versioned independently of other components. There exists no need to recompile and redeploy the entire application. The ease of upgrading and maintenance can easily cope with the ever increasing complexity of today's software applications. The ease of deployment allows software vendors to release the new features to their customers quickly.

Component-based software lowers the barriers to market entry. Since the unit of software is a component, not a whole application, software vendors with minimal staff can design and implement shrink-wrapped components and sell them as off-the-shelf software.

Software Component Infrastructure provides interoperability in distributed environments. It maximizes code reuse and provides a better approach for software maintenance and upgrades. SCI facilitates deployment and lowers the barriers to market entry.

We can formulate an application in terms of components, frameworks, and an object bus. This formulation of an application is drastically different than the traditional approaches to software engineering that result in monolithic applications. Figure 1.1 illustrates our conceptualization of an application.

In Figure 1.1, the application is the entire area that is filled with a gray shade. This area contains the entire framework, the ensemble within the framework, the security service provided by the object bus, the user interface horizontal facility, and part of the object bus itself. The included part of the object bus does not refer to a particular piece of software within the bus: The entire functionality of the bus is required for interoperability. However, we can think of the grid area as all the software required to network the hardware platforms that are running the different pieces of the application. The user interface facility is a value-added functionality that is provided for the users of the object bus. This facility itself can be thought of an application built on top of components and frameworks. Therefore, our formulation of an application can be generalized to include more than one framework. The security service is a core functionality that is provided by the bus. This service is itself a component. Horizontal and vertical facilities and bus services are covered in detail in the subsequent sections. The framework

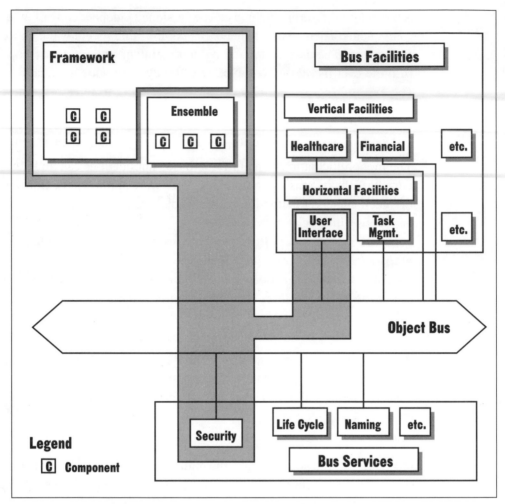

Figure 1.1 The formulation of an application in terms of components, frameworks, and an object bus.

in the grid area provides the structure of the application. The ensemble in the framework represents the development effort that is required to build an application (a precise definition of an ensemble is given in the Framework Section). This effort is unique to this particular application and denotes the variant portion of the entire application. The rest of the grid area represents the invariant part of the application. The power of SCI becomes evident if we realize that the invariant part might be as large as 80 percent of an application while the variant part may be only 20 percent of the application. The ideas presented here are fleshed out in the subsequent sections.

An application can be formulated to comprise multiple frameworks, components, and an object bus. This formulation allows software vendors to focus on value-added features of applications, while SCI provides the generic structures and functionality.

Component

The monolithic nature of mainframe-based applications can no longer cope with the increasing complexity of software applications. Conventional client/server methodologies have been an attempt to partition an application into a client and a server side, thus reducing the complexity of the application. However, these paradigms ultimately end up with two monoliths for an application instead of one. Traditional client/server techniques may indeed successfully result in server applications that have well-defined interfaces (services) and allow clients to access their services. However, They do not prescribe nor enforce any techniques to further divide clients and servers into sub-partitions. These monolithic clients and servers are usually extremely costly for software vendors to maintain and upgrade.

Another inherent issue with classical client/server techniques is the lack of plug and play. The client side of an application must be written with the specific knowledge about the server side. Only such clients can interoperate with the server. It is not feasible for independently developed applications to invoke the services of existing servers.

Component-based software development is a new direction in client/server computing that attempts to rectify the shortcomings of the traditional client/server technology. It is estimated that by the end of 1996 66 percent of all developers will be developing software using components (Strategic Focus 1995). The rest of this section covers components in detail.

Traditional client/server applications cannot cope with the increasing complexity of software applications. They cannot take part in plug and play environments.

What Is A Component?

We define a component as the quantum (unit) of software. This quantum should be large enough so that the component is functional and can be packaged and deployed. However, the quantum should be small enough so that it can be maintained and upgraded.

 A component is the quantum of software. It is big enough to be functional and deployable, but small enough to be maintainable.

A component has the following properties:

- **Deployable**—A component is an off-the-shelf, packaged piece of software that can be purchased from a vendor.

- **Maintainable**—A component is small enough so that it can be easily maintained and upgraded.

- **Functional**—A component is large enough so that it behaves in a desired, useful manner.

- **Specificity**—A component is designed to perform a very specific task. It represents a piece of an overall application. This piece can be fine-, medium-, or coarse-grained.

- **No direct communication path to other components**—A component should not directly communicate with another component. This lack of direct communication is essential for components to be maintainable and upgradable. Moreover, it allows them to be used in distributed environments. Note that this property does not imply that a component cannot invoke the services of another component. Rather, it emphasizes that the actual mechanism to invoke the service is done by another entity (an object bus or a framework).

- **Self describable**—A component can describe the services it provides to the rest of the system. This description is usually provided through a declarative, implementation-independent interface definition language.

- **Target framework**—A component is usually built for a particular framework. Such components may not work within other frameworks. For example, a Java Bean component cannot directly be used in the ActiveX environment. However, object wrappers can be used for such cross-framework functionality.

- **Target object bus**—A component that interfaces directly with an object bus may not be used with another object buses. Gateways are used to provide interoperability between two different object buses.

The above characterization of components provides a mechanism to partition an application into components. Each component provides a very specific functionality. It also describes itself to the rest of the infrastructure so that other components can access its functionality. The description is accomplished via a declarative language, which essentially separate the interface of a component from its implementation. This separation is critical in order for the component to operate in a distributed environment.

Since components do not directly interact with each other, the natural question to ask is the following: how do components cooperate with each other to form an application? The answer is through the use of frameworks or an object bus.

Components are extremely useful for distributed computing. They are of tremendous value to software developers. However, due to their specificity, they may not be as valuable to end-users. End-users usually have a need to deal with components that map directly to entities in the real world, such airplane, cars, and hotels. These real-world components are called *business components*.

Framework

There has been a lot of interest in applying object-oriented techniques to solving real world problems. Class libraries are proliferating in the software industry. After more than thirty years since its conception, object technology has found its way into production systems and mission-critical applications. Object technology has indeed delivered on the promises of information hiding and data abstraction. However, it has not been as successful in providing a mechanism for a high degree of code reuse.

It is true that class libraries provide fine-grained objects that can be shared across applications. However, these fine-grained objects only account for a part of an entire application. They entirely fail to capture the logic that pieces these objects together. Figures 1.2, 1.3, and 1.4 provide high-level representations of procedural-, object-, and framework-based applications.

The inherent flaw with procedural and class libraries is their passiveness. An application based on procedures (functions) comprises a number of

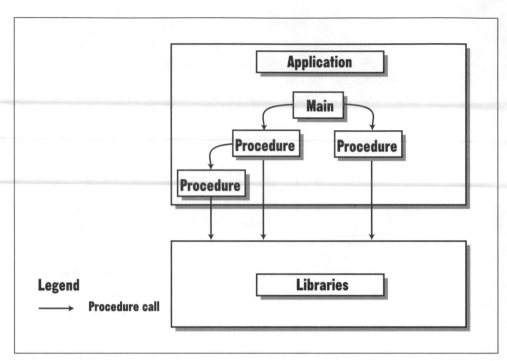

Figure 1.2   An application based on procedures.

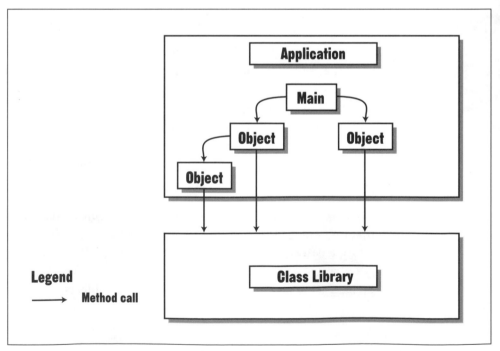

Figure 1.3   An application based on objects.

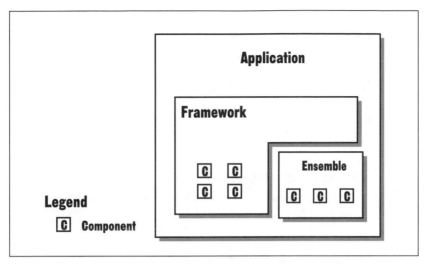

Figure 1.4 An application based on frameworks.

procedures that call each other (see Figure 1.2). These functions are usually coarse-grained objects, and therefore, they cannot be reused in other applications. Furthermore, the logic that is required to paste these procedures together to form an application is not captured by any function. The logic is scattered around in the application. An object-oriented application replaces the coarse-grained procedures with fine-grained objects. The procedure calls are replaced with method calls (see Figure 1.3). These objects, due to their fine granularity, may be reused in other applications. However, the objects are still passive: they still require a structure (flow of control) to connect them together. Because this structure is not captured by any object, it cannot be shared with other similar applications.

 Class libraries are inherently passive. They still require a structure that provides flow of control.

It turns out that many applications, especially in the same domain, share the same structure. This structure, if captured, provides structure reuse across applications in addition to object reuse. Figure 1.4 illustrates an application that is built inside a framework. The framework captures the structure of the application. The components (objects) no longer invoke each other methods. Instead, the framework calls the methods. Not only can the components can be shared with other applications, but the framework itself can be shared with other applications in the same domain. In essence, the framework provides a generic solution to a set of similar problems. This level of code reuse goes well beyond code reuse based on passive class libraries. The success of object technology requires an infrastructure that provides the following (Shebanow 1995):

- Changes developers' mindset to design general solutions.

- Enables software design to be more reusable and maintainable.

- Creates innovative software that addresses business problems.

 A framework captures the structure of many similar applications. The framework calls the objects instead of objects calling each other.

What Is A Framework?

A framework provides a generic design. It may also provide facilities (user interface, storage, etc.) that are useful to all applications. A framework is a partial (incomplete or generic) solution to a set of similar applications. The task of a developer is to take this incomplete solution and add the necessary code to create a compete application. The power of frameworks becomes evident now. A framework represents a part of an application. This part is designed by domain experts and has been coded and tested. The developer only needs to add the value-added code to the framework. This value-added code might be only 20 percent of the whole application; the framework supplies the other 80 percent of the functionality. The use of frameworks compares to the use of classes. In object-oriented design, a developer designs a class with the intent to instantiate the class a number of times. All instances (objects) share a similar structure with each other. However, each instance has its own state. The class is designed and tested only once. It can be used over and over by instantiating it with proper state variables. A framework is very much like a class. It is designed and tested once. It provides the structure for a set of similar applications. A developer creates a particular application by adding the behavior to the framework necessary to differentiate it from other similar applications.

An application in a domain comprises two partitions: *invariant* and *variant*. The invariant partition is the part that the application shares with all the other applications in the same domain. The variant partition is the portion that makes the application unique in its domain. A framework captures the invariant solution of the set of all problems in a domain. A developer must add the variant code to a framework to capture the behavior that makes this application unique in its domain. The invariant part of an application is also called an *ensemble*. An ensemble is precisely defined as (Andert 1994): "An ensemble incorporates the domain knowledge, expertise, rules, and policies of a particular solution. It is the part of the solution that varies from one problem to another within the domain, as opposed to the framework, which captures the invariant parts of a solution for that domain. The ensemble code conforms to the protocols established by the framework and extends or completes it for the specific solution."

 An application encompasses an invariant and a variant part. The invariant part is captured by the framework. The variant part is captured by the application developer.

Frameworks provide different levels of invariant knowledge depending on whether they are targeted at a particular domain or a number of domains. We investigate three frameworks: *horizontal*, *compound document*, and *vertical*.

Horizontal Frameworks

A horizontal framework is a framework that does not target a specific domain. Therefore, it can be used to solve a wide range of problems. Since a horizontal framework does not target a particular domain, it cannot contain a high level of invariant behavior. A good example of a horizontal framework is Microsoft's Visual C++ (MSVC) environment in conjunction with Microsoft Foundation Classes (MFC). MFC corresponds roughly to components, even though they do not satisfy all the properties formulated for components. MSVC is the horizontal framework: it is capable of solving a wide range of problems. Through the use of wizards, MSVC is capable of creating templates for different types of applications. These templates correspond to the invariant knowledge of the framework. A developer creates a unique application from a template by deriving specialized classes from MFC. The difference, in terms of behavior, between parent MFC classes and specialized classes is the variant knowledge. Note that the template determines the structure and flow of the control of the application. Therefore, the developer need not be concerned with the structure of the application. However, in practice, the developer may need to make changes to the template.

Compound Documents Frameworks

Compound documents framework is the most active and rewarding among all types of frameworks. It is the most active since the most well-known frameworks (OpenDoc, ActiveX, and now Java Beans) are geared toward compound documents. It is the most rewarding since these frameworks bring the power of frameworks right to the desktop. The term desktop here denotes the ordinary use of computers by millions of end users.

The term *compound document* refers to a document that can manage disparate types of data. The creating tool of each type of data might be a word processor, an audio tool, a video tool, and so on. However, the compound document can manage all types of data, created by different tools, in a seamless manner. The different pieces of information that a compound document manages are not required to reside locally on a desktop. Rather, a compound document can manage data across in a distributed environment. Moreover, not all the processing is required to be performed locally. For example, a piece of a compound document may be a graph that displays statistics. The calculations needed to come up with the statistics may be best performed on a server machine. The compound document hides the distributed nature of the graph and presents a seamless interface to the user. The above observations lead us to envision a distributed environment in which servers serve compound documents to users. The compound documents are the clients. They manage the distributed nature of data and processing and present a uniform user interface to desktop users. Compound documents become the ultimate desktop clients.

 A compound document manages data from different sources and handles the distributed nature of data and computation. It presents a coherent view to a user. Server applications serve compound documents to desktop users. Compound documents are the ultimate desktop clients.

We can think of a compound document as having two parts: a *container* and a number of components. The container hosts the components. A compound document is created by dropping components in a container and customizing the components.

A compound document framework usually utilizes an event-based *producer-consumer* model to capture the structure of an application. In this model, components register their interests in certain events with the container. When a component triggers an event, the container catches and delivers the event to all the components interested in that event.

The challenge of compound document frameworks is to allow different components in a framework to collaborate with each other in order to present a harmonious view of an application to a user. For example, all components that have a user interface must share the graphical window of the application in a seamless way. Furthermore, these frameworks must also anticipate new types of data that will come in the future. In other words, compound document frameworks must have an open architecture and cannot be limited to the existing types of data. Compound document frameworks have a number of key features that enable them to meet the aforementioned challenge. These features are covered in the next subsections.

STRUCTURED STORAGE

A compound document stores its data in a file. However, as already mentioned, a compound document consists of many components. Each component might manage a different kind of data. The format and structure of the data managed by a component makes sense only to that component. Each component is responsible for writing and reading the data it manages to and from a storage medium. The framework itself takes a passive role and never attempts to interpret, read, or write the data that belongs to its components. This passiveness is essential for the framework to accommodate new component types in the future.

Since a compound document contains a number of components each of which potentially manages a different type of data, the compound document storage file can no longer be flat. It has to be a segregated file. The file becomes a hierarchical file, very much like a directory, and the data associated with each component becomes a file within this structured file. Each component manages its portion of data within the storage. The framework provides a mechanism for components so that they can read and write their data within a structured storage.

The data associated with a component in a structured file can be either *embedded* or *linked*. Embedded data indicates that the data is stored in the storage and does not depend on data anywhere else in the network.

Linked data implies that the data resides somewhere else (perhaps inside another structured storage) and only a link to that data is stored in the storage. Consequently, any changes made to the actual source of the data (the source of the link) changes the linked data inside the hierarchical file.

UNIFORM DATA TRANSFER (UDT)

The lack of a uniform mechanism for programmers to transfer data between applications had always been a source of grief. For example, data transfer between two applications using clipboard cut-and-paste and drag-and-drop is fundamentally the same. However, programmers had to handle and code each case differently. A compound document framework provides a single protocol for data transfer between applications regardless of the exact method used to accomplish the transfer the data.

SCRIPTING

Scripting provides a mechanism for end users to customize their compound documents. An end-user can associate a script with a component so that the script runs when certain events transpire. For example, upon storing its contents, a script associated with a component can send an email to a group of people and notify them of the availability of new data.

USER INTERFACE

Compound document frameworks provide a powerful and seamless user interface for applications. They allow many components to share the graphical window associated with an application. They also manage *in-place activation*. Compound documents create a consistent interface across all the components that they host. In-place editing takes this concept one step further. When a user edits the data associated with a component, the component merges its menu with the container's menu and provides editing capabilities within the container's window. The alternative to this feature is for the component to invoke its creating tool, open a new window, and force the user to edit the data in the newly opened window. Once the editing phase is finished, the user must close the window and activate the original compound document window.

Vertical Frameworks

Vertical frameworks are well beyond the scope of this book. We present the following definition for vertical frameworks (Cotter with Potel 1995): "A [vertical] framework embodies a generic design, comprised of a set of cooperation classes, which can be adapted to a variety of specific problems within a given domain."

Object Bus

Object bus is the third link in the SCI. Components provide units of software and frameworks plug these components together and create applications. However, these applications are still bound to a single machine. The object bus extends the power of components and frameworks into the open networks. They allow millions (or possibly billions) of independent pieces of software to seamlessly interact with each other in an environment that consists of different operation systems, languages, hardware platforms, and compilers. Most notable examples of an object bus are CORBA (Common Object Request Broker Architecture) by the Object Management Group (OMG) and DCOM (Distributed Component Object Model) by Microsoft. These object buses are covered in detail in the next two chapters. Java Beans utilizes Remote Method Invocation (RMI) to create a native object bus. It also provides interoperability with CORBA. Chapter 5 covers the details.

It is not necessary for two objects that communicate with each other to understand each other's language. It is only sufficient for them to understand a common language. In SCI, this common language is the language of an object bus. The object bus provides a mechanism for every object to describe itself to the bus. This mechanism is through a declarative, implementation-independent interface definition language (IDL). Therefore, the object bus becomes the glue that connects all objects together through IDL.

When a client object invokes a service of a remote server object, the object bus receives the request, locates the server in the network, marshals the arguments, calls to the desired service of the server, receives the results, and transfers the results back to the client. The bus performs all these activities transparently on behalf of the client and server objects. The client is not aware that the request is fulfilled by an object in a different address space on a different machine. The server is not aware that the request is coming from a remote object. Note that the object bus also provides transparency in the location of the server.

Object bus is the ultimate middleware. It allows billions of objects that understand IDL to interact with each other. This interaction is totally transparent to the objects.

The advantages of an object bus goes beyond establishing connectivity between remote objects. It can also provide a set of core services (object services) that are useful to all the objects on the bus. For example, life cycle is a service that is potentially useful to a lot objects. The object bus defines this service once and allows all other objects to use the services of the life cycle server. Examples of other services are: security, licensing, persistence, naming, etc.

An object that communicates with an object bus may not be able to interact with another object bus. The reasons are twofold. First, the interface definition language that the object uses to describe itself to the bus may not be the same as the language of the other object bus. Second, the object requires a skeleton that allows the object bus to handle some of the details of remote invocation. These skeletons may be object bus specific.

Ideally, there will be only one object bus in the open networks. However, if both CORBA and DCOM continue to dominate different segments of the software market, we can employ two methods to provide interoperability between these buses. The first method is to wrap objects of one type into other types through object wrappers. The second approach is to provide a gateway between these two buses. The gateway can completely hide the two object buses from a client object: The client makes a request, and depending on the request, a DCOM server that sits on a DCOM bus or a CORBA server that resides on a CORBA bus fulfills the request.

Further Readings

Shebanow, Andrew. *The Power of Frameworks*, Addison-Wesley, 1995.

Cotter, Sean with Mike Potel. *Inside Taligent Technology*, Addison-Wesley, 1995.

Orfali, Robert, Dan Harkey, and Jeri Edwards. *The Essential Distributed Objects Survival Guide*, Addison-Wesley, 1996.

Orfali, Robert, Dan Harkey, and Jeri Edwards. *The Essential Client/Server Survival Guide*, Wiley, 1994.

Chapter 2

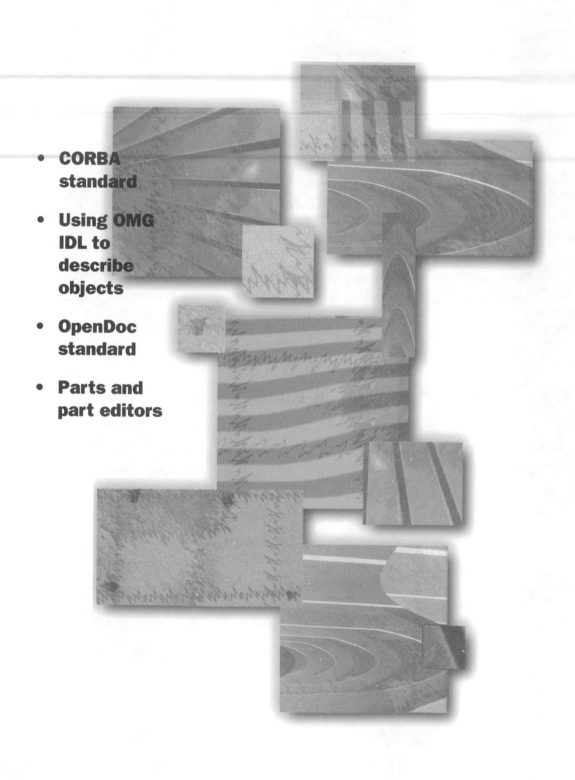

- **CORBA standard**

- **Using OMG IDL to describe objects**

- **OpenDoc standard**

- **Parts and part editors**

OpenDoc/
CORBA

This chapter presents OpenDoc/CORBA, the first real-world implementation (out of the three discussed in this book) of the Software Component Infrastructure. In this implementation, CORBA is the object bus, and OpenDoc is the compound-document framework. Here, we'll provides concrete examples for the abstract ideas presented in Chapter 1.

Even if you think you are solely interested in Java Beans, you should read this chapter for a number of reasons. First, an understanding of OpenDoc paves the way for grasping the ideas behind Java Beans, because both are frameworks for compound documents. Second, because OpenDoc is a more mature technology, familiarity with it will allow you to better understand and predict the future of Java Beans. Third, Java Beans provides an interface to OpenDoc so that beans can run as OpenDoc parts (which are explained in this chapter); an OpenDoc container can then host both OpenDoc parts and Java beans. As this chapter is being written, in fact, Apple and IBM are in the process of building the bridge between OpenDoc and Java Beans. Finally, Java Beans interoperates with CORBA through the Internet Inter-ORB Protocol (IIOP).

The first part of this chapter covers CORBA, which represents one the most ambitious efforts ever taken by hardware and software vendors to define an interoperability standard for distributed computation in a heterogeneous environment. CORBA, commonly known as the Object Management Group (OMG), includes more than 600 members. This chapter provides a technical overview of this technology, with an emphasis on such Java Beans-related features as the OMG Interface Definition Language (IDL) and IDL servers.

OpenDoc takes the power and vision of CORBA to the desktop. OpenDoc is a specification and an implementation that facilitates the creation of compound documents; in particular, it is an ideal environment for creating multimedia documents. This chapter includes a technical analysis of OpenDoc.

CORBA

Common Object Request Broker Architecture (CORBA) is a technology that facilitates rapid software development in a heterogeneously distributed environment. CORBA facilitates software development by providing a mechanism for decoupling the task of software specification from software implementation. This separation allows the architect of a product to break up the system into smaller pieces and assign each piece to a group. As we shall see later, the mechanism for this decoupling is the OMG IDL.

CORBA has defined and implemented a set of core services (life cycle, naming, persistence, and so on) that are potentially useful to a large number of applications. A software developer can rapidly incorporate these services into his or her programs through inheritance, thereby saving coding and testing efforts. These services are discussed in slightly more detail in a later section.

CORBA hides the complexities of client/server programming from a programmer. In traditional client/server methodologies, the programmer needs to use sockets or Remote Procedure Calls (RPCs) in order to allow two processes on different platforms to communicate with each other. In CORBA, however, the developer only deals with object references. Two separate processes communicate by invoking methods on object references; CORBA manages the gory details of interprocess communications. Furthermore, if the processes are on different operating systems or hardware platforms, CORBA performs all the necessary conversions between different data representations. These ideas are further explored in this chapter.

CORBA Object Bus: ORB

The Object Request Broker (ORB) is the object bus in CORBA. Clients and servers interoperate with each other through an ORB; see Figure 2.1.

As shown in the figure, a client and a server program never communicate directly. As a matter of fact, the client may not even be aware that the server program is a remote process running on a different machine. The client only has access to an object reference, which represents the server that the client is interested in. The client may have obtained this handle during some initialization routine, or perhaps as the result of a service invocation on another object reference. At any rate, the client proceeds and invokes a service of the server.

ORB intercepts the service request call. It then identifies the location of the server in the network. If the server is not running, ORB activates it and waits until it is ready to accept service requests. ORB automatically resolves any differences in data formats (such as byte ordering) of the client and server machines and hands the request over to the server. If the service request requires any data to be returned to the client, ORB translates the data back into the native representation on the client platform and returns the results to the client. All of these activities are carried out without any knowledge (code) on the client side.

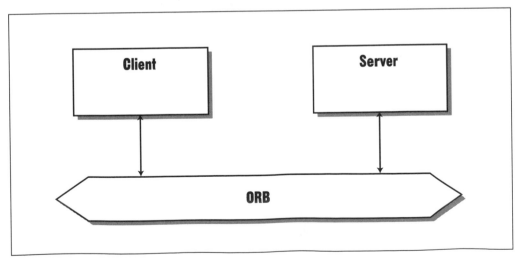

Figure 2.1 ORB provides interoperability between a client and a server program.

ORB provides interoperability for clients and servers in an heterogeneously distributed environment by locating servers and translating between different data formats. Clients are not even aware that servers may be running on a remote process.

The above characterization of ORB allows a client program to be developed without addressing the following issues:

- **Server programming language**—The actual language used to implement the server is immaterial; for example, it can be implemented later in Smalltalk, C, or C++. The actual implementation language does not affect the client program in any way.

- **Server platform**—The hardware architecture and the operating system of the platform hosting the server do not play a role. ORB automatically translates between different data formats.

- **Location transparency**—The actual location of the server (local or remote) is hidden from the client. Furthermore, the server program can be moved from one platform to another without affecting the client. This property is called *object forwarding* or *object migration*.

- **Network protocols**—ORB handles the different network hardware and protocols situated between the client and the server. The client program is not in any way aware of such protocols.

Because the client program does not have any knowledge of any of the aforementioned issues, it follows that ORB decouples the client development from the server development. All the client needs to know is a description of the services that a server is capable of performing. A server advertises these services through a declarative language called Interface Definition Language (IDL). In this book, we use IDL to refer generically to any Interface Definition Language. We'll use OMG IDL to refer to CORBA IDL when the distinction is necessary.

IDL

IDL is a declarative language that is used to specify the *interface* of an object. The notion of an interface essentially separates the behavior of an object from its implementation. The object is contractually bound to implement the behavior specified in its interface. There is no commitment on the part of the object, however, to use any particular language for the implementation.

An object only advertises its interface to the external world. This interface provides a number of key benefits. First, a developer can work on a client program without necessarily having access to the actual implementation of the object; all he or she needs to know is the interface. The implementation object can be developed later and be plugged into the object bus. Second, ORB uses the interface description of an object to translate between different data formats in a heterogeneous environment. Third, an IDL compiler can map the interface directly into a target language, greatly enhancing code development.

IDL provides a way to isolate the interface of an object from its implementation. The user of an object can then focus on that object's behavior without worrying about implementation details.

As a matter of fact, IDL has a far greater benefit, because it can be used to ensure the validity of the design of a product in a systematic way. In this model, every subsystem is represented by its IDL interface and is assigned to a group of developers. The task of each group is to determine whether they can implement their subsystem based on other subsystems' interfaces. This approach can successfully uncover design flaws. After the interface of each subsystem is firmed up, development work can proceed in parallel. (For a thorough treatment of this concept, see Mowbray with Zahavi, 1995.)

The usefulness of IDL is not limited to CORBA; it can be used in a systematic way to design large-scale applications.

OMG IDL is a subset of ANSI C++ extended with some constructs to account for the distributed nature of the environment. Consider the domain of geometric shapes consisting of rectangles and squares. The model in Listing 2.1, expressed in OMG IDL, captures a very simplified representation of this domain.

Listing 2.1 A very simplified model expressed in OMG IDL for shapes.

```
/* This module defines a rectangle and a square */
module shapes
{
   /* Definition of a rectangle */
   interface Rectangle
   {
      attribute integer length;
      attribute integer width;

      integer area();
      void draw();
      void translate(in integer x, in integer y);
   }

   /* Definition of square */
   interface Square: Rectangle
   {
   }
}
```

In OMG IDL, the keyword **module** introduces one level of scoping. The keyword **interface** collects a number of related operations; it might naturally map into a class. Note that the shapes module defines two interfaces: rectangle and square. The square interface inherits from the rectangle (note the use of a colon, **:**, to specify inheritance), but it does not define any new operations or data. The keyword **attribute** identifies a data member that has a **get/set** pair of accessor functions. The reserved word **readonly** can be used to designate a data member as read only. The IDL compiler automatically generates the **get/set** functions.

Note the use of **in** to specify that an argument to a function is an input argument and its value will not be changed during the function call (other possible values are **out** or **inout**). ORB uses these directives to determine which arguments need to be transferred across the network; for example, there is no need to transfer an argument of type **out** to the remote side. Also note that an argument type must be followed by an actual name, which is not mandatory in C/C++ style prototype declaration. OMG IDL also allows an operation to raise exceptions. These exceptions are mapped to the target language by the IDL compiler. (A more detailed analysis of OMG IDL is far beyond the scope of this book. The OMG IDL is described in about 40 pages in OMG 1995.)

In order to invoke a service on a server object, a client needs to know two pieces of data: the service name and the object reference. The server exposes its services via IDL. The IDL compiler maps the exposed services into a target language (like C or C++) and makes them available to the client. How does the client obtain the object reference? This question is answered in the next section.

Object References

A client specifies an object implementation (server) via its object reference and accesses the object implementation's services via its IDL interface. The IDL interface shields the client from changes in the implementation details of the server. The object reference protects the client from changes in the location of the server in the network.

An object reference isolates a client from changes made to the location of the object. Similarly, an object IDL interface isolates a client from implementation details of the object.

An object reference identifies a resource (server or object implementation) in a network. CORBA has standardized what an object reference does, but it has not specified any implementation details. CORBA vendors are free to implement object references in any manner they choose. Because object references are not interoperable in a federation of ORB systems, ORB gateways must translate between different implementations.

A couple of methods exist for obtaining an object reference. The first is through calls to **list_initial_services** and **resolve_initial_references** functions. The function **list_initial_services** returns the list of available service names. A service name in the returned list can then be passed to **resolve_initial_references** to obtain an object reference for that service. Another approach is via the CORBA Naming and Trader services, which take a service name and return a corresponding object reference (CORBA services are covered later in this chapter).

CORBA specifies two functions, **object_to_string** and **string_to_object**, to convert an object reference into a string and vice versa. The string form of an object reference can be saved in a file and later be converted to an object reference. Even though this approach is acceptable in certain situations, the preferred way of obtaining object references is through the Naming and Trading services.

Now that you understand IDL interfaces and object references, you are ready to delve more into different ways of invoking a service.

Static And Dynamic Invocations

A client can either specify the service that it wants to use at compile time (*static invocation*) or defer the decision until runtime (*dynamic invocation*). Dynamic invocation is quite useful for situations where new types of services are added to the network and clients want to dynamically discover and bind to these services. As you shall find out, however, there is a price to pay for this level of flexibility.

OMG received two different proposals on interface invocation. One proposal (backed by DEC and HyperDesk) suggested dynamic invocation, whereas the other one (sponsored by Sun and HP) opted for static invocation. OMG provided a *common* architecture for both methods, resulting in the letter *C* in CORBA.

This section covers static and dynamic invocation interfaces, and it provides a comparison between them. Please use Figure 2.2 for reference throughout the rest of this section.

STATIC INVOCATION INTERFACE (SII)

A client can select a particular object implementation (server) and a particular method of the object at compile time. In this scenario, the client might pass a *predefined* name to the CORBA Naming service, retrieve an object reference associated with the server, and then invoke a predefined method on the object reference. If the Naming service does not have any knowledge of the service name, it raises an exception.

In this paradigm, the client knows *a priori* the exact service that it is interested in. If a better, similar service is added to the network in the future, the client cannot dynamically use the new service. SII precludes clients from leveraging the new services added to a network.

SII is achieved through three distinct components in the ORB: *static IDL stubs*, the ORB core, and *static IDL skeletons* (refer back to Figure 2.2). The client invokes a method of an object implementation by statically

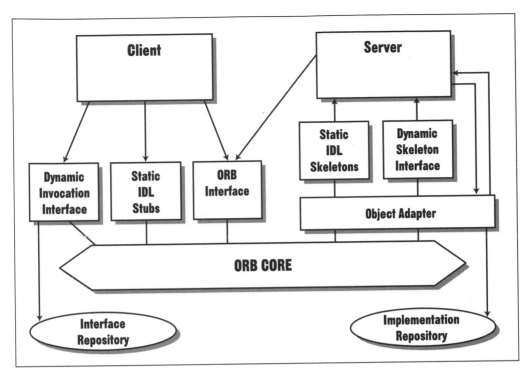

Figure 2.2   The structure of the ORB.

calling into a static IDL stub. The stub translates between different data formats and then calls into the ORB core. The core finds the location of the object in the network, activates the object, and then calls into a static IDL skeleton. The skeleton translates the data to a representation suitable for the object implementation and invokes the desired method of the object. Any data returned by the object is propagated back to the client in the reverse order.

The static IDL stubs and skeletons are generated automatically by an IDL compiler. Note that this detailed view of a method call reveals the fact that a client and a server are separated from each other by three layers. These three layers are accountable for the versatility of the ORB in a heterogeneously distributed environment.

A client invokes a method of an object implementation by calling into a static IDL stub. This call emerges on the other side of the ORB by a static IDL skeleton, calling upward into a method of the object implementation.

Dynamic Invocation Interface (DII)

A client can defer the selection of an object implementation, interface, and operation until runtime. This flexibility can result in creation of very adaptable systems. These systems discover the services available in the network at runtime and choose the service that maximizes some criterion (such as performance or usability). Such systems are essentially self-managing and self-upgradable.

There is a price to pay, though, for this degree of flexibility. The client needs to go through the following four steps:

1. Identify the object implementation.

2. Identify the interface of the object.

3. Construct the method invocation.

4. Invoke the method.

The client interacts with the Dynamic Invocation Interface component and the Naming (or Trading) service to perform these steps. DII uses the *Interface Repository* database (and other modules providing runtime information) and provides the client with sufficient information to invoke a method dynamically. Once the client invokes the method, the ORB core takes the method call and invokes the corresponding method of the object implementation through an upward call in the static IDL skeleton component.

The skeleton can never find out whether the method was invoked statically or dynamically. In other words, even though SII and DII have different implementations on the client side, only one implementation exists on the server side.

 A client can have complete flexibility in choosing a target object implementation, interface, and operation at runtime. The server side of the ORB cannot distinguish between static and dynamic method calls.

SII Vs. DII

This section provides a terse comparison between static and dynamic method calls.

- **Ease of programming**—SII is the natural procedure of method invocation for most programmers.

- **Ease of understanding**—Because it is easier to understand, SII should result in more reliable code than DII.

- **Performance**—SII should result in faster code compared to DII.

- **Type checking**—The IDL compiler can type check the arguments in static method calls.

- **Flexibility**—SII cannot take advantage of new services introduced into a network (many applications do not require this level of flexibility). DII can result in extremely adaptable systems.

- **Invocation semantics**—DII has a *deferred synchronous* invocation semantic, which is nonblocking with return result, in addition to *synchronous* and *asynchronous* invocation semantics. An asynchronous method invocation is nonblocking—a client does not have a standard way to synchronize with the message delivery to the target object, and, therefore, cannot receive any results. A deferred synchronous invocation, on the other hand, does not block, but it allows a client to receive results from an object implementation,

The treatment of the client side of the ORB is almost complete. We have described the various ways that a client can invoke a service, and the manner in which a client can obtain object references. So far, we have assumed that the server which a client is interested in is running and ready to receive requests. In reality, there is another component in the ORB—namely, object adapters—that deals with issues such as server activation and deactivation. The next section introduces object adapters and completes the discussion on the architecture of the ORB.

 *We have not discussed the ORB Interface and Dynamic Skeleton Interface (DSI) components. The ORB Interface provides some generic ORB services that might potentially be useful to clients and servers. DSI provides a way to access object implementations that do not have static IDL skeletons.*

Object Adapters

A different number of ways exist to activate an object implementation. The object implementation can be a part of the client process itself. In this case, the computation is not distributed, but the object implementation can be transported to other systems without affecting the client code. Such an object does not require any external activation; the implementation runs when the client code starts up. An object implementation may require external activation if it is on a remote system and has not been started yet. It also is possible for an object to reside in another system, such as an object-oriented database. In this case, the object may require a very specific form of activation.

Different activation policies exist as well. Some objects can fulfill only one request at a time; other requests must be queued up until these objects are ready to accept them. Another set of objects do not require queuing and can handle many requests. Yet, you might also start a new object implementation for every incoming request.

Once an object implementation is activated, an object reference needs to be assigned to the activated instance. Any future requests targeted at this object reference should be mapped to the correct instance.

Object adapters are responsible for all of the aforementioned behavior. As shown in Figure 2.2, object adapters separate the ORB core from the static IDL skeleton and Dynamic Skeleton Interface components. Because different object implementations may require different activation polices, there can be a proliferation of object adapters. To cope with this situation, CORBA specifies a *Basic Object Adapter* (BOA) that can be used for most object implementations; please refer to Siegel (1996) for more details.

Object adapters handle different activation policies for object implementations. They instantiate new objects at runtime and assign object references to them.

The CORBA Services

The CORBA services (also known as object services) correspond to the bus services in the Software Component Infrastructure of Chapter 1. A detailed description of these services is beyond the scope of this book; if you would like to know more about them, refer to the "Further Readings" section at the end of this chapter. Although in this section we only list the names of the services, each name provides a good indication of what the service might do.

OMG has specified the following eleven services:

- Life Cycle
- Naming
- Persistence
- Event
- Transaction
- Concurrency
- Relationship
- Externalization
- Query
- Licensing
- Properties

In addition, OMG is in the process of standardizing five other services:

- Security
- Secure Time
- Trader
- Collection
- Startup

The CORBA Facilities

CORBA facilities, also know as common facilities, extend the concept of CORBA services up to the level of system integrators and application vendors. These services provide common functionality for a wide range of vertical applications. These common services might very well be the last type of services that OMG will try to standardize, because any attempt to provide standards for top-level application objects will most likely fail. CORBA facilities consist of horizontal and vertical facilities, as described below.

HORIZONTAL CORBA FACILITIES

These facilities are potentially useful to all market segments. Vertical application vendors can leverage off of these standard facilities and add domain-specific, variant behaviors to create market-specified applications (refer to Chapter 1 for the definition of variant knowledge). Currently, OMG has standardized the following four horizontal facilities:

- User Interface

- Information Management

- Systems Management

- Task Management

VERTICAL CORBA FACILITIES

OMG is in the process of defining the vertical facilities. So far, it has specified Healthcare and Financial facilities, and more work is in progress at the time of this writing. Interested readers should refer to the *Common Facilities Architecture Guide,* published by OMG in 1995.

OpenDoc

After reading about the CORBA horizontal and vertical facilities, you might wonder why OpenDoc is needed at all. As mentioned in Chapter 1, compound documents are the ultimate clients for desktops. Servers serve compound documents to desktops; these documents are capable of managing different kinds of data, handling data in different locations in the network, and performing distributed computation. CORBA, though, does not provide a compound-document framework. The CORBA horizontal facilities are high-level services useful to application developers, and the CORBA vertical facilities are geared at very specific market segments.

This section introduces the reader to OpenDoc. Due to its similarity with Java Beans, OpenDoc provides valuable insights into the capabilities of Java Beans. Because it also firms up a number of concepts presented in Chapter 1, we strongly encourage you to go back and revisit that chapter after reading this one.

OpenDoc supports compound documents, can be used in a network environment, is customizable, and is available on a wide range of platforms. OpenDoc documents accept all kinds of multimedia data, including some that have yet to appear. An OpenDoc document can consist of many parts, each of which may represent a particular kind of data (text, image, video, and so on). These parts are hierarchically organized and can contain other parts.

OpenDoc parts are potentially transferable across platforms and can be dragged and dropped. Each part is equipped with the software that can display and modify it, and it can be edited in place without opening a new window. In fact, because an OpenDoc comprises many different parts and each part has its own software, it no longer makes sense to associate a creating tool with the whole document. OpenDoc changes the monolithic applications into part-centered documents. If any of these statements sound strange; review Chapter 1, in which we presented them.

Most of the capabilities of OpenDoc are based on a few simple concepts: *documents*, *parts*, *part editors*, and *frames*.

OpenDoc shifts the focus of a user from an application-centered model to a document-centered model.

Documents

In OpenDoc, documents are *containers*; they host parts. A document does not have an associated application, but it does have a corresponding file that comprises the data in all of the contained parts. A document can contain an arbitrary number of parts organized in a hierarchical structure.

Parts

In OpenDoc, components (see Chapter 1) are called parts. A part is the unit of operation; it contains data and the software that manipulates the data. A part is a self-contained entity. A developer creates a (compound) document by assembling parts, each of which represents a kind of data (graphics, text, spreadsheet, and so on) and a tool that manages the display and modification of the part. Because parts can contain other parts, it is possible to create arbitrary complex documents.

A part can be a *container part*, which can embed other parts, or it can be a *noncontainer part,* which cannot contain other parts. Every document has a *root part*, which is the top-level part that embeds all of the other parts in the document. Most parts are container parts, but some parts (such as clocks) may not have any reason to embed other parts.

A developer can purchase off-the-shelf parts from vendors, add custom parts, and assemble the results quickly into OpenDoc documents. He or she can even replace the software that manages a part with other software. The software that manages a part is called *part editor*, which is described in the next section.

Part Editors

A part is very much like an object in object-oriented paradigms. The state of an object corresponds to the data in a part; the behavior of an object maps to the part editor in a part.

Part editors are responsible for displaying their parts on a display screen, editing these parts, and storing their states. If a document has a number of parts that all share the same part editor, only one copy of the editor needs to reside in memory. A *part viewer* is a special part editor than can only render (display or print) a part; it cannot modify the state of a part.

Frames

A part is displayed in a frame. The hierarchical nature of parts in a document naturally results in a hierarchy of frames within the display window. A part is responsible for selecting, deselecting, moving, or deleting its contained frames. Frames are not required to be rectangular and can have arbitrary shapes.

Part Kinds And Categories

A part binds to a part editor through a *part kind*. A part kind determines the format of data that is managed by a part editor. A part editor can handle more than one part kind. Similarly, a part can have more than one part kind.

A part has a *preferred part editor*; the part editor that originally created or last edited the part. Because a compound document can have a large number of parts, each of which may be a unique part kind, the compound document may require the presence of all the preferred part editors. OpenDoc relaxes this requirement with *part categories*, which specify the general description of the data format of a part. It follows that the relationship between part kinds and part categories is many-to-one. A user of a compound document can associate a part editor for a part category; OpenDoc uses this part editor if the preferred part editor for a part in that category is missing.

Presentation

A part in OpenDoc may have more than one view. In this case, the part editor displays all of the views, with each one having its own frame. For example, consider a part that represents the expenditures of a household. The part editor can display the expenditures as text, in table form, or by drawing a pie (or bar) chart. Each of these forms represents a presentation of the part and has its own view.

User Interface

One of the challenges of OpenDoc is to provide protocols that allow different parts—which may not know anything about each other—to collaborate and share the document window of a compound document. In OpenDoc, a container part dictates the positions, shapes, and sizes of the embedded frames. An embedded part must negotiate with its containing part before it can make any changes to its frames.

OpenDoc provides two standard menus: the *Document menu* and the *Edit menu*. A part editor can introduce new menus, or it can modify the standard OpenDoc menus.

Event Handling

OpenDoc follows the event-handling methodology that we set forth in Chapter 1. All user interactions with the different parts of a compound document are delivered to the *document shell*. Based on the location of the event and ownership of other resources, the shell determines the part editor that must handle the event. The shell then delivers the event to the part editor through a *dispatcher*.

A part editor never polls for events, nor does it directly communicate with other parts. Instead, it waits passively until it is notified of an event by the dispatcher. As we emphasized in Chapter 1, a compound-document framework imposes the structure and the flow of control of an application. Therefore, the job of a developer is to assemble and customize these components into an application, as opposed to providing a logic for the structure of the application.

Uniform Data Transfer (UDT)

OpenDoc provides protocols for uniform data transfer between parts. There is no restriction on the source and the destination of UDT; they can be two parts in the same document or in different documents. UDT refers to providing the same behavior for various ways of transferring data (primarily, clipboard and drag-and-drop).

OpenDoc supports both linking and embedding concepts. In *linking*, the data in a part is actually stored in another place; in *embedding*, the data is copied, and the relationship between the source and the destination of UDT is lost.

Storage

The basics of structured storage have been outlined in Chapter 1. OpenDoc supports structured storage by allowing multiple part editors to share a single file. OpenDoc uses *storage unit* to organize its storage. The part editor of a part stores the part's data in (at least) one storage unit. This unit is distinct from all the other units used by other parts. Storage units can have links to other storage units.

Scripting

Scripting is only one of the several ways to extend the capabilities of OpenDoc. A complete overview of extensibility in OpenDoc is beyond the scope of this book. OpenDoc supports a scripting model to enhance the communications between parts. In this model, scripting events are delivered from a scripting system to a part editor. For example, a user can attach a script to a part; he or she can then invoke the script through a button. The button generates a scripting event, which is delivered to the part and causes the part to run the script. OpenDoc supports the *Open Scripting Architecture* (OSA). Examples of OSA on Mac OS are AppleScript and Frontier.

As you can see, OpenDoc provides the technology to change a user's desktop to essentially a compound-document client. All the different components of the document collaborate with each other to present a seamless user interface to the user. How do these components invoke services of other objects distributed in the enterprise? The answer is through CORBA. OpenDoc has embraced CORBA to provide interoperability among compound documents and object servers. The marriage of OpenDoc and CORBA is essential to bridge the gap between desktops and the enterprise and capture the software infrastructure.

Further Readings

The Common Object Request Broker Architecture and Specification; Revision 2.0. Object Management Group, 1995.

Siegel, Jon. *CORBA Fundamentals and Programming*. Object Management Group, 1996.

Mowbray, Thomas, and Ron Zahavi. *The Essential CORBA*. Object Management Group, 1995.

OpenDoc Programmer's Guide. Apple Computer, 1995.

Chapter 3

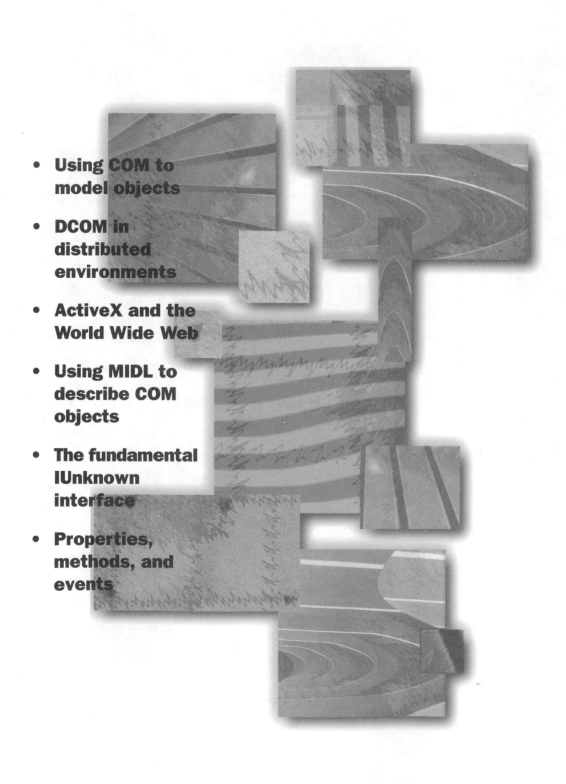

- **Using COM to model objects**

- **DCOM in distributed environments**

- **ActiveX and the World Wide Web**

- **Using MIDL to describe COM objects**

- **The fundamental IUnknown interface**

- **Properties, methods, and events**

Chapter

3

ActiveX/ DCOM

This chapter presents another embodiment of the Software Component Infrastructure (SCI) model: ActiveX and the Distributed Component Object Model (DCOM). These two technologies, along with myriad others that are built on top of COM and DCOMs and provide other core features, form the strategy that Microsoft is using to dominate the SCI enterprise, from back-end servers all the way up to desktops.

It is intriguing that Java and DCOM, two technologies from competing vendors, can be used together for application development. The incarnation of DCOM in a programming language is in some ways closer to Java than C++. For example, DCOM exposes the services of an object through one or more interfaces. Java has the notion of an interface and allows an object to implement more than one interface—a feature that can be used to implement COM objects. Another synergic use of Java and DCOM is the use of "garbage collection" in Java to eliminate the need to do reference counting on DCOM objects. (Reference counting, discussed later in this chapter, is the mechanism that DCOM uses to manage an object's life cycle.)

Through a bridge from Java Beans to ActiveX, beans can be wrapped into first-class ActiveX components that can be instantiated in an ActiveX container. As we have already mentioned, Java Beans provides similar bridges to OpenDoc and CORBA objects. (The creators of Java Beans apparently have left no stone unturned in terms of ensuring the interoperability of Java Beans with other dominant technologies.)

This chapter provides enough of an overview of ActiveX/DCOM for you to understand the implications of the Java Beans/ActiveX bridge. It starts with COM and then explains the importance of DCOM in distributed environments. Because COM is the foundation of several other Microsoft technologies (DCOM, Automation, Uniform Data Transfer, Monikers, OLE, and ActiveX), the majority of this chapter is dedicated to COM. At the end, we'll provide an overview of ActiveX controls.

COM In General

Component Object Model (COM) is the cornerstone of the "reusable software component" paradigm. The distributed version of COM—DCOM—is the object bus in the SCI for ActiveX/DCOM; it provides a uniform mechanism for a client to invoke the services of an object regardless of the location of the object (local or remote), the server type (dynamic-link library or standalone executable), or the language used to implement an object. (Note that in this chapter, we use the term *object*, instead of *server*, to refer to a piece of software that provides services to a client.)

In other words, COM provides location, server type, and language transparency. COM accomplishes this uniformity by specifying the manner in which an object exposes its services to the outside world, a binary interface for service invocation, a method to manage the life cycle of an object, ways to reuse an object, and a mechanism to transfer data across different address spaces. The rest of this section explores these ideas in detail.

Even though COM provides location transparency, it cannot be used to access remote objects. As we will explain later, COM is not network aware and is confined to a single machine. DCOM, the network version of COM, actually provides access to remote objects.

Because this distinction is not necessary when presenting concepts, however, we will sometimes use COM to refer to both versions.

Interfaces

The notion of an interface is fundamental to the component software technology. This is because the process of component creation is different than that of component instantiation. Components (also known as *controls*) are usually created by third-party vendors in accordance to certain specifications. To build an application, developers purchase these off-the-shelf components and instantiate them in a control container. The only viable mechanism for developers to identify the services of a component generically is through interfaces. The idea of using interfaces to define the services of an object is not new to COM; as noted in Chapter 2, CORBA uses a similar approach (OMG IDL).

A COM object advertises its services through one or more interfaces. Figure 3.1 depicts a COM object with two interfaces: **IUnknown** and **IExample**. (In COM, it is customary to begin the name of an interface with the letter *I*.) Because **IUnknown** is a standard interface that all COM objects must support, any COM object has at least one interface. This interface is explained further in a subsequent section. The COM object in Figure 3.1 exposes another set of services via its second interface, **IExample**.

In order for interfaces to be useful, there must be a standard method for a control to describe its interfaces, a way for a client to identify which interface it desires to use, and a way for a programming language to invoke the methods of an interface. Each of the above methods is described in the following sections.

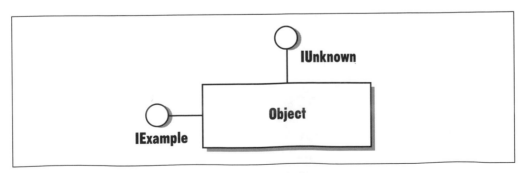

Figure 3.1 A COM object that has two interfaces.

INTERFACE DESCRIPTION: MIDL

A component uses the Microsoft Interface Definition Language (MIDL) to advertise the methods that it provides. MIDL is based on the IDL used in Open Software Foundation's Distributed Computing Environment (OSF DCE). Like the OMG IDL, MIDL is a declarative language that an object can use to precisely define its interfaces, the methods in each interface, and the parameters of each method.

COM does not mandate the use of MIDL for an object to define its interfaces. The critical requirement is for the object to adhere to the COM's binary interface standard, which is explained in a later section. However, MIDL is frequently used for interface description.

The model in Listing 3.1 describes an object that provides an implementation for rectangles. (In fact, a rectangle should probably be an object with different interfaces, each exposing a set of related functionality, but this example is presented solely to explain the syntax of MIDL.)

Listing 3.1 A simplified model expressed in MIDL for rectangles.

```
[ object, uuid(12345678-1234-1234-1234-123456789ABC) ]
interface IRectangle : IUnknown
{
  import "unknwn.idl";
  HRESULT Area([out] OLEINT *res);
  HRESULT Draw();
  HRESULT Translate([in] OLEINT x, [in] OLEINT y);
}
```

In the model in Listing 3.1, the term *object* signifies that MIDL is using the extensions made to the DCE IDL. The keyword **uuid** (explained in the next section) and the accompanying hexadecimal number uniquely identify the **IRectangle** interface, which inherits the fundamental methods from **IUnknown** via the inheritance operator ":". The import statement is required so that a MIDL compiler can locate the **IUnknown** interface. MIDL uses a data type called **HRESULT** to capture the errors returned by methods. The use of the keywords **[in]** and **[out]** is very similar to OMG IDL. These keywords are required in a distributed environment so that COM can correctly transfer the parameters across different address spaces.

In COM, interfaces are *immutable*. In other words, once a component defines an interface, it should not change that interface. This is a reasonable constraint, because any client using the interface would cease to operate after it was changed. Of course, there is no mechanism to prevent a developer from changing the interface of a control, but such practices are strongly discouraged.

Note that the above restriction does not imply that the *implementation details* of an interface cannot be changed. If an object needs to modify or add new methods to an interface, it can do so by implementing a new interface. For example, an object that provides an implementation for **IRectangle** can provide another interface, possibly named **IRectangle1**, that has some added methods. Any client that is using **IRectangle** will not be affected by the new interface, but new clients can leverage **IRectangle1** to perform tasks that were not feasible with the older one.

INTERFACE IDENTIFICATION: GUID, IID, UUID, CLSID

A client needs a way to identify a particular interface of an object whose methods it wishes to invoke. As described in the previous section, an interface has two names: a human-readable name (such as **IRectangle**) and a UUID, which is more suitable for a machine. COM uses a 16-byte value, called a globally unique identifier (GUID), for this purpose. The entity identified can be an object, an interface, or something else.

Interface GUIDs are usually called interface identifiers (IIDs). For historical reasons, however, MIDL uses the keyword **uuid** (which stands for "universally unique identifiers") to name an interface. GUIDs used to identify the class of an object are called class identifiers (CLSID). The important point to keep in mind is that GUID, IID, UUID, and CLSID are all 16-byte hexadecimal numbers and are used to identify an entity uniquely.

Providing unique names for interfaces is important. A software developer who wishes to develop an application for displaying and manipulating rectangles, for example, can then consult a catalog of off-the-shelf components that implement two-dimensional objects. This catalog might list all the different implementations (IIDs) of **IRectangle**. The developer can then purchase the desired control. (This example is for illustration only and is used to underscore the fact that an interface can have a number of different implementations.)

Note that each implementation of **IRectangle** might actually provide a different set of methods, or perhaps the same methods with different parameters. This situation is unavoidable unless there is a standard that precisely defines **IRectangle**. In this case, each control vendor would provide a different implementation for the same interface, and controls can be interchanged without disturbing the rest of an application.

INTERFACE IMPLEMENTATION: VTABLES

COM separates the interface (behavior) of an object from its implementation language. A client can use a language such as Microsoft's Visual Basic to invoke the methods of a COM object, but the object itself can be implemented in any language, such as C or C++. A client can invoke a method of a COM object written in an arbitrary language, because COM mandates a binary interface standard for all COM objects. The crucial part of this binary standard is the notion of a *vtable*.

In order for a client to invoke a method in an interface of an object, it needs to acquire a pointer to the desired interface. Assume a client has already acquired such an interface pointer to **IRectangle** of an object. (The process of acquiring interface pointers is described in a subsequent section.) Figure 3.2 illustrates this situation.

As shown in Figure 3.2, the memory allocated to an instantiated object (which resides in memory) does not actually contain any methods. Instead, the object maintains a pointer to each method. All of these pointers are organized in tables called vtables. A client's interface pointer actually refers, via an internal pointer in the object, to the beginning of a vtable for that interface.

Because all interfaces inherit from **IUnknown**, the first three pointers in each vtable are reserved for **IUnknown** methods—namely, **QueryInterface()**, **AddRef()**, and **Release()**, which are discussed in the next section. The rest of the pointers refer to the methods that the particular interface provides. In Figure 3.2, these pointers identify the methods of **IRectangle**.

All COM objects are required to implement their interfaces via vtables, regardless of the language that is used for implementation. A client of a COM object may have to be aware of vtables, depending on the language used to implement the client. For example, a client of **IRectangle** that is written in C must be aware of the chain of pointers to the

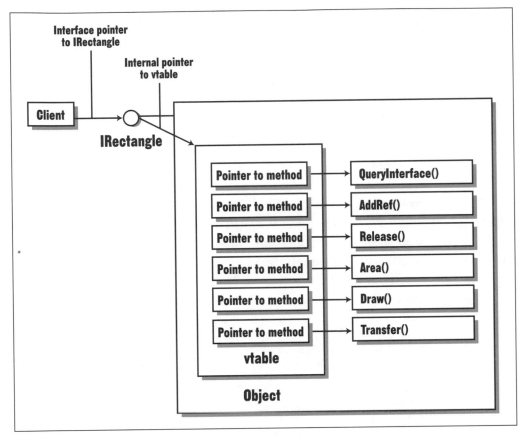

Figure 3.2 Binary implementation of an object.

IRectangle vtable. Therefore, the client must first de-reference the pointer to **IRectangle** and then invoke a method, such as the **Area()** method, via the internal vtable pointer.

A C++ client does not have to worry about vtables, however, because C++ compilers create memory layouts for objects that are very similar to vtables. The compiler thus implicitly accounts for the chain of pointers, relieving a C++ programmer from de-referencing an interface pointer first. Visual Basic masks vtables in a similar manner.

All COM objects are internally implemented via vtables. A client has to be aware of vtables if the client's programming language does not account for them.

IUnknown

IUnknown is the most important interface in COM. All COM objects must support this interface, and all interfaces must inherit from it. The importance of **IUnknown** can be underscored by observing that an object is a COM object if it adheres to the binary standard specification and supports **IUnknown**.

IUnknown provides three methods for querying about different interfaces of an object and managing its life cycle: **QueryInterface()**, **AddRef()**, and **Release()**. When a client creates an instance of an object, it normally requests a pointer to the object's **IUnknown** interface. The client can then query the object to find out whether the object supports a particular interface by calling **QueryInterface()** and passing the IID of the desired interface. If **QueryInterface()** returns a NULL, the client concludes that the object does not support the desired interface and can either exit gracefully or attempt to search for another similar interface. Otherwise, the client can proceed to invoke the methods in the interface of the object.

QueryInterface() allows clients to discover the capabilities of objects and adapt themselves dynamically. For example, consider an object with three interfaces: **IUnknown**, **IRectangle**, and **IRectangle1** (an improved form of **IRectangle** added to a later version of the object). Clients that are written to the older version of the object know only about **IRectangle** and use **QueryInterface()** to get a pointer to this interface. Clients that are aware of the new version, however, can ask for **IRectangle1**. If such clients are deployed in a production environment that has the new version of the object, they can take advantage of the added **IRectangle1** features. Otherwise, if the environment only supports an older version of the object, they receive a NULL pointer when they attempt to access **IRectangle1**. These clients can then fall back on the previous version and acquire a pointer to **IRectangle**. As a result, they are still functional and behave very much like the clients that are written to the older version.

COM solves the problem of software versioning through immutable interfaces and QueryInterface().

The other two methods that **IUnknown** provides are used to manage the life cycle of an object. The next section explores these methods.

Reference Counting

When a client creates a new instance of an object, COM activates the object and returns to the client a pointer to one of the interfaces of the object. The object activation might cause a dynamic-link library (DLL) to be loaded in the process space of the client or a standalone executable to be started in a different process space. When the client is finished with an object, COM may have to deactivate the object. But how does the client know that the object is no longer required and should be deactivated? It doesn't. The reason is that when the client instantiated an object, COM may have reused an existing object in use by another client. This situation is common with DLLs, because one DLL can serve many clients. Managing the life cycle of an object gets even more complicated, because a client can pass an interface pointer to another client without ever going through COM.

In fact, the only entity that knows when an object is no longer needed is the object itself. An object maintains a count of the total number of its reference pointers that are in use. When a client asks COM for an interface pointer, COM increments the reference count by issuing a call to **AddRef()** on behalf of the client. When a client passes an interface pointer to another client, it must explicitly increment the reference count itself. Finally, when a client no longer needs a pointer, it must decrement the reference count through **Release()**. When an object discovers that its reference count is zero, it knows that it is no longer needed, and it destroys itself.

In COM, a client is responsible for managing an object's life cycle. If a client forgets to inform an object that it no longer is needed, the object is doomed to remain in memory until the machine is powered down.

Server Types

The actual implementation code for an object is in a server. A server can define one or more classes. Furthermore, for a class, a server might support only one running object (instance) or more. COM supports three kinds of servers: in-process, local, and remote.

An *in-process server* is a DLL. When a client creates an instance of an object that is implemented in a DLL, COM loads the DLL into the process space of the client if it is not already loaded. A *local server* is a standalone executable that runs on the same machine as the client. A local server can support one or more clients. A *remote server* (which can be either a DLL or a standalone executable) runs on a machine different than the client's machine. Note that COM does not support remote servers, but DCOM provides support for all types of servers.

COM and DCOM support in-process, local, and remote servers. A client, however, is typically oblivious to the type and location of a server; it always obtains an interface pointer to an object and invokes the interface's methods.

Marshaling

If the object is implemented in an in-process server, COM loads the server's DLL in the process space of a client when the client instantiates an object. The interface pointer that the client acquires as a result of instantiation is indeed a pointer to the vtable of the object. Any method invocation in the interface is as fast as a C++ virtual method invocation.

The interface method invocation, however, is more complicated if the object is implemented in a local server. Note that two processes that are in different address spaces can communicate only through an interprocess communication (IPC) scheme. Therefore, it is not possible for an interface pointer to point directly to the object's vtable in this case, because the object resides in a different address space. An additional problem is the transfer of parameters between the client and server processes. The parameters need to be packed in a suitable format, shipped to the other process, and unpacked. This process of packing and unpacking of parameters is called *marshaling* and *unmarshaling*. Figure 3.3 depicts how a client invokes a method of a local server.

As Figure 3.3 illustrates, the interface pointer that a client has to an object in a different process is actually a pointer to a proxy object. When the client invokes a method in the interface, the proxy object marshals the parameters and ships them to the stub in the server process. The stub unmarshals the arguments and invokes the method on behalf of the client. Any data that needs to be shipped back to the client traverses from the stub to the proxy.

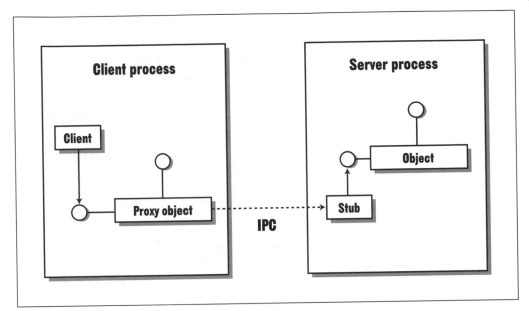

Figure 3.3 COM uses a proxy object and a stub for cross-process method invocation.

Note that as far the client is concerned, the process of invoking a method is the same as it is for an in-process server, although the client might notice a slight performance degradation. (The case of a remote server is discussed in the later section on DCOM.)

It is constructive to point out that CORBA accomplishes the same behavior through the use of static IDL stubs and static IDL skeletons (see Chapter 2). Both CORBA and COM use the information contained in IDL files to create these ancillary programs.

Marshaling and unmarshaling are the processes of packing and unpacking parameters for an across-process transfer. COM creates a proxy object and stub to manage the implementation details of this transfer.

COM Object Creation

The examples so far have assumed that the client has already obtained an interface pointer to an object. Once it has done this, it can use **QueryInterface()** to obtain other interface pointers. But how does the client obtain the very first interface pointer?

The answer to this question requires an understanding of *system registries*. A client designates an object that it instantiates by passing COM the CLSID of the object. COM needs a way to map this CLSID to the location of the server that implements the object. This mapping, along with other useful information, is stored in a system registry. For Microsoft Windows and Windows NT, COM uses the registry native to those systems. COM does not mandate the use of a particular registry, but any COM-compliant registry must provide the following information for a COM object, as shown in Table 3.1.

A client uses **CoCreateInstance()** to request an interface pointer of an object from COM. (It can also obtain an interface pointer by using the class factory of the object.) The client passes the CLSID and IID of the desired object and the desired interface as the parameters to this function. Note that **CoCreateInstance()** is a global function directly provided by COM, *not* a method in an interface.

In response to this function call, COM searches the system registry of the client's machine and retrieves the type and the location of the server that implements the object. COM activates the server if it is not running, or if it cannot support multiple clients, and then passes the desired interface pointer to the client. Once it returns the interface pointer to the client, COM is oblivious to further interactions between the client and the object.

 A client requests an interface pointer from COM by supplying the CLSID and IID. COM consults the system registry, finds the location of the server, activates the server if necessary, returns the interface pointer, and then drops out of the picture. Future interactions of the client and the object are not mediated by COM.

Table 3.1 Required information for a COM object.

Information	Description
CLSID	The class identifier, which serves as the key to the table.
Server type	The type of the server that contains the object code (namely, in-process, local, or remote).
Server location	The pathname to the in-process or local server (or, if the server is remote, the identification of the remote machine).

DCOM

COM only supports in-process and local servers; it cannot support remote servers. Microsoft introduced DCOM in 1996 to provide cross-machine method invocation.

Distributed COM introduces a few issues. First, unlike COM, it must be concerned about security and access control. COM correctly assumes that if a user can run a client application on a machine, then a server can also be activated on that machine. This assumption, however, is not true for remote servers; a machine usually limits access (such as activating a server) to its resources by remote clients. A second issue is the transfer of data across two machines. Third, the manner to signal DCOM that a server needs to run on a remote platform must be determined.

Remote Object Creation

DCOM utilizes system registries to locate remote objects. As noted earlier, a system registry has a entry for an object, which is indexed by the object's CLSID. Also recall that the entry must provide a location for the server that implements an object. If the location of the server is another machine instead of a pathname, DCOM consults the system registry on the specified remote machine and obtains the pathname to the remote server.

If the remote server is a DLL, DCOM creates a *surrogate process*, loads the DLL in the surrogate process, and returns an interface pointer to a proxy object to the client. If the remote server is a standalone executable, DCOM simply runs the executable instead of creating a surrogate process.

*A client calls **CoCreateInstance**() and passes CLSID of the object and IID of the interface to DCOM. If the location of the server in the system registry on the client machine is another machine instead of a pathname, DCOM activates a remote server for the client. The client is oblivious to the fact that the server is run on a remote machine.*

Remote Object Access

Once a remote object is created, DCOM requires a mechanism to access the remote object and invoke its methods. You may recall that an interface pointer to an in-process object directly points to a vtable; therefore, object access boils down to accessing a C++ object. For local servers, COM needs to set up proxy objects and stubs and use IPCs to invoke methods across different address spaces.

Accessing a remote object is slightly more complicated because the object resides in not only a separate process but also a separate machine. IPC (interprocess communication) is no longer sufficient; a full-blown remote procedure call (RPC) is required. DCOM uses MS RPC, which is based on OSF DCE (Open Software Foundation's Distributed Computing Environment) RPC, for remote method invocations. Like COM, DCOM uses proxies and stubs to manage the details of access to remote objects, but it uses RPC in place of IPC.

 DCOM uses MS RPC to access remote servers. A client might notice an even greater performance degradation compared to accessing local servers, but it cannot determine the location of the servers.

Marshaling

Transferring data across machines is a more complicated undertaking than doing so across processes on the same machine. Different hardware platforms have disparate ways of representing data. For instance, many systems use ASCII to represent characters, whereas IBM uses EBCDIC for its mainframes. There are different specifications for floating-point numbers, and an integral type might differ in byte ordering and length on different machines.

Marshaling translates parameters into a machine-neutral format, called Network Data Representation (NDR), before packing them for shipment to a stub on a remote machine. The stub in turn unpacks the data, translates it from NDR format into the local machine's format, and performs method invocations.

 Data is translated to and from NDR when shipped between different machines.

Security

DCOM needs to address two fundamental security issues: *activation policy* and *call policy*. The former is a policy to determine who can remotely activate servers on a given machine. Furthermore, once a server is activated, the machine needs the latter policy to determine who can remotely call methods of the server.

Activation policy is captured via a machine's registry. The registry can allow everyone to launch servers on the machine, or it can entirely disallow remote server activation. Between these two broad settings, the registry can use *access control lists* (ACLs) to grant permission to individual clients.

Once an object is started, it is ready to receive calls from clients. The object, however, might want to limit access to certain authorized users. Furthermore, the communications between a client and the object may need to be protected from eavesdropping if the communication channel is not secure. In order to support a wide range of requirements, DCOM provides the following security services:

- **Authentication**—Authentication proves that a *principal* (such as a client, an object, or a user) is who it claims to be.

- **Authorization**—Authorization is used to guard resources from unauthorized accesses. An object can use ACLs to associate a list of clients that are authorized to access its resources.

- **Data integrity**—This service ensures that the data an object or a client receives is not tampered with.

- **Data privacy**—This service performs encryption before it sends data to insecure networks. Data privacy is essential for cases when a client is transmitting sensitive data, such as credit card numbers, to an object over open networks.

ActiveX Controls

So far in this chapter, we have been using the term *component* or *control* without defining exactly what one is. Components can be different things, depending on their type, but the kind that is emerging as an open standard is called *ActiveX controls*.

Controls did not originate with COM. Rather, the first generation of controls were designed to work exclusively with Visual Basic. These controls were called VBXs (Visual Basic Extensions), and they had a lot of features in common with ActiveX controls. The inherent problem with VBXs was that they limited the choice of a *control container* to Visual Basic containers—in other words, it was not possible to use them inside other control containers, such as Visual C++ or Web containers. The OLE Controls specification addressed this problem by specifying all of the interfaces that a COM object must support. These interfaces implemented everything that a control would ever want to do: providing a user interface, sending events, managing properties, and much more.

The OLE Controls specification was a step in the right direction, but it went too far. Not all controls have user interfaces, nor do they need to let containers set their properties. Because of the specification, though, OLE control implementers had no choice but to support all the mandated interfaces. This approach may have not been as fatal if World Wide Web (WWW) pages did not emerge as another type of control containers. In order to add dynamic behavior to static HTML pages, Web content developers needed to embed these controls directly into their pages, but the time it took to download these pages from Web servers turned out to be excessive. As a result, OLE controls were simply not efficient for deployment through the Web.

ActiveX Controls specification addressed the inefficiency issue. This standard requires that a control implement only **IUnknown**, and that it can register itself in a system registry. This self-registration allows a control container to discover the capabilities of a control dynamically by accessing the system registry. The ActiveX Controls specification continued to standardize all the capabilities of controls, but controls are not mandated to implement the interfaces that they do not intend to support.

*An ActiveX control only needs to implement **IUnknown** and register itself in a registry. In essence, an ActiveX control is very much like a COM object. Any additional features that an ActiveX control provides, however, must follow ActiveX Controls standards.*

The ActiveX Controls specification identifies the following four main categories of functionality for ActiveX controls:

- **User interface**—A control may provide a user interface to a container.

- **Properties**—A control can have a set of properties, which can be modified by a container. Furthermore, a control can inquire about its container's properties.

- **Methods**—A control may have a number of methods, which can be invoked by a container.

- **Events**—A control can generate and send events to a container.

The rest of this section explores these features.

Component Categories

How can a control container determine the capabilities of an ActiveX control? It can no longer assume that the control implements all of the possible interfaces; the ActiveX Controls specification has removed this rigid mandate.

A container needs to discover the features of a control for two reasons. First, if the control does not support certain features (such as allowing the container to set its properties), the container can disable those features by graying out appropriate menus. Moreover, a container might delay the actual loading of a control until it is really needed if the container can find out certain information about the control. Second, the container might even elect not to instantiate the control if it is not capable of interacting with the control. As mentioned earlier, there are different types of containers, each with its own set of capabilities. An application does not need to be a full-fledged container to instantiate ActiveX controls; ActiveX controls can even be containers for other controls. As a result, there might be cases where a container cannot interact with a control, and knowing the capabilities of a control prior to instantiating it allows the container not to load the control if there is a problem.

A control advertises its features by enumerating its category identifiers (CATIDs) in the registry. A CATID is a GUID; it allows a control to identify the interfaces that it supports, or even a particular set of methods within an interface. A container can then access the registry and determine the functionality of the container before loading it. For CATIDs to be useful, there must be an agreement within the ActiveX community on the features that each CATID represents. Component categories are not widely used, however, and some containers (such as Visual Basic 4) do not support them.

User Interface

A control can provide a full-blown user interface by implementing all the interfaces specified by ActiveX Controls specification (including **IOleInPlaceActiveObject**, **IViewObject2**, and **IOleCache2**, to name a few). For several reasons, however, a control does not usually implement all of the prescribed interfaces.

Most ActiveX controls are implemented as in-process servers. Because the DLL associated with a control is directly loaded into a container's address space, the control can directly write to the container's window. Also, controls follow the *inside-out activation* policy. In this policy, a control is activated with a single mouse click regardless of how deeply it is nested in a container; this is the behavior that a user expects, because a control is an integral part of an application. In contrast, OLE compound documents follow the *outside-in activation* policy, in which a user has to activate each contained document to reach a nested document.

Properties

A control usually has a set of properties that allow a user to change its presentation or behavior. For example, a control might have a property for its foreground color, a property for the thickness of its border, and a property to enable or disable a feature.

If a control defines properties, it must implement the **IDispatch** interface to allow its container to get the values of properties or set their values. The ActiveX Controls specification defines *property pages*, which provide a standard user interface to change the properties of a control. Supporting property pages is a rather complex task for a control, but the end result is that a container can pop up a tabbed dialog box, letting a user modify a control's properties in an efficient manner. (Visual Basic also provides a window, called a *property window*, for modifying properties.)

It is useful for a control container to define *ambient properties*. Controls can access these properties and use them to provide a consistent presentation across all controls in a container. For instance, a container can define a background and a font property. Controls in the container can then inquire about the values of these properties and set their corresponding properties to the same values, providing a consistent background and font to a user.

Methods

A control may also have methods that are invoked by a container. The ActiveX Controls specification dictates that a control must implement the **IDispatch** interface to allow its methods to be invoked through the **IDispatch::Invoke** method.

A container can access a control's *type library* to determine the list of all the methods that the control supports, and their parameters. The container can then present this list to a user as a visual programming aid. A type library is a binary file that is generated by a MIDL compiler through parsing the MIDL description of a control. The information in a type library includes the list of all the methods that a control supports and the description of their arguments. A container can access a type library through well-defined interfaces (such as **ITypeLib** and **ITypeInfo**) and generate a list of methods.

A separate language, called ODL (Object Description Language), was previously used to define a type library. A tool called MkTypLib would then parse an ODL file and generate a type library. ODL and MkTypLib are things of the past, and their capabilities have been absorbed into MIDL and MIDL compilers, respectively.

Events

Events are different than methods. To cause an action in a control, a container invokes a *method* in the control. To cause an action in a container, a control sends the container an *event*. Once a container receives an event from a control, it is free to take whatever course of action that it deems necessary. The container can ignore the event, handle the event itself, or deliver it to another control that has expressed an interest in this event.

Further Readings

Chappell, David. *Understanding ActiveX and OLE*. Microsoft Press, 1996.

Brockschmidt, Kraig. *Inside OLE, Second Edition*. Microsoft Press, 1995.

Chapter 4

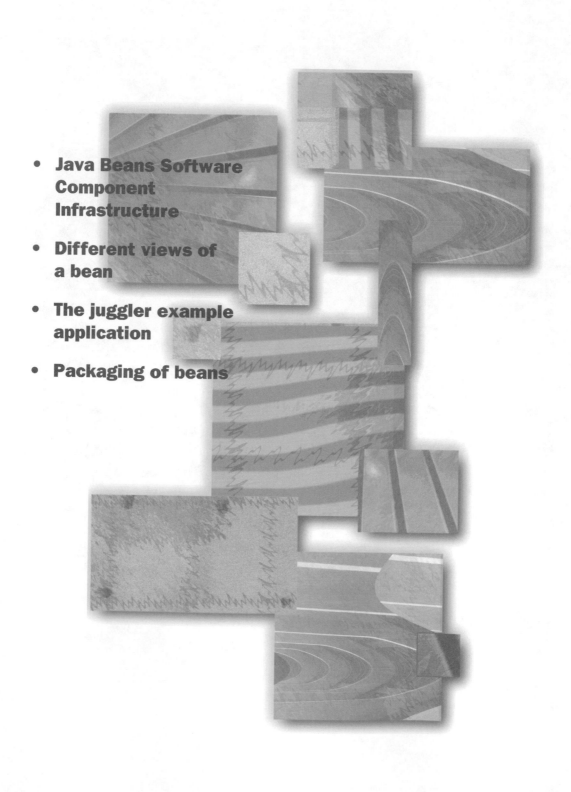

- **Java Beans Software Component Infrastructure**

- **Different views of a bean**

- **The juggler example application**

- **Packaging of beans**

Chapter 4

Java Beans

This chapter covers the fundamentals of Java Beans technology. As you will see, this technology is similar to the OpenDoc/CORBA and ActiveX/DCOM technologies, and it follows the general concepts presented in Chapter 1.

You can use Java Beans to implement beans (reusable software components that can be manipulated visually in a framework), which can be used in two ways. First, you can instantiate the beans in containers and customize them to create *composite applications.* This chapter provides a detailed example of building a composite application. Alternately, you can use coarse-grained beans, such as spreadsheets and word processors, and assemble them into *compound documents*. Although Java Beans supports compound documents, it does not provide the same degree of functionality for them as do other compound-document centered frameworks, such as OpenDoc.

A bean can reside in a wide range of different environments. It can be embedded in a native Java Beans container; it can be wrapped as an ActiveX object and instantiated in containers such as Microsoft's Visual Basic or Microsoft's Internet Explorer; it can be integrated with LiveConnect inside Netscape Navigator; or it can be used as an OpenDoc part. Regardless of the environment, the bean preserves its state through properties, fires events, and services other objects via its methods. One of the design goals of Java Beans has been the interoperability of beans with other component models, most notably OpenDoc, ActiveX, and LiveConnect. This interoperability is transparent to end users and is accomplished through bridges.

After you read this chapter, you might wonder when you should design beans instead of class libraries. Class libraries provide general-purpose APIs to services without usually supplying any GUI. You may use these APIs programmatically to develop an application; you cannot use them in a visual builder tool. You can, however, use such a tool to assemble beans into an application visually.

As a general guideline, you should design a service as class libraries if it does not benefit from visual manipulation. For example, you should design a class library for general-purpose database access because this library can be used programmatically in other applications for database access. You can, however, provide a database access bean on top of this library so that a developer can use a visual framework to instantiate and customize this bean to perform a specific task, such a database query.

Java Beans Infrastructure

Java Beans technology provides a collection of standard classes and methods, which can be used by framework builders and bean developers to design and build Java Beans frameworks and off-the-shelf beans. Each framework will undoubtedly provide different ways for users to assemble beans into applications; all framework and bean developers, however, should adhere to the Java Beans specification so that all beans are operable in all frameworks. For example, the specification prescribes a set of design patterns that a bean can follow to identify supported properties to a framework. A framework can then use these design patterns to gather the list of a bean's properties and allow a user to modify them through a graphical user interface.

A common use of Java Beans is to build non-distributed applications. Java Beans also defines various object buses (see Chapter 1 for the definition of this term) that a Java Beans application can use to connect to a server on a remote machine. With the introduction of object buses,

Java Beans technology becomes a full-fledged Software Component Infrastructure (SCI), extending from a local machine to the Internet and intranets. The current 1.0 specification of Java Beans provides for three object buses: *Remote Method Invocation* (RMI*), Internet Inter-ORB Protocol*(IIOP), and *Java Database Connectivity* (JDBC) database protocols. Please refer to Figure 4.1 for a pictorial representation of beans in a distributed environment.

A bean can communicate with other beans in the same JVM, or it can access remote objects in the network via RMI, IIOP, or JDBC.

RMI

RMI introduces a distributed programming mechanism for Java clients to invoke services of remote Java servers. RMI provides a pure Java solution to the problem of heterogeneous distributed computation: Java is used to define the distributed system interfaces, and it is used to implement the clients and servers that implement the interfaces.

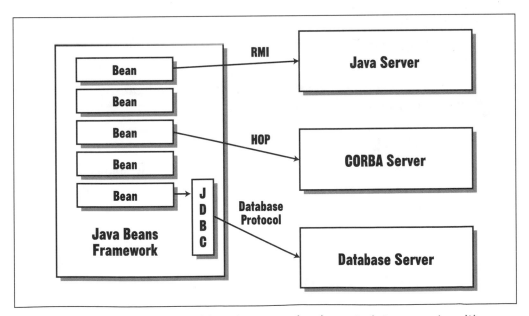

Figure 4.1   Java Beans provides three mechanisms to interoperate with remote objects.

IIOP

CORBA 2.0 stipulates an interoperability protocol between different ORBs that an ORB must implement in order to be considered CORBA 2.0 compliant. This protocol is called IIOP, which is the *General Inter-ORB Protocol* (GIOP) over TCP/IP. GIOP consists of three specifications: the Common Data Representation (CDR) definitions, GIOP message formats, and GIOP transport assumptions. GIOP is simple, inexpensive, and scaleable; it can even be scaled to the Internet. GIOP can be implemented on any reliable, connection-oriented protocol (such as Novell Netware's IPX), not just TCP/IP, although IIOP (GIOP over TCP/IP) is the only protocol that all ORB vendors are mandated to support. IIOP creates a federation of ORBs out of individual CORBA 2.0 ORBs designed by different vendors. A client can invoke the services of a server anywhere in the federation, not just a server in the same ORB as the client.

The use of IIOP is not limited to ORBs—any system that can communicate in IIOP can hook itself up to a CORBA 2.0 object bus and access CORBA servers. Java supports OMG IDL and provides an IDL compiler. The compiler generates Java stubs from IDL files; these stubs are analogues to CORBA static IDL stubs and COM proxy objects. Java stubs marshal the parameters of method calls and invoke the services of remote CORBA objects through IIOP.

A bean can access the services of a CORBA object in any CORBA 2.0-compliant ORB.

JDBC

JDBC is a specification for developing database applications that do not target a specific data source. At runtime, a JDBC application determines the database driver that it needs to load to connect to a specific data source. Many database connectivity vendors have committed to developing database drivers for JDBC. A very useful and easy-to-implement driver is a bridge from JDBC to ODBC. Because a variety of ODBC drivers currently exist, this bridge can connect JDBC applications to almost all different data sources.

A bean can use JDBC to connect itself to a data source. This data source can be on the same machine that the bean is running, or it can be somewhere else in the network. It is important to note that JDBC itself does not have any notions of remote processing—drivers use database protocols to access remote database servers.

Beans

As noted earlier, Java Beans defines a bean as a reusable software component that can be manipulated visually in a framework. There are a variety of frameworks, including Web pages, visual applications, GUI layout tools, and compound-document frameworks. Frameworks provide different ways for users to assemble beans into applications. For example, they may provide purely visual methods or allow users to write Java code that manipulates beans.

Beans have different levels of granularity, as we mentioned briefly at the start of this chapter. A bean can be fine-grained, medium-grained, or coarse-grained. Beans have different characteristics, depending on whether they operate at the design-time stage or the runtime stage. For example, a bean may provide substantial design-time functionality, which allows an application developer to instantiate and customize the bean in an application. This bean, however, need not present the same design-time behavior to an end user because the bean has already been customized. This distinction between different views of a bean is important; it will be discussed further in the next section.

As we pointed out in Chapter 3, because an ActiveX control is (usually) implemented as a DLL, it resides in the same process space as its container. As we will discuss in a later section, beans have a similar behavior. Like components in SCI, beans have properties, methods, and events. The subsections that follow explain the above topics in more detail, and they also introduce you to issues such as multi-threading and security.

 A bean is a reusable software component that can be visually instantiated and customized in a framework.

Different Views Of A Bean

Three different groups of people interact with beans: implementers (who create the beans), developers (who assemble the beans into applications), and end users. It is very important that you understand the distinction among the views of each of these groups.

A Bean Implementer's View

An implementer creates a bean according to requirements that prescribe (among other things) the graphical representation of the bean, the properties and methods that it supports, the events that it fires, and potentially an explicit customizer. The implementer adheres to the Java Beans specification to ensure that the bean can be used in all Java Beans frameworks. For example, the specification identifies a set of conventions for naming methods and interfaces, referred to as *design patterns*, so that a framework can infer information about a bean's properties, methods, and events. Failure to follow the specification will limit the use of a bean.

An implementer can use low-level programming APIs to create a bean. This approach might be practical for simple beans. For more complex beans, the implementer might use a visual tool.

It is important that you do not confuse the visual tool that an implementer uses to create a tool with the visual tool that an application developer employs to assemble beans.

We expect that bean implementers will have access to a wide range of bean builder tools, similar to the tools that ActiveX control implementers have at their disposal, such as the Control Development Kit (CDK) and the Control Wizard included in Microsoft's Visual C++. In addition to facilitating the process of bean development, a visual tool helps an implementer in adhering to the Java Beans specification. For instance, the implementer might use a dialog box to specify the properties of a bean to the tool; the tool then automatically generates properly named access methods for the properties.

A bean implementer is concerned with creating beans that meet functional requirements and adhere to the Java Beans specification. The customer of an implementer is an application developer.

An Application Developer's View

As an application developer, you build an application for end users that needs to meet certain requirements. You do not, however, start from scratch; you use a collection of off-the-shelf beans to assemble your application. As you saw in Chapter 1, this approach is fundamentally different from other approaches (such as procedural or object-oriented paradigms), and it can result in a tremendous code reuse.

You will use prefabricated beans to build the application. In some cases, however, you may not find a bean that meets your needs—if so, you'll require a *custom bean*. As we have already mentioned, the processes of bean creation and application development are fundamentally distinct. In a software organization, there are usually two groups of people: one group that develops custom beans, and one that uses the off-the-shelf and custom beans to build applications.

There are a number of commercial frameworks for assembling beans into applications (Chapter 5 presents a list of currently available frameworks). The Java Beans Developer's Kit (BDK) 1.0 also contains a rather simplistic framework, shown in Figure 4.2. This framework includes a container called BeanBox, a collection of beans organized in a

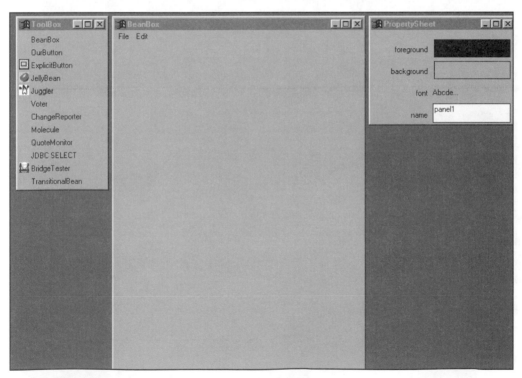

Figure 4.2 The BDK 1.0 framework includes a container, a toolbox, and a property editor.

toolbox, and a property editor called PropertySheet. All of these frameworks provide some level of visual aids for the instantiation and customization of beans. We will use the BDK framework to illustrate the process of application development using beans.

The application you'll build is a juggler animation. The juggler starts juggling by clicking a button labeled "start"; it is not required to stop the juggler from juggling. First, invoke the BDK framework and examine the list of available beans in the ToolBox. You'll notice that the ToolBox contains a Juggler bean and a ExplicitButton bean. If the ToolBox had not included either of these two beans, you would have to look in a catalog for other third-party beans or design a custom bean. You can click on the Juggler bean in the ToolBox and instantiate it somewhere in the BeanBox container (see Figure 4.3).

The container displays a visual representation of the Juggler bean. The instantiated bean is the current selection, and the PropertySheet lists the properties of the bean, such the foreground color, the background

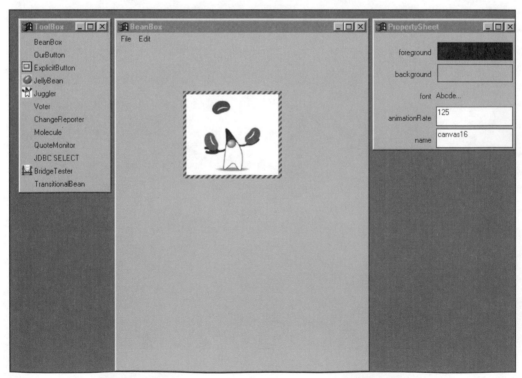

Figure 4.3 The BeanBox container after the instantiation of the Juggler bean.

color, and the animation rate. Now choose the ExplicitButton bean and instantiate it under the Juggler bean. The container displays the graphical representation of the button and chooses it as the current selection. Figure 4.4 illustrates the result.

Use the PropertySheet to change the label of the button from "press" to "start," as shown in Figure 4.5. The changes made to the label of the button in the PropertySheet are reflected in the instantiated bean as they are being made.

Now you'll use the visual features of the container to connect the button to the juggler. From the Edit menu, choose Edit|Events|button push|actionPerformed, as shown in Figure 4.6. The container provides a rubber-banding mechanism so that you can select the bean that should receive this event. Select the Juggler bean.

The container presents a dialog box (shown in Figure 4.7), asking the developer to select a target method in the Juggler bean that should be

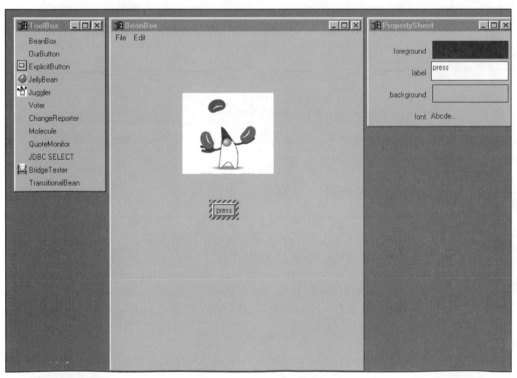

Figure 4.4   The container following the instantiation of the Juggler and ExplicitButton beans.

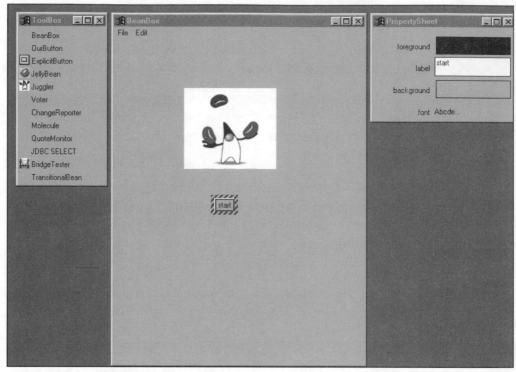

Figure 4.5 The container after changing the label of the button from "press" to "start."

invoked when the button fires a push event. Select "start" and click on OK in the dialog box. The container internally generates code to invoke the start method of the juggler when a user clicks on the button.

The application is now complete. Click on the start button, which will cause the juggler to start juggling.

This example illustrates the primary advantage of frameworks: a tremendous amount of code reuse. You started with prefabricated software components and used the framework to instantiate and connect the beans. You did not provide the structure of the application; the framework generated the architecture. The framework is written once and reused across many applications. (These ideas were discussed thoroughly in Chapter 1.)

Of course, this example is rather simplistic. In a real-world application you may not have located all the controls that you need. Furthermore, the process of customizing the controls is more complex than what we

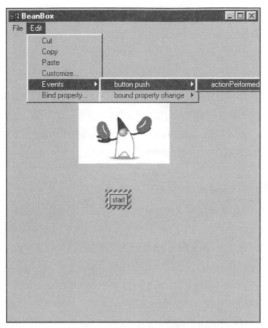

Figure 4.6   Attempting to connect the button to the juggler.

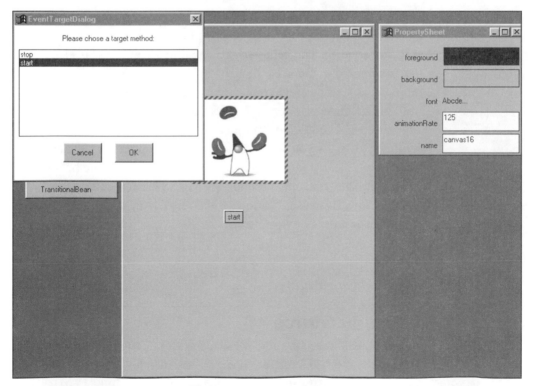

Figure 4.7   The dialog box listing the stop and start methods of the Juggler bean.

did together, and may involve writing Java code. As more beans and better frameworks become available, however, we can expect this process to become reasonably simple.

An application developer is concerned with assembling and customizing beans into applications. The customer of a developer is an end user. The implementer's view is also referred to as the design-time view.

AN END USER'S VIEW

For an end user, a Java Beans application is an ordinary application. You, as an end user, may not be able to infer that the application actually consists of a number of beans, or distinguish between the container and the beans. In the case of the juggler application, the application developer clicks on the start button and notices that the figure starts to juggle. As an end user, you are entirely oblivious to the fact that the application developer has connected the push event of the button to the start method of the juggler.

Because an end user usually does not need to customize an application, a bean does not need to have the same behavior in its developer's and end user's views. The behavior of a bean to an end user is also called the *runtime view*. Because the design-time behavior of a bean is not required at runtime, the code that implements the design-time view need not be present to run an application. For some beans, the code to support design-time views is much more than the code to support the runtime views. As you shall see later in this chapter, Java Beans specification has clearly separated the design-time and runtime behavior of a bean into different classes, allowing a browser to speed up the download of a Java Beans application by not transferring the classes required for the design-time environment.

An end user views a Java Beans application as an ordinary monolithic application.

Address Space

A bean runs in the same address space as its container. If the container is an application (as opposed to an applet), then both the container and contained beans run in the same Java Virtual Machine(JVM). If the container is an applet in a Web page, then the contained beans run in the JVM associated with the browser rendering the page. This JVM itself runs in the same address space as the browser.

A bean and its container run in the same Java Virtual Machine.

Invisible Beans

A visual representation constitutes an integral part of a bean. The bean implementer creates this GUI representation and associates it with the bean. A developer uses this representation to instantiate and customize the bean, while an end user uses it to interact with the bean.

A bean, however, may not have a GUI representation. Lack of a GUI might be useful for server applications, which do not have user interfaces. A bean's visual representation can be turned off at runtime; this feature allows an application to turn its GUI off if it is running as a server. Note that even though they lack graphical representations at runtime, invisible beans are still manipulated inside frameworks.

Beans that run in server applications usually do not have runtime visual representations.

Multi-Threading

Similar to other Java objects, beans run in a multi-threaded environment. In this environment, more than one thread of execution can invoke a bean's methods or set its properties. Therefore, beans implementers must ensure that their beans are thread-safe.

Internationalization

Java programs work in terms of locale-independent programmatic names. For example, a method calls another method by using its programmatic name, regardless of the current default locale. It is not a client's responsibility, however, to convert certain strings to the current locale. For example, imagine a class that returns the name of the default background color. This class is responsible for passing the localized color name to its callers. In general, a package should localize any appropriate strings (according to the current default locale) prior to passing it out through its public APIs.

The same guideline applies to beans. Because beans expose the names of their methods and properties to developers through frameworks, these methods and properties should be localized if they use the **FeatureDescriptor** class. In particular, the "display name" and "short help" strings supported by the **FeatureDescriptor** class need to be localized (the **FeatureDescriptor** class is covered in a later chapter).

A package is responsible for localizing appropriate variables before passing them out through its public APIs.

Properties

You have already been exposed to properties in Java Beans in the juggler example. We changed the label for the button from "press" to "start" by modifying the label property in the PropertySheet.

Java Beans introduces *bound* and *constrained* properties. When the value of a bound property changes, the bean owning the property sends out a notification message to all the beans that have expressed their interest in the property. A constrained property is similar to a bound property, except that other beans can veto a change in its value. Chapter 6 covers properties in detail.

Methods

A bean can have methods, which are similar to the methods of a Java class. Beans export their methods explicitly or implicitly through design patterns. For example, the Juggler bean described earlier exports two methods: start and stop. A framework can associate the events that a bean fires with methods in other beans; in this case, the firing of an event by a bean causes a method in another bean to run. Although we do not dedicate a chapter to methods, you will see many examples of method usage throughout this book.

Events

Events are the mechanism by which a bean informs other beans that something interesting has happened. In the juggler application, for example, the start button fires an event when pressed. Through the use of an *event listener*, the **start** event triggers the start method of the Juggler bean. Events are explained in detail in Chapters 7 and 8.

Security

As you know by now, a bean runs in the same process space as its container. Therefore, it is subject to the same security constraints as that container. Java Beans does not introduce any changes to the standard Java security model, which currently distinguishes three types of programs: *standalone applications*, *signed (trusted) applets*, and *unsigned (untrusted) applets*. Standalone applications and signed applets are not subject to any security restrictions; they can access local files and open network connections to any host in the network. Unsigned applets are subject to the Java sandbox model. Because they do not have permission to access local files or open socket connections to arbitrary hosts, they can only open up socket connections to the hosts that they originated from. There are three areas, however, that Java Beans developers need to pay special attention to: introspection, persistence, and menubar merging.

Beans running in full-fledged applications do not have any security constraints. Beans in an unsigned applet are constrained by a browser's security manager, which usually prevents the beans from accessing local files and opening arbitrary network connections.

INTROSPECTION

Introspection is the process of discovering a bean's properties, methods, and events at runtime. Framework developers can assume that they have unlimited access to the high-level introspection APIs and the low-level reflection APIs in the design-time environment (these APIs are explained in Chapter 9). In particular, standalone applications and signed applets can use the above APIs to discover all the data members and methods of a bean, including the private fields. Unsigned applets can only discover the public data members and public methods.

PERSISTENCE

Beans can store their internal states in both the design-time and runtime environments. For instance, as an application developer, you usually change the state of a bean through the process of customization after instantiating the bean in a container; this bean should save its design-time state for future invocations. Similarly, an end user may further customize the bean in the application, which causes the bean to store its runtime state for future use. As a bean implementer, you should keep in mind that at runtime you may not have access to local files if a bean is running in an unsigned environment. In this case, another application, such as a browser, might use the serialization techniques to read or store the state of the bean.

MENUBAR MERGING

Beans inside a standalone application or a signed applet can merge their menubars with their application or browser. Beans in an unsigned applet can merge their menubars with the applet; they cannot, however, do any kind of GUI merging with the browser running the applet.

Uniform Data Transfer (UDT)

UDT allows the transfer of structured data objects within the same application or between process boundaries through the clipboard or drag-and-drop. The AWT package in JDK 1.1 provides a number of new interfaces and classes to support UDT. For example, the Transferable interface defines abstractions for transferring data, and the **DataFlavor** class identifies the type of data.

Packaging

Unlike a class, a bean usually requires more than one file for its definition. For example, a bean may have an image file, a customizer file, a help file, and a file containing the behavior of the bean. It is critical that all of the files associated with a bean be packaged into a single archive file so that it can be easily transferred to application developers or downloaded by browsers.

Java Archive (JAR) is the utility that is used to package beans. A JAR file has a ZIP format and may contain a manifest file, which describes the contents of the JAR file. A single JAR file can contain more than one bean, and it may be signed by the private key of the person or vendor who has developed the bean. A browser can verify this signature when it downloads the bean and grant it additional privileges.

Packaging is the process of archiving all the files associated with a bean into a single ZIP file.

Conclusion

In this chapter we laid the groundwork for Java Beans. We introduced you to the Java Beans SCI and explored the three different object buses: RMI, IIOP, and JDBC. We then discussed beans and emphasized the three different views of beans; we also took you through the step-by-step development of the juggler example. We finally introduced you to multi-threading, security, properties, events, properties, and packaging in Java Beans.

We are going to shift gears in Part II of this book. We have dedicated each chapter to covering one aspect of Java Beans in gory detail and providing numerous code segments. In the next chapter, you will develop your first Java Beans application: the HelloWorld program.

PART 2

Fundamentals Of Java Beans

Part II of this book will introduce you to the principles of the Java Beans technology. Chapter 5 demonstrates the famous HelloWorld application built on top of Java Beans. Chapter 6 is dedicated entirely to discussing properties. You'll see single-valued, indexed, bound, and constrained properties with numerous code samples.

Chapter 7 focuses on the advantages of the JDK 1.1 delegation-based event model. Chapter 8 explains event handling in extended AWT components. Chapters 7 and 8 will be useful to AWT programmers who need to understand the new event model.

Chapter 9 covers the object serialization techniques, covers the Object Serialization facility of Java Beans and presents design guidelines for bean persistence. Chapter 10 discusses the Java Core Reflection API. It shows you how to write programs that examine the data members, member methods, and constructors of a class. An understanding of the Reflection API sheds light on the automatic analysis process, which is used to deduce the properties, methods, and events of a bean.

Chapter 11 shows you how to provide explicit information about your beans. This information can be used instead of, or in conjunction with, any implicit information obtained by the automatic analysis process. Finally, Chapter 12 teaches you how to provide custom property editors for your beans.

Completing Part II of this book will familiarize you with the fundamentals of Java Beans, and you will be ready to apply them to developing Java Beans applications.

Chapter 5

- **HelloWorld program**

- **Simple PushButton and HelloDisplay custom beans**

- **Manual assembly of beans**

- **Visually-aided assembly of beans**

- **Currently available frameworks**

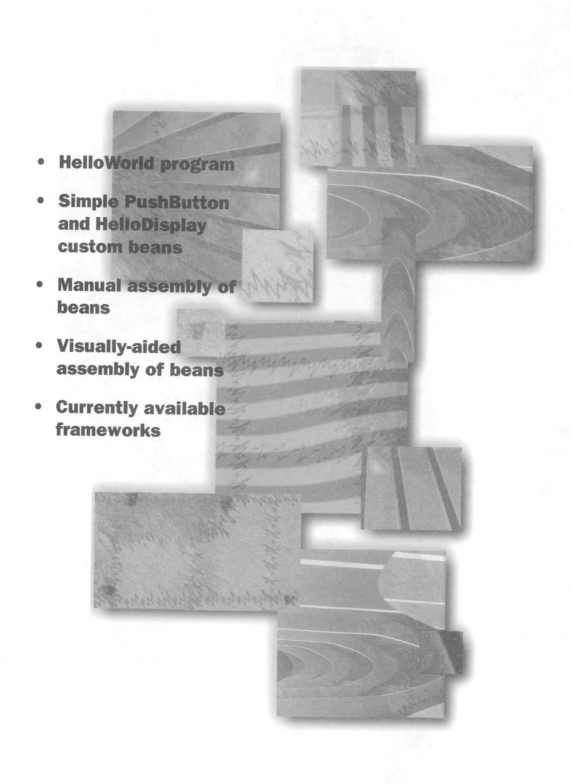

HelloWorld Bean Application

This chapter presents the HelloWorld program, which is one of the simplest applications built with beans. This program provides a user interface that consists of three beans: a display bean and two button beans. Clicking one of the buttons causes the message "Hello World" to appear in the display bean; clicking the other button clears the display bean. The HelloWorld program illustrates many important concepts of the Java Beans technology, including bean creation, properties, events, event listeners, and methods.

This chapter also provides two simplified examples of custom beans. These beans are created from scratch by extending appropriate classes in AWT and packaged by the jar facility available in JDK 1.1.

There are two methods for assembling beans into applications: programmatic and visual. In the programmatic approach, a programmer develops an application by writing Java code that instantiates beans, customizes them, and connects the instances together. This approach is fundamentally similar to other object-oriented software development techniques and has the drawback that the programmer must supply the structure of the application. In the visual method, a developer usually uses drag-and-drop to instantiate beans and works with the menu bar and the property sheet editor to customize them. In this case, the framework automatically supplies some or all of the program structure, resulting in increased productivity. In this chapter, we use both the programmatic and visual methods to develop the HelloWorld example.

The availability of high-performance Java Beans frameworks is critical to developing real-world bean applications. These frameworks should provide visual methods for developers to instantiate and customize beans into applications. Additionally, frameworks need to allow developers to customize the beans further by directly entering Java or scripting code in the framework. This chapter provides a quick survey of some of the currently available frameworks.

Java Beans Frameworks

This section provides an overview of the Java Beans frameworks that were available or advertised as this book went to press. This list is not comprehensive, and we do not intend to endorse any particular framework. You can use the Web sites listed in the "Further Readings" section at the end of this chapter to research these frameworks further and choose one that meets your specific requirements. Note that these frameworks are not specifically designed for Java Beans; rather, they are integrated design environments (IDEs) that have been enhanced to support the Java Beans architecture.

We have decided to use the BeanBox framework for application development. This decision has its advantages and disadvantages. BeanBox is simple and does not have the sophistication of other frameworks, but it is free and we can assume that you have access to it. Another advantage of BeanBox is that it allows you to focus on the fundamentals of Java Beans without getting bogged down into particularities of any specific framework.

AppletAuthor

AppletAuthor provides a palette of beans that can be dropped into a container and assembled together to form an applet. The palette of beans includes multimedia sounds and animations, effects (such as stock ticker tapes), buttons, and lists. It also provides a JDBC bean that can be used for database access. AppletAuthor is marketed by IBM Corporation and should be commercially available in the first quarter of 1997.

Java Workshop

The current 1.0 release of Java Workshop provides Web-centered development tools, a GUI builder, an integrated toolset, multiple-platform support, and publication tools. The next release of Java Workshop will support Java Beans and provide other enhancements, such as remote debugging and just-in-time (JIT) compilers. Java Workshop is developed by SunSoft, a division of Sun Microsystems, Inc., and is anticipated to be available in the first half of 1997.

JBuilder

JBuilder provides visual design tools and wizards to create custom beans. You can visually instantiate and link custom, out-of-the-box, or off-the-shelf beans into applications. The JBuilder's DataDirector contains database beans, which allow you to develop database applications quickly. Some of the subsystems of JBuilder's environment, such as the component designer and the two-way tool engine, are built on top of Java Beans. JBuilder is a product of Borland International, Inc.

Mojo

Mojo comprises two parts: a GUI designer and a coder. The designer provides a visual mechanism for building Java applications, whereas the coder provides direct access to all aspects of coding. The Mojo 2.0 Enterprise Edition, slated for release by the end of 1996, will support only the transitional Java Beans model. This model is a temporary solution for bean application development until JDK 1.1 becomes available. Mojo 3.0, scheduled for release in the first quarter of 1997, will fully support the Java Beans architecture. Mojo is developed by Penumbra Software.

Project Studio

Project Studio in an integrated visual assembly environment for creating, accessing, and publishing HTML content and Java applets. This framework includes a powerful set of business beans for charting, graphing, database access, spreadsheets, white boards, and chatting. SunSoft, a division of Sun Microsystems, Inc., expects to deliver Project Studio in the first half of 1997.

VisualAge

VisualAge is geared toward client/server application development. It assists users with the user interface and network aspects of distributed programs, thereby allowing them to focus on the logic of their applications. VisualAge, scheduled for release in the summer of 1997, is marketed by IBM Corporation.

Visual Café

Visual Café provides a library of standard beans to be visually linked with applications. Visual Café also includes an extensive set of source code development tools that are integrated seamlessly into the visual tools. Symantec Corporation develops and markets this framework.

BeanBox

You should already be familiar with the BeanBox framework from the previous chapter. As noted earlier, BeanBox is very simple and does not include many of the features available in the other frameworks; as a result, it is not suitable for developing complex applications. BeanBox is freely available as a part of BDK 1.0, however, and is adequate for certain applications. Because the current 1.0 beta release of BeanBox cannot save a bean application as a class file, you must always use it to run BeanBox-generated applications—you cannot run them in a browser or as standalone applications. This is obviously a limitation and may be fixed in a later release.

If you are planning to use BeanBox, you need to install both the JDK 1.1 and BDK 1.0 releases, because the current 1.0 beta release of BDK is not packaged with JDK. The "Further Readings" section of this chapter includes Web sites for information on JDK and BDK.

 *You must install JDK 1.1 to use BDK 1.0. The previous releases of JDK are not compatible with BDK 1.0.*

Coding Standards

We do not intend to present a formal treatment of Java coding standards, because this book is not about the Java programming language. We will, however, introduce you to some guidelines that we have followed in all of our sample examples.

Coding standards are established to promote consistency in coding among a group of programmers and facilitate understanding of programs written by other people. Many of the choices made in defining these standards are arbitrary; they often do not signify any advantage over other alternatives.

We employ the convention of capitalizing class names and starting the names of variables and methods with lowercase letters. Variables that are declared **final** must be entirely in uppercase letters. So, for instance, class **Foo** has a final variable **PI** and a method **fooBar**, which has a local variable called **bar**. We also adhere to the Java Beans guidelines for naming event and listener classes: we end the name of an event class with **Event** and the name of a listener class with **Listener**. Therefore, **ActionEvent** is a valid name for an event class and **ActionListener** is a properly named listener class. Listener classes are explained later in this chapter.

We also introduce certain guidelines of our own. All of the Java interfaces must start with **I**, and all of the exception classes must begin with **E**. Furthermore, the name of a non-static data member of a class starts with **m_**. For example, the interface **IFoo** throws an exception of type **EBar**, which has a data member called **m_reason**. The curly brackets { and } must always appear on a line by themselves to enhance code readability.

In addition, for publishing reasons, we adhere to a requirement that code listings must not exceed 55 characters per line. As a result, we need to break the lines in places that we would otherwise not do so. This requirement has also forced us to limit the length of some identifiers; for example, in most situations we have chosen the name **l** for a variable of type Listener instead of the more intuitive **listener**.

HelloWorld Beans

The HelloWorld example needs two kinds of beans: a button and a display bean. The button is the source of events, and the display bean responds to the events generated by the button. One of the early tasks of a bean application developer is to identify and locate all the controls that are needed. These controls can be out-of-the-box beans provided by the framework, off-the-shelf-components supplied by third-party control vendors, or custom beans.

For the HelloWorld application, BDK 1.0 already provides an OurButton bean, which fires events of type **ActionEvent**. We, however, implement our own PushButton bean for two reasons. First, the OurButton bean does not adhere to the JDK 1.1 event handling model. Second, because it is a more complex bean than PushButton, it is not very suitable for being analyzed as an introductory bean. A display bean that can display the "Hello World" text does not come with the BeanBox framework, and we, therefore, implement a custom HelloDisplay component. These beans are explained in details in the subsequent sections.

You need to design custom beans if you cannot find the controls you need in your framework's palette of beans or third-party component catalogs.

PushButton Bean

In this section we implement a PushButton bean from scratch. When clicked, this button generates an **ActionEvent**. Other beans can express their interest in this event to the PushButton bean; they will then get notified when a user clicks on the button. PushButton also provides a property called **label**, which can be changed programmatically or visually within a framework. Listing 5.1 presents this bean.

Listing 5.1   The PushButton bean.

```
package mybeans.pushbutton;

import java.awt.*;
import java.awt.event.*;
import java.util.Vector;
import java.beans.*;
```

```java
/**
 * A simple push button bean.
 * This bean has a label property and fires an
 * ActionEvent when pressed.
 */
public class PushButton extends Canvas
{
  // List of all listeners who are interested in the
  // push event generated by this component.
  //
  private Vector m_pushLs = new Vector();
  private String m_label;

  // Constants to control the display of the label.
  //
  static final int XPAD = 10;
  static final int YPAD = 8;


  /**
   * Constructs a PushButton with a default label.
   */
  public PushButton()
  {
    this("push");
  }

  /**
   * Constructs a PushButton with a specified label.
   * @param label the label of the button
   */
  public PushButton(String label)
  {
    super();
    setFont(new Font("Dialog", Font.PLAIN, 12));

    m_label = label;

    // Inform the superclass that this component
    // is interested in mouse events.
    //
    enableEvents(AWTEvent.MOUSE_EVENT_MASK);
  }
```

```
/**
 * Returns the label of the button.
 *
 * @see #setLabel
 */
public String getLabel()
{
  return m_label;
}


/**
 * Sets the button's label and changes its size to
 * fit the label.
 *
 * @see #getLabel
 */
public void
setLabel(String label)
{
  m_label = label;
  sizeToFit();
}



/**
 * Informs the component that this ActionListener
 * is interested in the action events generated by
 * this component.
 *
 * Note: the JavaBeans specification does not
 * require ActionListeners to run in any
 * particular order.
 *
 * @see #removeActionListener
 * @param listener the ActionListener
 */
public synchronized void
addActionListener(ActionListener l)
{
  m_pushLs.addElement(l);
}

/**
 * Informs the component that this ActionListener
 * is no longer interested in the action events
 * generated by this component.
 *
```

```java
 * @see #addActionListener
 * @param listener the ActionListener
 */
public synchronized void
removeActionListener(ActionListener l)
{
  m_pushLs.removeElement(l);
}



/**
 * Paints the button.
 * The label is centered in both dimensions.
 *
 */
public synchronized void paint(Graphics g)
{
  int width = size().width;
  int height = size().height;

  g.setColor(getBackground());
  g.fillRect(1, 1, width - 2, height - 2);
  g.draw3DRect(0, 0, width - 1, height - 1, true);

  g.setColor(getForeground());
  g.setFont(getFont());

  g.drawRect(2, 2, width - 4, height - 4);

  FontMetrics fm = g.getFontMetrics();
  g.drawString(m_label,
    (width - fm.stringWidth(m_label)) / 2,
    (height + fm.getMaxAscent() -
    fm.getMaxDescent()) / 2);
}



/**
 * Processes the mouse events.
 * This method generates an ActionEvent in
 * response to a mouse click and calls
 * processActionEvent to handle the event.
 */
protected boolean
processMouseEvent(MouseEvent eve)
{
  switch(eve.getId())
    {
```

```
      case MouseEvent.MOUSE_CLICKED:
      {
        ActionEvent actEve;
        actEve = new ActionEvent(this, 0, null);
        processActionEvent(actEve);

        break;
      }

      default:
      {
        break;
      }
    }

    // It is important to call the superclass event
    // handling method somewhere in the code.
    //
    return super.processMouseEvent(eve);
  }


  /**
   * Processes the action of clicking on the button.
   * This method calls the actionPerformed() methods
   * of all the listeners who have expressed their
   * interest by calling addActionListener().
   */
  protected void
  processActionEvent(ActionEvent eve)
  {
    Vector ls;

    // All the listeners who have expressed their
    // interest at the time the component triggers
    // an event must get notified.
    // Therefore, you must clone the listeners in a
    // synchronized block to ensure that a listener
    // who had expressed its interest before the
    // trigger gets notified if it is removed from
    // the list of listeners by another thread.
    //
    synchronized (this)
    {
      ls = (Vector) m_pushLs.clone();
    }
```

```java
      for (int i = 0; i < ls.size(); i++)
      {
        ActionListener l;
        l = (ActionListener)ls.elementAt(i);
        l.actionPerformed(eve);
      }
    }


    /**
     * Calculates and returns a suitable size for
     * the button.
     */
    public Dimension getPreferredSize()
    {
      FontMetrics fm = getFontMetrics(getFont());
      Dimension dim;
      dim = new Dimension(fm.stringWidth(m_label) +
                    XPAD,
                    fm.getMaxAscent() +
                      fm.getMaxDescent() + YPAD);
      return dim;
    }

    /**
     * Calculates and returns the minimum size of
     * the button.
     */
    public Dimension getMinimumSize()
    {
      return getPreferredSize();
    }

    /*
     * Resizes the button to fit the label.
     */
    private void sizeToFit()
    {
      Dimension d = getPreferredSize();
      resize(d.width, d.height);

      Component comp = getParent();
      if (comp != null)
      {
        comp.invalidate();
        comp.layout();
      }
    }
}
```

You might be wondering about the length of this code in contrast to that of the HelloWorld program written in C or in Java without using beans. If so, keep in mind that PushButton is a reusable software component built from scratch; it can potentially be used in any application that requires **ActionEvent**s. Its code is no more complicated than an AWT widget that has similar functionality. Actually, this bean is indistinguishable from an ordinary AWT component, although this situation will change as we add more features to the bean. Second, the PushButton code is quite straightforward: it extends the **Canvas** class and displays a GUI, supports one property, and fires an action event.

EXTENDING THE AWT COMPONENT CLASS

A bean usually extends the AWT **Component** class or one of its subclasses. The PushButton bean, for instance, extends **Canvas**, which is a direct subclass of **Component**.

The new event model in JDK 1.1 is fundamentally different than the previous releases of JDK. According to this model, a custom class extended from **Component** does not receive any events unless it either registers a *listener* class with its superclass or explicitly enables the delivery of events. A listener class implements a callback method, which can be invoked when an interesting event occurs in a component. The **PushButton** class calls **enableEvents(AWTEvent.MOUSE_EVENT_MASK)** to express its interest in receiving mouse events.

 *A custom bean usually calls **enableEvents()** to express its interest in receiving certain events, which are designated by the argument passed to **enableEvents()**.*

The PushButton bean displays a graphical user interface to a user by overriding the **paint()** method, which draws a rectangle and displays the label of the button. As we mentioned in Chapter 4, a bean may elect not to provide a GUI. Such invisible beans are used as shared resources or in server-side applications. PushButton, however, is always used on the client side and supplies a visual representation.

SUPPORTING THE LABEL PROPERTY

PushButton supports a property that keeps track of its label. You probably have already used properties in your Java programs. A property is very much like a regular data member of a class, although there are some distinctions. First, its value can be accessed or modified through accessor methods. Second, it usually represents an aspect of the visual representation or functionality of a bean. Third, the accessor methods that manipulate a property must adhere to certain naming conventions (design patterns).

The PushButton bean supplies two accessor methods for **label**;the names of these accessor methods, **getLabel()** and **setLabel()**, follow the Java Beans naming guidelines. A framework can use the introspection API to inquire about the methods that this bean supports and conclude that PushButton supports the **label** property. The framework can then display this property in a property editor and allow a user to manipulate it. Note that the framework determines the name of a property by analyzing the names of its accessor methods, not the actual name of the data member. The PushButton bean, for example, internally uses the variable **m_label** for the **label** property; this name, however, is never used by a framework. Please refer to Chapter 6 for a detailed discussion of properties.

*A framework analyzes the names of **getLabel()** and **setLabel()** methods and determines that PushButton supports a read/ write property called **label**.*

FIRING ACTION EVENTS

PushButton has asked for the delivery of mouse events by calling **enableEvents()**, but how should these events be routed to it? According to the JDK 1.1 event model, **PushButton** can override **processMouseEvent()** and supply its own event handling routine. This method takes **MouseEvent** as a parameter, which contains the type of the mouse event, such as pressing, releasing, or clicking, and other useful information, for example, the number of the clicks.

PushButton is only interested in the mouse clicks; it therefore checks the ID of the event and, if it is that of a mouse click, it creates an event of type **ActionEvent** and calls **processActionEvent()** for further processing. Although **PushButton** ignores all other event types, it calls its superclass **processMouseEvent()** and gives its parent a chance to run its event handling code.

The **processActionEvent()** method simply notifies all the listener classes by invoking their **actionPerformed()** methods and passing the specific instance of the event. The mechanism that Java Beans uses to propagate events is called *callback*, which is identical to callback classes in Java and function pointers in C and C++. In this model, an object supplies a callback function pointer or object to another object, which in turn calls the callback when an interesting event transpires. Note that because Java does not have function pointers, only classes can be supplied as callbacks. PushButton keeps track of all the callbacks in its internal data member **m_pushLs**. PushButton first clones this variable and then retrieves and invokes all the callbacks in its own thread. The cloning of callbacks is important; it ensures that a listener who has been registered at the time an event occurs will get notified if it is removed from **m_pushLs** by another thread before **processActionEvent()** has had a chance to invoke the callback.

So far, you know how a bean receives events from Java environment and the manner in which it dispatches the events to all the interested listener classes. You may not know, however, how a bean allows a class to register its interest in an event generated by it. For every event that it fires, a bean should provide a pair of properly named methods that add and remove listeners to the list of callbacks interested in that event. **PushButton** supplies **addActionListener()** and **removeActionListener()**. The argument to these methods is an **ActionListener** object, which implements the **actionPerformed()** method. These two methods simply update **m_pushLs**.

A framework concludes that a bean fires an event of type <listener-type> if it sees a pair of methods, **add<listener-type>(<listener-type>)** and **remove<listener-type>(<listener-type>)** (In the PushButton bean, for example, the listener type is **ActionListener**). Furthermore, the framework can determine the names of the callback methods in a listener object and present a graphical list to a user. The ins and outs of events and the new model in JDK 1.1 are discussed in Chapter 7.

 A custom bean needs to provide a pair of add/remove methods for every event type that it generates.

COMPILING

Compiling a bean is very similar to compiling a Java class. A bean, however, usually consists of more than one class: it can have an icon, a customizer, a **BeanInfo** class, and so on. Therefore, all of the bean class files and all other resource files must be packaged and delivered as a unit. JDK 1.1 provides a utility, called *Java archive* (JAR), that supports the ZIP format and can bundle a number of files into one flat JAR file.

Another complication when compiling a bean is the configuration management. Because a bean comprises more than one file, we need to ensure that proper versions of files are packaged together and that the JAR file is recreated whenever any of the bean's files changes. The best way to manage this complexity is through the use of makefiles. We have provided makefiles for Windows 95 for all the sample beans in this book; you can easily change these makefiles to run on UNIX platforms. To run the makefiles, you need to have access to the **nmake** utility (which is available in many of Microsoft's development environments, such as Visual C++). Listing 5.2 shows the PushButton makefile.

Listing 5.2   The PushButton Makefile.

```
NAME= PushButton

CLASSFILES= \
  PushButton.class

GIFFILES=

JARFILE= ..\..\jars\pushbutton.jar

all: $(JARFILE)

# Create a JAR file with manifest.

$(JARFILE): $(CLASSFILES) $(GIFFILES)
  echo Manifest-Version: 1.0 > manifest.tmp
  echo.  >> manifest.tmp
  echo Name: $(NAME).class >> manifest.tmp
  echo Java-Bean: True >> manifest.tmp
  jar cfm $(JARFILE) manifest.tmp *.class $(GIFFILES)
  @-del manifest.tmp


.SUFFIXES: .java .class
```

```
.java.class :
  javac $<

clean:
  -del *.class
  -del $(JARFILE)
```

The PushButton bean currently consists of only one Java source file, PushButton.java. The PushButton makefile, pushbutton.mk, first compiles this file and then creates a manifest file for PushButton. JAR utility and manifest files are explained in detail in Chapter 12. The makefile packages the class file and the manifest file into pushbutton.jar, which is saved in a directory called jars.

All of the beans developed in this book are located in the mybeans directory in the CD-ROM. Each bean has its own directory and defines a package mybeans.<bean-name>. The PushButton bean, for example, is located under mybeans\pushbutton and is packaged into mybeans.pushbutton. The beans' JAR files are all located in the jars directory, which is in the same place as the mybeans directory.

You can copy the sample files from the CD-ROM and run pushbutton.mk makefile, shown in the following code segment. Make sure that you have the JDK 1.1 bin directory in your path and have set the CLASSPATH environment variable to include both the JDK 1.1 and BDK 1.0 class files.

```
e:\coriolis\cdrom\mybeans\pushbutton>nmake pushbutton.mk

Microsoft (R) Program Maintenance Utility    Version 1.61.6038
Copyright (C) Microsoft Corp 1988-1996. All rights reserved.

        javac PushButton.java
        echo Manifest-Version: 1.0 > manifest.tmp
        echo.  >> manifest.tmp
        echo Name: PushButton.class >> manifest.tmp
        echo Java-Bean: True >> manifest.tmp
        jar cfm ..\..\jars\pushbutton.jar manifest.tmp *.class
Deleting E:\coriolis\cdrom\mybeans\pushbutton\manifest.tmp
    1 file deleted        16,384 bytes freed
```

```
e:\coriolis\cdrom\mybeans\pushbutton>cd..\..\jars

e:\coriolis\cdrom\jars>dir

 Volume in drive E is unlabeled      Serial number is 3294:E277
 Directory of  E:\coriolis\cdrom\jars\*.*

12/24/96   9:13        <DIR>    .
12/24/96   9:13        <DIR>    ..
12/26/96   9:05             864  hellodisplay.jar
12/27/96  15:06           2,136  pushbutton.jar
        3,000 bytes in 2 files and 2 dirs     32,768 bytes
allocated
   315,260,928 bytes free

e:\coriolis\cdrom\jars>jar tf pushbutton.jar
META-INF/MANIFEST.MF
PushButton.class

e:\coriolis\cdrom\jars>
```

HelloDisplay Bean

The PushButton bean generates events of type **ActionEvent** when a
user clicks on it. We need another bean that can react to these events
and display the "Hello World" text or clear it. Therefore, we create
another custom bean, called HelloDisplay; it has two methods, **on()**
and **off()**, that turn its display screen on and off. Listing 5.3 shows the
entire **HelloDisplay** source code.

*HelloDisplay is not a general-purpose bean; we have
solely designed it to facilitate the comprehension of Java
Beans concepts.*

Listing 5.3   The HelloDisplay bean.

```
package mybeans.hellodisplay;

import java.awt.*;
import java.awt.event.*;
import java.beans.*;


/**
 * This class displays the "Hello World" text in a
 * text field.
```

```
 * It provides two services for ActionEvents: on()
 * off(). The on() method turns the display on while
 * the off() method clears the display.
 */
public class HelloDisplay extends TextField
{
  private String m_text = "Hello World";

  public HelloDisplay()
  {
    super("", 11);
    setEditable(false);
  }

  public void on(ActionEvent eve)
  {
    setText(m_text);
  }

  public void off(ActionEvent eve)
  {
    setText("");
  }
}
```

When you visually connect an event fired by a bean to a target bean, a framework generates and displays the list of only those methods in the target bean that accept the same event type as the argument. For example, when connecting the PushButton **actionPerformed()** method to HelloDisplay, BeanBox lists only the **on()** and **off()** methods because they take one argument of type **ActionEvent**.

Programmatic Assembly Of HelloWorld Beans

The PushButton and HelloDisplay beans must be linked together to create the HelloWorld application. Although a framework is the natural choice for carrying out the linking process, Java Beans does not mandate the use of frameworks. Instead, a bean application developer can instantiate and connect the components in a program—that is, by supplying the programming structure and flow of the control. To illustrate the programmatic linkage of beans, we have created the HelloWorld applet, which is shown in Listing 5.4.

Listing 5.4   The handmade HelloWorld applet.

```java
import java.awt.*;
import java.awt.event.*;

import mybeans.pushbutton.*;
import mybeans.hellodisplay.*;


/**
 * This class assembles three beans into an applet:
 * a display bean, an "on" button and an "off" button.
 * The beans are hooked up so that the pushing of the
 * "on" button causes the message "Hello World" to
 * appear in the display bean. The "off" button turns
 * the display off.
 */
public class HelloWorld extends java.applet.Applet
{
  HelloDisplay hellodisp;

  public void init()
  {
    setLayout(new FlowLayout());

    // Add the display.
    //
    hellodisp = new HelloDisplay();
    add(hellodisp);

    // Add the "on" button.
    //
    PushButton btnOn = new PushButton("on");
    btnOn.addActionListener(new OnButtonListener());
    add(btnOn);

    // Add the "off" button.
    //
    PushButton btnOff = new PushButton("off");
    btnOff.addActionListener(new OffButtonListener());
    add(btnOff);
  }


  /*
   * This class calls the "on" method of the display
   * bean.
   */
```

```
class OnButtonListener implements ActionListener
{
  public void actionPerformed(ActionEvent eve)
  {
    hellodisp.on(eve);
  }
}


/*
 * This class calls the "off" method of the display
 * bean.
 */
class OffButtonListener implements ActionListener
{
  public void actionPerformed(ActionEvent eve)
  {
    hellodisp.off(eve);
  }
}
}
```

The HelloWorld applet creates an instance of the HelloDisplay bean and adds it to the applet container. It then instantiates PushButton and calls the button's **addActionListener()** method to express its interest in receiving action events from PushButton. This first button will act as the "on" button. As an argument to **addActionListener()**, HelloDisplay must supply an object that implements the **ActionListener** interface.

Note that all the listeners defined by Java Beans are interfaces, not classes; it is impossible to define generic listener classes. HelloDisplay, for instance, defines **OnButtonListener**, which implements the **ActionListener** interface and defines the **actionPerformed()** method to invoke the **on()** method of HelloDisplay. The **OnButtonListener** class performs a similar task, mapping the click on the "off" button to the **off()** method of PushButton.

Let's go through the sequence of steps that takes place when a user clicks the "on" button. When a user uses a mouse to interact with the PushButton bean, the Java event system calls the bean's **processMouseEvent()** to process the mouse event. This method checks to determine whether or not the mouse event is a click; if so, it goes through the list of all the listeners that have been added to its internal list through calls to

addActionListener(). (Actually, an internal method within PushButton performs this task). It finds only one listener, **OnButtonListener**, and invokes the listener's **actionPerformed()** in its own thread. This method, in turn, calls the **on()** method of HelloDisplay, causing the "Hello World" text to appear. At this point, **actionPerformed()** returns, and PushButton discovers that there are no more listeners. As the final step in the sequence, PushButton calls its superclass **processMouseEvent()** method and then stays idle until it is notified by the Java event system about further mouse events.

In the new event model in JDK 1.1, a component stays idle until it is notified about an event in which the component has expressed interest. This new model should result in considerable performance increase over the older event model.

Compile and run the HelloWorld applet. You can use the **appletviewer** tool in JDK 1.1 or use a browser that is compatible with JDK 1.1. Listing 5.5 lists a sample HTML file that you can use, and Figure 5.1 shows the applet running in **appletviewer**.

All the sample programs for a chapter that are not beans are located in a directory named Chap<n>, where <n> is the chapter number.

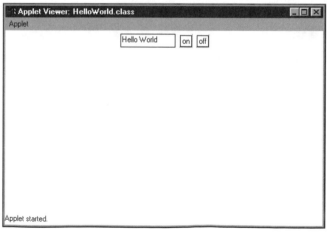

Figure 5.1 The HelloWorld applet.

Listing 5.5   A sample HelloWorld HTML file.

```
<HTML>
<HEAD>
<TITLE>Hello World</TITLE>
</HEAD>
<BODY>
<APPLET code="HelloWorld.class" width=500 height=300>
</APPLET>
</BODY>
</HTML>
```

When you look at the code for the HelloWorld applet, you might wonder how programming using beans is different than using regular AWT widgets. In fact, aside from the new event model and increased performance, there is not much difference. If you programmatically assemble beans into an application, you have to supply the structure of the application. If you use a framework, however, the framework visually assists you in assembling your beans, and it generates the flow of control for you.

Visual Assembly Of The HelloWorld Beans

Two tasks are required in order to build the HelloWorld program visually. First, you need to add the custom PushButton and HelloDisplay beans to your framework. Second, you need to assemble the beans in the framework.

Adding Beans To A Framework

A framework almost always comes with a palette of beans, but it should also allow you to add custom or third-party controls to the palette. There is no standard way of adding controls; each framework might provide a different procedure. Consult the manuals of the framework you are using to understand its procedure.

BeanBox looks into the contents of the jar directory (which is located in the same directory as the beanbox directory) and compares the beans located in that directory to the beans in its ToolBox. If the jar directory contains a new bean or a newer version of an existing bean, BeanBox updates its ToolBox. You can copy the jar files that you created for

PushButton and HelloDisplay into the BeanBox jar directory and run the makefile located in the beanbox directory:

```
d:\beans\beanbox>nmake run
```

The above command updates the beans in the ToolBox and runs the BeanBox. You should see the PushButton and HelloDisplay bean at the end of the ToolBox. If you are on a UNIX platform, you must use the supplied GNUmakefile.

If you want to simply run the BeanBox without updating the ToolBox, you can also use the run.bat file for Windows or run.sh for UNIX.

Assembling The HelloWorld Application

After you have updated the BeanBox framework, choose the PushButton bean from the ToolBox and instantiate it in the BeanBox container. Notice that the PropertySheet displays the **label** of the button, in addition to the other properties that have been defined in the PushButton superclasses. BeanBox has determined the presence of the editable **label** property by the virtue of the fact that PushButton has defined the **getLabel()** and **setLabel()** methods. Figure 5.2 shows the BeanBox after the instantiation of PushButton. Change **label** to "on," create a second "off" button, and instantiate the HelloDisplay bean.

You now need to connect your beans. Select the "on" button and choose Edit|Events|action|actionPerformed from the menu bar (see Figure 5.3). The BeanBox can determine that the button generates an "action" event by the presence of the **addActionListener(ActionListener)** and **removeActionListener(ActionListener)** methods defined in PushButton. Note that in Figure 5.3, BeanBox displays "action" when it lists the events; the "listener" part of **ActionListener** is superfluous. The other events shown in Figure 5.3 are inherited by PushButton from its parents. Also note that BeanBox has listed the name of the callback **actionPerformed()** method defined by the **ActionListener** interface.

Visually connect **actionPerformed()** to the HelloDisplay bean. The BeanBox framework pops up a dialog box, shown in Figure 5.4, that lists all the potential target methods in HelloDisplay. The framework

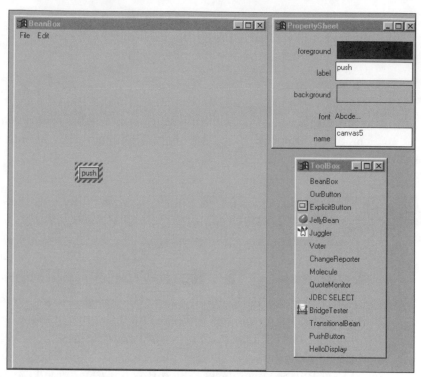

Figure 5.2 The BeanBox after the instantiation of PushButton.

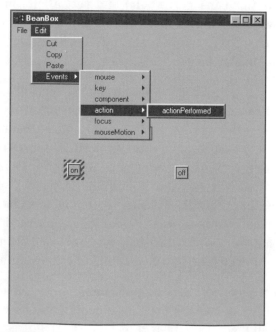

Figure 5.3 The BeanBox lists all of the events fired by PushButton.

Figure 5.4 The dialog box listing the target methods of HelloDisplay.

generates this list by going through all the public methods of HelloDisplay and keeping the ones that take one argument of type **ActionEvent**, which is the argument type taken by **actionPerformed**().

Conclusion

The HelloWorld application clearly shows the power of frameworks. You visually use the framework to instantiate and link your beans; internally, the framework generates the structure of your application. In HelloWorld, for example, the framework generates all the code you would have to otherwise write yourself.

This chapter has introduced you to a very simple bean application. We deliberately eliminated a lot of details from this chapter so that you could focus on the concepts. The next chapters, however, will take you through the ins and outs of all the important aspects of Java Beans. You will learn about properties, the first of these aspects, in the next chapter.

Further Readings
Web Resources

AppletAuthor: http://www.ibm.com/Java

Java Workshop: http://www.sun.com/workshop/java

JBuilder: http://www.borland.com

Mojo: http://www.PenumbraSoftware.com

Project Studio: http://www.sun.com/workshop

VisualAge: http://www.software.ibm.com/ad/vajava

Visual Café: http://www.symantec.com

JDK: http://java.sun.com

BDK: http://splash.javasoft.com/beans

Chapter 6

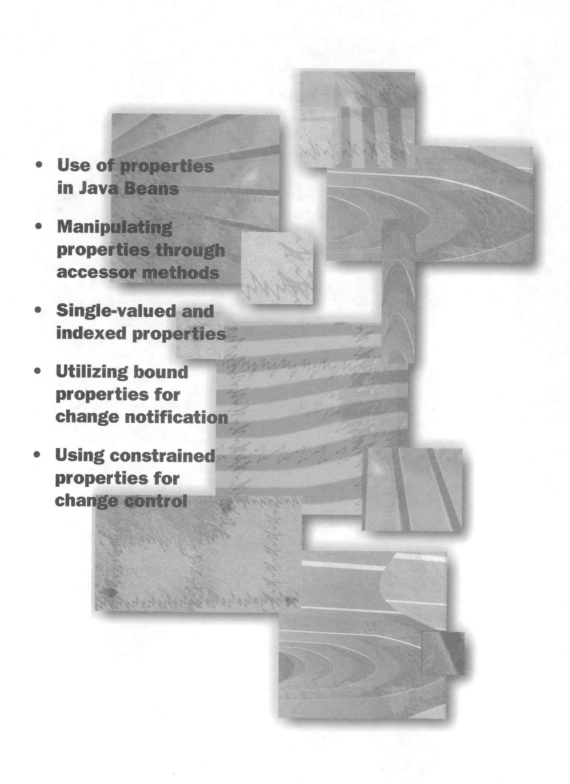

- **Use of properties in Java Beans**

- **Manipulating properties through accessor methods**

- **Single-valued and indexed properties**

- **Utilizing bound properties for change notification**

- **Using constrained properties for change control**

Properties

This chapter provides an in-depth discussion of properties in Java Beans. Properties are an integral part of the Java Beans technology, and they are used to control the appearance or behavior of a bean. A bean usually makes its properties persistent by serializing them into a file, and it reloads them when it is invoked.

Properties are manipulated in a number of ways. Properties can be visually accessed and modified in a framework. The framework examines a target bean and deduces the properties that the bean supports. It then displays the properties in a property sheet editor and allows a user to modify them. Properties can also be programmatically manipulated by other beans through calling their accessor methods. Finally, properties may also be exposed and changed in a scripting environment.

Java Beans supports two basic types of properties: *single-valued* and *indexed*. A single-valued property contains only one value. For example, the **label** property of the PushButton bean developed in Chapter 5 holds one value of type **String**. An indexed property contains multiple values, usually in the form of an array.

Java Beans also introduces *bound* and *constrained* semantics. These semantics prescribe the levels of control that a bean has over a change in the value of a property in another bean. These semantics are independent of the basic property types; a property always has a basic type, and it may have a semantic type as well.

In the rest of this chapter, we discuss all of the aforementioned concepts in detail and provide numerous code segments. We also develop a new version of PushButton, called PushButton1, that represents a bean with many different property types. We build some simple applications in the BeanBox framework with this bean that demonstrate the use of properties.

Property Accessor Methods

A bean defines internal properties and exposes them to other beans through accessor methods. It is possible to designate a property as **public**, allowing other objects to access it directly. This approach, however, has a number of drawbacks.

First, **public** data members violate the information hiding and data encapsulation principles of object-oriented programming (OOP). If you define a property as **public** and later change its name, you break all the programs that have accessed that property by using its name. Second, a **public** data member can never be a *computed property*—that is, one whose value depends on other variables. For example, a class representing circles may elect to export its area as a property and keep its radius internal. A user can then directly specify a value for its area by calling an accessor method that internally computes and sets the corresponding value for the radius; the circle never explicitly keeps track of its area, but it gives the user the illusion of having an "area" property. Third, a **public** property cannot trigger an action when its value is not changed through an accessor method. You cannot, for instance, repaint a bean to reflect its current foreground color if you allow direct access to its foreground property. Finally, **public** properties without accessor methods prevent a framework from examining methods and deducing the properties that a bean supports.

 *Define your properties as **private** or **protected** and expose them through a pair of accessor methods.*

There are two types of accessor methods: *getters* and *setters*. A getter gets the value of a property, whereas a setter sets the value to a new value. A bean should almost always define getters for its properties; in contrast, setters are optional and allow a user to modify properties. Both getter and setter methods may throw exceptions and should follow the Java Beans naming convention (as explained in the remainder of this chapter).

A read-only property provides only a getter accessor method, whereas a read-write property defines both a getter and a setter.

Property Types

As noted earlier, a property can be single-valued or indexed. A single-valued property contains only one value, while an indexed property can hold one or more values. In addition to having one of these basic types, a property can be read-only or read-write and can have a semantic type.

Single-Valued Properties

A single-valued property is the most common type. In this case, you define a data member that holds only one value and export it via a pair of getter/setter methods. You can limit the write-access to a property by not providing a setter method. You should follow the convention of naming your accessor methods **get<PropertyName>()** and **set<PropertyName>()**, where <PropertyName> is the actual name of a property.

Listing 6.1 shows the definition of a single-valued read-write property exported as **label**.

All the code segments in this chapter are taken from the PushButton1 bean. You should add this bean to your framework so that you can carry out the demonstrations in this chapter.

You internally define the property as **m_label**; a framework examines the **getLabel()** and **setLabel()** method names and deduces that PushButton1 has a property called **label**. Note that the class type (or data type) returned by a getter method must be the same as the argument type taken by the corresponding setter method. You can internally name the property whatever you like—Java Beans does not mandate any relationship between the name of a property and the names of its accessor methods. You should also note that **setLabel()** triggers an action after it sets the value of **label** to its new value.

Listing 6.1   A single-valued, read-write property.

```
// Label property.
// This is a single-valued, read-write property.
//
private String m_label;

/**
* Returns the label of the button.
*/
public String getLabel()
{
  return m_label;
}

/**
* Sets the button's label.
*
* @param label the new label for the button
*/
public void setLabel(String label)
{
  m_label = label;
  sizeToFit();
}
```

You can disallow write-access to a property by defining only a getter method, leaving out the setter method. For example, PushButton1 has a **count** property, which is read-only; it keeps track of the number of buttons (of type **PushButton1**) that have been instantiated in a framework. A framework deduces that a property is read-only when it encounters a getter method without its setter counterpart. Listing 6.2 displays the **count** property.

Listing 6.2   A single-valued, read-only property.

```
// Count property.
// This is a single-valued read-only property,
// that contains the number of instantiated
// buttons.
//
private static int m_count = 0;
```

```
/**
 * Returns the label of the button.
 */
public int getCount()
{
  return m_count;
}
```

 The beta 3 release of BeanBox 1.0 cannot handle read-only properties. Therefore, you do not see the **count** property in the PropertySheet when you instantiate PushButton1.

 A single-valued property contains only one value and can be read-only or read-write.

BOOLEAN PROPERTIES

A special kind of a single-valued property, a Boolean property, has a Boolean value and, therefore, has only two states. Java Beans introduces an additional way of naming the getter method of a Boolean property—namely, the **is\<PropertyName>**() syntax. PushButton1, for instance, has a **pushed** Boolean property that indicates whether the button should be drawn in the up or down position. Listing 6.3 presents the code segment that implements the **pushed** property. The getter accessor methods for this property is named **isPushed**() instead of **getPushed**() (the setter method still has the usual **setPushed**() name). Note that the **is\<PropertyName>**() syntax can be provided in addition to **get\<PropertyName>**(). In this case, however, the Java Beans specification does not elaborate exactly which method gets called when a framework retrieves the value of a Boolean property. Even though the exact behavior might depend on the framework, both methods should result in the same returned values.

 A Boolean property is a single-valued property that has a value of either *true* or *false* value.

Listing 6.3   A single-valued, Boolean, read-only property.

```
// Pushed property.
// This is a single-valued Boolean read-write property
// that controls the position of the button.
```

```
// A value of true causes the button to be displayed
// is the down position.
//
private boolean m_pushed;

/**
 * Returns the pushed position of the button.
 * true: button is in the down position.
 * false: button is in the up position.
 */
public boolean isPushed()
{
  return m_pushed;
}

/**
 * Sets the button's pushed position.
 *
 * @param pushed the new position for the button
 */
public void setPushed(boolean pushed)
{
  m_pushed = pushed;
}
```

After making sure that you have added PushButton1 to BeanBox (or your favorite framework), run the framework and instantiate this bean in its container. The PropertySheet editor displays the **pushed** property with its current **false** value. Note that PropertySheet uses a Boolean editor, which provides a choice between only **true** and **false**. Figure 6.1 shows the BeanBox after the instantiation of **PushButton1**.

You can name your getter method for a Boolean property is<PropertyName>() instead, or in addition to, get<Property-Name>() if it better describes the usage of your property.

Indexed Properties

In addition to single-valued properties, Java Beans also provides for multi-valued properties. A multi-valued property supports a collection of values instead of only one; the collection can have zero or more items. Because you typically have to identify the exact item by providing an index into the collection, Java Beans refers to such properties as *indexed properties*.

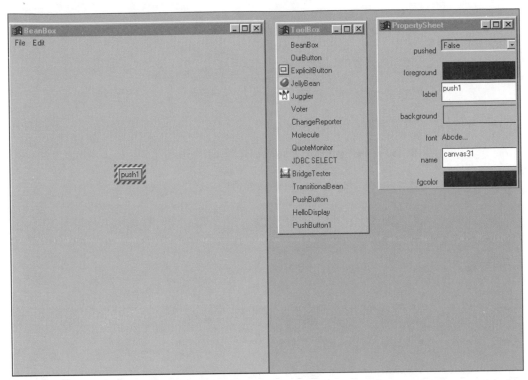

Figure 6.1 BeanBox uses a special Boolean editor for the **pushed** property.

You can use the syntax for accessor methods of single-valued properties to retrieve the entire collection of values of an indexed property or set its collection to a new collection. Java Beans supports an additional syntax that you can use to retrieve an arbitrary element of a collection or set an element to a new value (this syntax is similar to the original syntax, except that both the getter and setter methods take an extra argument of type integer). Listing 6.4 illustrates a multi-valued property called **labels** that implements both types of accessor methods, while Listing 6.5 shows the general syntax.

Listing 6.4   An indexed, read-write property.

```
// Labels property.
// This is an indexed read-write property.
//
// Note: This property does not affect the
//  appearance or the functionality of the bean.
//
private String[] m_labels;
```

```
/**
 * Return s the label of the button.
 */
public String[] getIndexedLabel()
{
  return m_labels;
}


/**
 * Sets the button's label.
 *
 * @param label the new label for the button
 */
public void setIndexedLabel(String[] labels)
{
  m_labels = labels;
}


/**
 * Returns the label of the button.
 */
public String getIndexedLabel(int index)
{
  return m_labels[index];
}


/**
 * Sets the button's label.
 *
 * @param label the new label for the button
 */
public void setIndexedLabel(int index, String label)
{
  m_labels[index] = label;
}
```

Listing 6.5   General forms for accessor methods of indexed properties.

```
<PropertyType>[] get<PropertyName>()
void set< PropertyName>(<PropertyType>[] values)
<PropertyType> get< PropertyName>(int index)
void set< PropertyName>(int index, < PropertyType> value)
```

Note that if you support the single-valued form of accessor methods, you have to implement your internal property as an array type. If you only support the multi-valued form, however, you are free to use any kind of collection for your property, not just arrays. For instance, you can implement an indexed property as a linked list; a user of the accessor methods is entirely oblivious to the internal representation.

You should not support the single-valued form of accessor methods for indexed properties unless this is a requirement. This form forces you to use arrays and exposes your internal implementations.

The current 1.0 release of Java Beans restricts the type of an index to be an integer. Although integers might represent the most common use of indices, there are cases where other types are more appropriate. Consider, for example, an indexed property that represents the collection of all students in a class. For this property, it might be more intuitive to index into the collection by a student's last name instead of a number. A future release of Java Beans may lift this limitation.

The accessor methods of a multi-valued property may throw a **java.lang.ArrayIndexOutOfBoundsException** runtime exception if a property is implemented as an array and an index is outside the array bounds. For other types of implementations, the accessor methods may throw similar exceptions. The setter method can also throw an exception if the provided new value of an element is not a valid input.

The beta 3 release of BeanBox 1.0 does not support indexed properties.

An indexed property has a range of values and can be read-only or read-write. Its accessor methods can throw exceptions.

Property Semantics

The single-valued and multi-valued properties by themselves do not support an *event-driven* notification system between beans. In an event-driven system, a source object notifies a target object when there is a change in the state of the source object in which the target object is interested.

To understand why you might need such a capability, suppose that you are developing a bean application. You need to ensure that all the beans fit seamlessly in the container by supplying the same background color for all the beans. Initially, all the beans might set their background color to the ambient background color of the container. When a bean changes its background color, you might want to transfer this change to the container and all the other beans. If you use the basic single-valued and indexed properties, you would have to poll for such changes; if you use an event-driven system, a bean can automatically notify other beans by invoking callbacks.

Java Beans provides two different change propagation semantics for properties, which are used in conjunction with the basic property types. These semantics dictate the level of involvement of a bean when the value of a property in another bean changes. The simplest case is when a property does not support any semantics; in this case, a change in its value does not involve any other bean. In the PushButton1 bean, for instance, a change of value in **label** does not trigger an action in another bean. A property can provide the bound semantics in which a change in its value causes notification messages to be sent to all the interested beans. In the case of constrained semantics (the highest level of control that a bean can impose on a property in another bean), the property cannot change unless the controlling bean approves the change.

 Bound and constrained properties provide semantics for single- and multi-valued property types. These semantics designate the level of involvement of a bean when a property in another bean changes.

Bound Semantics

A bound property notifies a target object when its value changes. The object can take whatever action it deems necessary to respond to the change; it cannot, however, prevent the property from changing its value. This semantics is called *bound* because it allows a component to bind special behavior to a change in the value of a property in another component. The process of creating a bean with bound properties entails the following steps:

1. Determining the bound properties

2. Supporting **PropertyChangeListener** listeners

3. Invoking the listeners' callbacks from a setter

A bound property sends a change notification message to all interested beans when its value changes.

DETERMINING THE BOUND PROPERTIES

You need to decide which properties of a bean should support the bound semantics. These properties are usually specified in the bean's requirement document.

Due to performance implications, avoid specifying a property as bound unless you can assume that another bean might want to receive change notifications when the value of the property changes.

PushButton1, for example, exports its background color as a bound property called **background**, as shown in Listing 6.6. Note that PushButton1 comments on **background** without actually defining a data member. As we already mentioned, a property is exposed by defining getter/ setter methods, not by defining a data member. Also note that **background** does not intend to provide a getter method, which is already inherited from its superclass. A framework can still successfully examine the PushButton1 methods and deduce the presence of **background**.

Listing 6.6   Bound background property in PushButton1.

```
// Background color property.
// This is a single-valued read-write bound
// property.
//
// Note: We inherit the superclass getBackground()
//   access method.
// Note: We do not define a new data member.
//
```

SUPPORTING PROPERTYCHANGELISTENER LISTENERS

The interface **PropertyChangeListener** must be implemented by any object wishing to be notified by a bean when the value of a bound property changes. As depicted in Figure 6.2, this interface is a direct descendant of **java.util.EventListener**, which is the root interface for all listener interfaces. **PropertyChangeListener** defines only one method, **propertyChange()**, which is called back by a bean. This method takes a **PropertyChangeEvent** object as an argument.

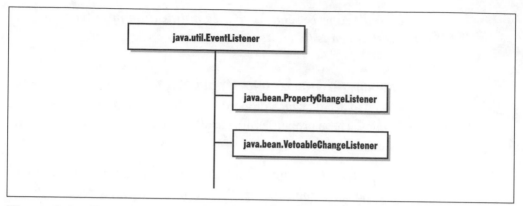

Figure 6.2 **EventListener** is the root interface for all event listeners.

This event object contains the name of the changed property, its old value, and its new value. It also defines three methods for retrieving these values: **getPropertyName()**, **getOldValue()**, and **getNewValue()**. The old and new values must be of type **Object**; therefore, if the property has built-in types, you must convert these values to their corresponding wrapper classes when you construct a **PropertyChangeEvent**. For example, you should use **java.lang.Integer** for an **int** value. You can use **null** if you do not know the true value of a property. You can also use **null** for the property name to indicate that an arbitrary set of properties have changed; in this case, the old and new values should also be **null**. The class **java.util.EventObject** is the parent of all event classes, as illustrated in Figure 6.3.

The name of the property in PropertyChangeEvent must be locale independent.

A bean with bound properties must maintain an internal list of **PropertyChangeListener** listeners and allow other beans to register and de-register their listeners. The bean can implement two methods for this purpose—namely, **addPropertyChangeListener()** and **removePropertyChangeListener()**. These methods take one parameter of type **PropertyChangeListener**. A framework can examine these methods and deduce that the bean supports bound properties; it then allows other beans to connect themselves visually to this bean and receive notification messages. You will see an example of this shortly.

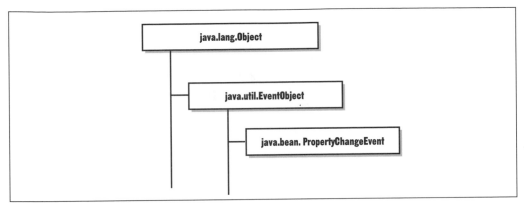

Figure 6.3 **EventObject** is the parent class for all event objects.

You can manage the list of **PropertyChangeListener** objects and add or remove elements from it when a bean registers or de-registers a listener. Alternatively, you may use the **PropertyChangeSupport** utility class, which is furnished by Java Beans. This class provides three methods: **addPropertyChangeListener()**, **removePropertyChangeListener()**, and **firePropertyChange()**. The first two methods simply take a **PropertyChangeListener** as argument, while **firePropertyChange()** requires three arguments—the name of the property whose value has changed (a **String**), the old value (an **Object**), and the new value (an **Object**). If you take this approach, simply use the add/remove methods for registration/de-registration, as illustrated in Listing 6.7.

Listing 6.7   The use of PropertyChangeSupport for registration/de-registration.

```
// This object keeps track of all the listeners who
// have registered their interest in a change in
// the value of any bound property and
// calls the listeners' propertyChange()
// callback methods.
//
private PropertyChangeSupport m_pcsGlob;

/**
 * A bean calls all the registered
 * PropertyChangeListeners' propertyChange callback
 * methods when the value of a bound property
 * is changed.
 *
```

```
 * Use addPropertyChangeListener() to register
 * your listener and removePropertyChangeListener()
 * to deregister a listener.
 *
 * Note: the JavaBeans specification does not
 *  require PropertyChangeListeners to run in any
 *  particular order.
 * Note: These listeners are global to all
 *  bound properties. You cannot use a listener
 *  registered in this manner to listen on a
 *  change of value in a specific property.
 *
 * @see #removePropertyChangeListener
 * @param l the PropertyChangeListener
 */
public void
addPropertyChangeListener(PropertyChangeListener l)
{
  m_pcsGlob.addPropertyChangeListener(l);
}

/**
 * Deregister this PropertyChangeListener.
 * This call is harmless if PropertyChangeListener
 * isn't on the list.
 *
 * @see #addPropertyChangeListener
 * @param l the PropertyChangeListener
 */
public void
removePropertyChangeListener(PropertyChangeListener l)
{
  m_pcsGlob.removePropertyChangeListener(l);
}
```

INVOKING THE LISTENERS' CALLBACKS FROM A SETTER

When a bound property changes value, you need to invoke the
PropertyChangeListener callbacks. Because the value of a property
can change only in its setter method (unless, of course, you have al-
lowed public access to it), all you need to do is to call all of the
PropertyChangeListener objects. If you are not using **Property-
ChangeSupport**, you have to create a **PropertyChangeEvent**, go
through the list of the registered listeners, and invoke their
propertyChange() methods. This approach is very similar to the way
that we invoked the callbacks of **m_pushLs** in PushButton.

*Java Beans specifies that a **PropertyChangeListener** be called only when the value of a bound property changes. If the old and new values of a property are the same, you must not invoke the listener.*

If you are using the **PropertyChangeSupport** class, you can simply invoke its **firePropertyChange()** method, which creates a **Property-ChangeEvent** object from its arguments and calls all the listeners with the change-event object as an argument. Listing 6.8 shows how the **background** property in PushButton1 uses this approach.

Listing 6.8 The background property uses PropertyChangeSupport for sending notifications.

```
/**
 * Sets the button's background color.
 * This property is bound and changing its value
 * results in a change notification being sent to
 * all registered listeners.
 *
 * Note: The new value of a bound property is set
 *  before invoking the callbacks.
 *
 * @param color the new color for the button
 */
public void setBackground(Color color)
{
  Color colorOld = getBackground();
  super.setBackground(color);

  // Invoke the callbacks.
  // m_pcsGlob will invoke all the callbacks on
  // behalf of this bean.
  //
  m_pcsGlob.firePropertyChange("background ",
    colorOld, color);
}
```

You must invoke a listener after you have changed the value of a bound property.

Using A Bound Property In A Framework

Once you have created a bean with a bound property, you can hook up other components to this bean in a framework so that these components receive automatic notification messages when the bound property changes value. In this section, you connect the PushButton1 bean, located on the CD-ROM, to ChangeReporter in the BeanBox framework.

The ChangeReporter bean is an out-of-the-box component that comes with BeanBox. It is a simple text field that extends the **TextField** class in AWT and defines a new method, **reportChange()**. This method accepts an argument of **PropertyChangeEvent** type and simply displays the new value of a bound property in its display field. This bean is provided by BeanBox so that you can experiment with bound properties.

Run the BeanBox and instantiate ChangeReporter and PushButton1. Select the button and execute Edit|Events|propertyChange|propertyChange from the menu bar, as shown in Figure 6.4. As you should know by now, BeanBox deduces that PushButton1 generates an event of type

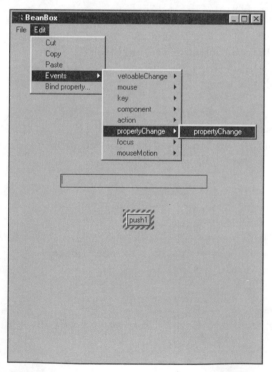

Figure 6.4 PushButton1 fires a **PropertyChangeEvent**.

PropertyChangeEvent because PushButton1 defines **addProperty-ChangeListener()** and **removePropertyChangeListener()**.

The process of sending property change notifications is accomplished by generating events.

Select the instantiated ChangeReporter as the target for this event. BeanBox pops up a dialog box, shown in Figure 6.5, listing all the potential methods in ChangeReporter that can react to bound property changes. Because ChangeReporter implements only one such method, this dialog box contains only one element, the **reportChange()** method. Accept this method and change the value of the **background** property in PushButton1. ChangeReporter reports the new value, as shown in Figure 6.6.

In practice, of course, you do not use ChangeReporter; you instantiate other suitable target beans that take more appropriate actions (such as changing their background colors) when a bound property changes. The important point to keep in mind is that all such target beans must implement one or more methods that take one argument of type **PropertyChangeEvent**.

USING A BOUND PROPERTY IN A HANDWRITTEN PROGRAM

Frameworks are the natural tools for building applications with beans that have bound properties; you can, however, create such applications programmatically. The procedure that you need to follow in order to do this is very similar to the way we programmatically created the

Figure 6.5 BeanBox displays the list of potential target methods.

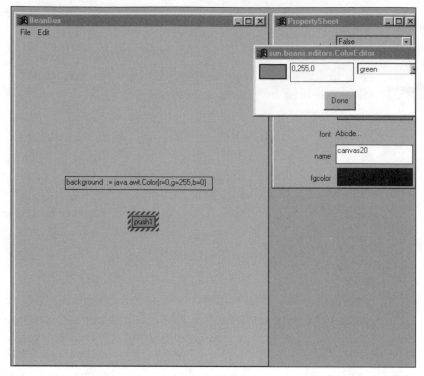

Figure 6.6 ChangeReporter displays the new value for **background**.

HelloWorld applet in Chapter 5. Basically, you need to create a listener hook-up class that implements the **PropertyChangeListener** interface and registers it with a source bean that has bound properties. In the **propertyChange()** method of the hook-up class, you need to call an appropriate method of a target bean, which is interested in receiving property change notifications. The procedure is straightforward, but you need to provide a hook-up class for each target bean.

Constrained Semantics

Constrained semantics support the maximum level of control that a bean can impose when the value of a bound property in another bean changes. In these semantics, the controlling bean can prevent the controlled bean from changing its constrained properties. The steps you need to follow to create constrained properties are very similar to those of bound properties: After you have identified the constrained properties, you need to support **VetoableChangeListener** listeners and invoke their callbacks when the value of a constrained property changes.

A bean can constrain the range of values that a constrained property in another bean can have.

SUPPORTING VETOABLECHANGELISTENER LISTENERS

The interface **VetoableChangeListener** is the interface that any object wishing to limit the value of a constrained property in a bean must implement. This interface is a direct descendant of **java.util.EventListener**, as shown in Figure 6.2. **VetoableChangeListener** defines only one method, **vetoableChange()**, which is called back by a bean when one of its constrained properties changes. This method takes a **PropertyChangeEvent** object as an argument and throws a **PropertyVetoException**.

A subclass of **java.lang.Exception**, **PropertyVetoException** defines one constructor that takes a **String** argument for a descriptive message and a second **PropertyChangeEvent** argument for the event that triggered the exception. This class also provides the **getPropertyChangeEvent()** method, which returns the offending event. A controlling bean throws this exception when it disapproves the proposed new value for a constrained property.

A bean with a constrained property must keep an internal list of **VetoableChangeListener** objects and allow a controlling bean to register and deregister its listeners. The bean can define two methods for this purpose—namely, **addVetoableChangeListener()** and **removeVetoableChangeListener()**, each of which takes one argument of type **VetobleChangeListener**.

You have two choices for managing the list of registered listeners. You can manage this list yourself and add listeners to it or remove elements from it when a bean registers or de-registers a listener, or you may use the **VetoableChangeSupport** class supplied by Java Beans. This utility class provides three methods: **addVetoableChangeListener()**, **removeVetoableChangeListener()**, and **fireVetoableChange()**. The add/remove methods take **PropertyChangeListener** as a parameter. The **fireVetoableChange()** method needs three arguments identical to **firePropertyChange()** defined in **PropertyChangeListener**. PushButton1 utilizes the second approach to support its constrained property **fgcolor**, as shown in Listing 6.9.

Listing 6.9 PushButton1 uses VetoableChangeSupport.

```
// This object keeps track of all the listeners who
// have registered their interest in a change in
// the value of any constrained property and
// calls the listeners' vetoableChange()
// callback methods.
//
private VetoableChangeSupport m_vcsGlob;

/**
  * A bean calls all the registered
  * VetoableChangeListeners' propertyChange callback
  * methods before the value of a constrained property
  * is changed.
  *
  * Use addVetoableChangeListener() to register
  * your listener and removeVetoableChangeListener()
  * to deregister a listener.
  *
  * Note: the JavaBeans specification does not
  *  require VetoableChangeListeners to run in any
  *  particular order.
  * Note: These listeners are global to all
  *  constrained properties. You cannot use a
  *  listener registered in this manner to listen on
  *  a change of value in a specific property.
  *
  * @see # removeVetoableChangeListener
  * @param l the VetoableChangeListener
  */
public void
addVetoableChangeListener(VetoableChangeListener l)
{
  m_vcsGlob. addVetoableChangeListener(l);
}

/**
  * Deregister this VetoableChangeListener.
  * This call is harmless if VetoableChangeListener
  * isn't on the list.
  *
  * @see # addVetoableChangeListener
  * @param l the VetoableChangeListener
  */
public void
```

```
removeVetoableChangeListener(
  VetoableChangeListener l)
{
  m_vcsGlob. removeVetoableChangeListener(l);
}
```

*You should use the utility class **VetoableChangeSupport** to manage the list of listeners for constrained properties unless you need special behavior.*

INVOKING THE LISTENERS' CALLBACKS FROM A SETTER

When you update the value of a constrained property in a setter method, you have to call all of the **VetoableChangeListener** callbacks. If you are not using **VetoableChangeSupport**, you need to go through the internal list that keeps track of these callbacks and invoke their **vetoableChange()** methods.

There is, however, an additional complexity when one of the listeners vetoes the change. In this case, you have to inform all the listeners that did approve the change about the veto so that they will have a chance to take appropriate actions. Suppose, for example, that you are seeking approval to change the foreground color of a bean. Controlling beans that approve the change might have set their foreground color to the new value. If another bean vetoes the change, you must give the beans that approved the change a chance to revert back to the old value.

You alert the beans about the reversion by constructing a new **PropertyChangeEvent** object and calling their **vetoableChange()** methods. If one of those beans vetoes the reversion, there is really nothing that you can do; just ignore the veto.

*Java Beans mandates that a **VetoableChangeListener** be invoked only if the new value of a bound property is different than the old value.*

Less work is involved, though, if you are using **VetoableChangeSupport**. All you need to do is to invoke its **fireVetoableChange()** method, which creates a **PropertyChangeEvent** object and calls all the listeners with the change event object as an argument if the proposed value of a constrained property is different than its current value. This utility class also handles the case when a proposed change is vetoed. Listing 6.10 shows the **fgcolor** property defined in PushButton1 and the use of **VetoableChangeSupport** in the **fgcolor** setter method.

Listing 6.10   The fgcolor setter method calls fireVetoableChange().

```
// Foreground color property.
// This is a single-valued read-write constrained
// property.
//
// Note: We cannot call this property "foreground"
//  because its setter method could not throw a
//  vetoable exception. In Java, a method redefined
//  in a subclass can throw exceptions of only the
//  types defined in its superclass.
// Note: We do not need to define a data member.
//

/**
 * Returns the foreground color of the button.
 */
public Color getFgcolor()
{
  return getForeground();
}


/**
 * Sets the button's foreground color.
 * This property is constrained and changing its
 * value results in a change notification permission
 * being sent to all registered listeners.
 *
 * Note: The new value of a constrained property is
 *  set after invoking the callbacks.
 * Note: This setter method throws an exception.
 *
 * @param color the new color for the button
 * @exception PropertyVetoException if the proposed
 *   color is vetoed
 */
public void setFgcolor(Color color)
throws PropertyVetoException
{
  // Invoke the callbacks.
```

```
    // m_vcsGlob will invoke all the callbacks on
    // behalf of this bean.
    //
    Color colOld = getForeground();  // old color
    m_vcsGlob.fireVetoableChange("foreground",
      colOld, color);

    // No one has vetoed this change.
    //
    super.setForeground(color);
}
```

Notice that we could not have designated the **foreground** property, which is inherited from the parents of PushButton1, to be constrained because the setter method **setForeground()** cannot throw a **PropertyVetoException**. This method is already defined in a superclass as a method that does not throw any exceptions, a behavior that cannot be modified by an extended class. Therefore, we had to create the new **fgcolor** property.

The **setFgcolor()** method delegates the task of invoking the listener callbacks to **VetoableChangeSupport** by calling its **fireVetoableChange()**. If any of the controlling beans vetoes the proposed change, this method throws an exception. Otherwise, **setFgcolor** updates the value of **fgcolor**.

You should change the value of a constrained property only after none of the listeners has vetoed the proposed change.

USING A CONSTRAINED PROPERTY IN A FRAMEWORK

In this section you connect PushButton1 to Voter, a control available in the BeanBox palette. An extension of class **Label** in AWT, Voter exports a boolean property, **vetoAll,** and has a method, **vetoableChange(PropertyChangeEvent)**. If **vetoAll** is set to true, this method throws a **PropertyVetoException**; otherwise, no exception is thrown.

In the BeanBox container, create an instance of Voter and PushButton1. As shown in Figure 6.7, select the button and execute Edit|Events| vetoableChange|vetoableChange from the menu bar. Note that BeanBox can conclude that PushButton1 supports constrained properties by examining the **addVetoableChangeListener()** and **removeVetoableChangeListener()** methods.

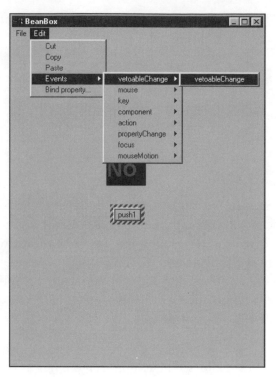

Figure 6.7 PushButton1 supports constrained properties.

After you choose the instantiated Voter as the target for this event, BeanBox brings up the dialog box shown in Figure 6.8, which lists all the potential methods in Voter that can respond to a change of value in a constrained property. This dialog box contains only one entry because **vetoableChange** is the only method that takes one argument of type **PropertyChangeEvent**. Accept this method and then attempt to

Figure 6.8 BeanBox pops up the list of all potential target methods.

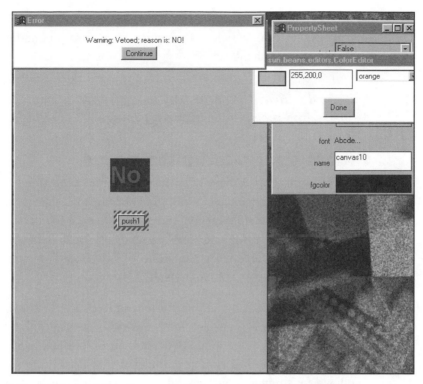

Figure 6.9   Voter vetoes the new proposed value for **fgcolor**.

modify the value of the **fgcolor** property in PushButton1. As illustrated in Figure 6.9, Voter vetoes the proposed change and causes the new value to be discarded.

You can exploit constrained properties to solve much more complex problems. For instance, you can design a credit card approval system based on constrained properties that rejects an applicant if certain factors are not met. You would most likely design these applications with a framework. You can also, however, create handmade programs that exploit constrained properties by programmatically supplying the structure of the programs and all the necessary hook-up classes.

Bound And Constrained Semantics

Bound and constrained semantics are not mutually exclusive. In other words, you can create a property that is both bound and constrained. All you have to do is to support both the **PropertyChangeListener** and **VetoableChangeListener** listeners by providing the appropriate add/remove methods. You also need to call both the **vetoableChange()** and **propertyChange()** methods when the value of a bound and constrained property changes.

 *You should always call **vetoableChange()** first, update the property, and then invoke **propertyChange()**.*

Global Vs. Specific Listeners

The procedures that we have been describing for supporting bound and constrained properties have a *global* scope. In this approach, a bean maintains one internal **PropertyChangeListener** list for all of its bound properties, and one **VetoableChangeListener** list for all of its constrained properties. Therefore, when the value of *any* bound or constrained changes, the bean calls all the registered listeners.

In this scheme, it is not possible for a bean to express its interest in a particular property. It is an all-or-nothing deal—the bean either receives callbacks from all of the bound/constrained properties, or it receives no callbacks at all. For example, imagine that PushButton1 had defined two constrained properties, and you connected this bean to a Voter. When you would change the value of any of the constrained properties, the Voter would receive callbacks and either decline or approve the change. You could not have created an application with two Voter beans, one set to reject all proposed changes, and the other to validate them all, connecting one of the constrained properties to a Voter and the other one to the second Voter.

 A global bound/constrained listener receives callbacks from all of the bound/constrained properties.

The global approach has two drawbacks. First, as already mentioned, it is not possible to connect a particular property to a target bean. Second, it might introduce a performance degradation because a bean gets events about property changes that it may not be interested in. The first shortcoming can be resolved if a target bean filters out the irrelevant events based on their property names. This scheme, however, may result in non-generic beans and slows down the system; for example, the **Voter** bean could no longer react to arbitrary constrained properties. For these reasons, Java Beans provisions specific listeners.

A *specific* listener is registered on a per-property basis and receives callbacks only from the property that it has been associated with. A specific listener is entirely oblivious to updates in the values of other properties. A bean can support specific listeners for a bound property by supplying the following two methods:

```
void add<PropertyName>Listener(PropertyChangeListener)
void remove<PropertyName>Listener
  (PropertyChangeListener)
```

Similarly, a bean supports specific listeners for a constrained property by providing the following methods to register and de-register listeners:

```
void add<PropertyName>Listener(VetoableChangeListener)
void remove<PropertyName>Listener(VetoableChangeListener)
```

A specific bound/constrained listener receives callbacks only from a designated bound/constrained property.

You are not required to support specific listeners for your beans; the support for global listeners might be sufficient. If you decide to provide a per-property listener, you can simply follow the general procedure we outlined for global listeners. You only need to ensure that you have correctly named your add/remove methods, and you need to keep an internal listener list for each property that supports specific listeners.

Do not support specific listeners unless you are convinced that they enhance the functionality of the suite of beans you are designing.

Conclusion

In this chapter, we introduced you to the concept of properties and showed you how to utilize them to manage the appearance and functionality of your applications. We classified properties as either single-valued or multi-valued, and we provided you with the general design patterns for naming their accessor methods. We also presented the bound and constrained semantics and showed you how to implement them. Finally, we discussed global listeners and told you how you might gain functionality and performance with specific listeners.

Properties are one of the cornerstones of Java Beans. In the next chapter we discuss events, the other fundamental part of Java Beans. We present all the relevant concepts and demonstrate their usage with numerous code segments.

Chapter 7

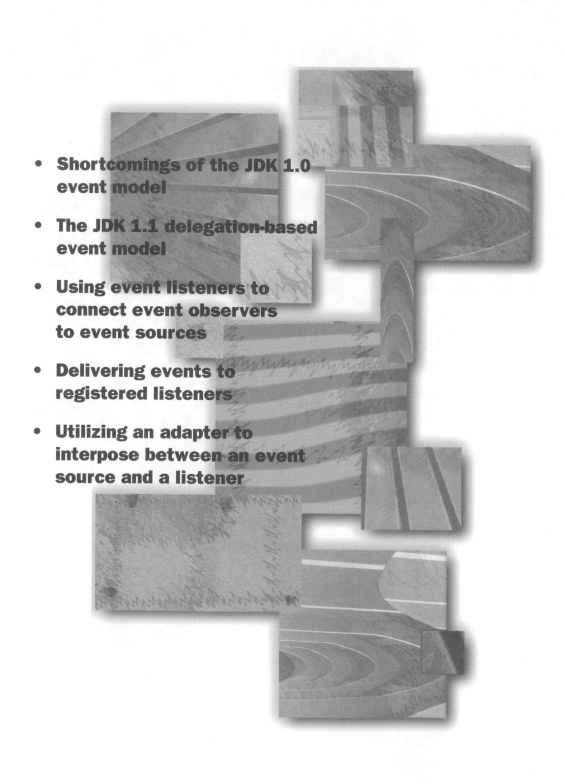

- **Shortcomings of the JDK 1.0 event model**

- **The JDK 1.1 delegation-based event model**

- **Using event listeners to connect event observers to event sources**

- **Delivering events to registered listeners**

- **Utilizing an adapter to interpose between an event source and a listener**

Chapter 7

The JDK 1.1 Event Model

Events are a general-purpose programming paradigm; they are used to transfer state-change information from one subsystem to another. One of the key applications of events is to model and design systems whose state changes may not be predictable. System failure is a good example of a behavior whose exact time of occurrence cannot be known in advance. If you are trying to design a system that responds to failures in a unit, you may want to use events to notify another unit that can take corrective actions.

Windowing environments utilize events to route user interactions (such as mouse clicks or keystrokes) with GUI widgets to appropriate branches of code that can respond to the interactions. A windowing application usually consists of two distinct but related parts: the GUI and the application logic. The GUI has a root window, which usually contains other windowing widgets organized in a hierarchy. When a user interacts with the root window, the windowing environment generates an event, determines the gadget in the hierarchy that should be receiving it, and sends it to that gadget. In response, the target GUI component executes a chunk of programming logic code to handle the event.

A good event model must be scaleable, have a fast response time, and separate the GUI portion of an application from the programming logic. These features allow new event handling units to be added to a system without distributing the system or degrading the performance.

In this chapter, we will present an overview of the JDK 1.0 event model. Although it is now obsolete, it provides a good example of an event model with flawed characteristics. This overview is followed by a discussion of the JDK 1.1 delegation-based event model.

We will discuss in detail the fundamentals of the event paradigm and show you its performance and scalability characteristics. We will precisely define events, event sources, event listeners, and event observers, as well as illustrate the life cycle of events (starting from their generation in event sources and their consumption in event observers). We will employ all the concepts and theory of the delegation-based event model to create an event-driven failure-recovery prototype system, which we call Failure Command System (FCM).

The JDK 1.0 Event Model

Although the Java Beans delegation-based event model is not based on the JDK 1.0 model, knowledge of the latter model can help you gain a better understanding of the Java Beans approach. This section presents an overview of the JDK 1.0 model and delineates its shortcomings.

Overview Of The JDK 1.0 Event Model

JDK 1.0 provides two entry points into its windowing event environment: **action()** and **handleEvent()** methods. You can override either of these two methods and insert your own programming logic for event handling. If you return **true** from either method, you signal the Java windowing system that you have consumed the event and it should not do any further processing. If you return **false**, Java propagates the event up through the hierarchy of GUI widgets until it is either consumed by a widget or the root window of the hierarchy is reached.

You can override the root container's **action()** or **handleEvent()** method and insert the event handling code for all your GUI components in the overridden method. This case requires a complex conditional statement to first determine the GUI widget that generated the event and then invoke an appropriate method to handle the event. All the event handling methods belong to the container and usually reside in the same source file that creates the front-end GUI.

Alternatively, you can use inheritance to subclass an AWT component and add the component-specific event handling code in the subclass. Even though this approach distributes the event handling code across many different subcomponents and does not have the complex conditional block of code, it results in a proliferation of AWT components whose sole purpose is to capture component-specific event handling logic.

Shortcomings Of The JDK 1.0 Event Model

The JDK 1.0 event model suffers from a lack of scaleability and performance, and it violates some software engineering design principles. Neither of the above approaches can result in a clean separation between the GUI code and the application logic code; you must integrate your event handling methods with the code that creates the GUI. For an application that has a large number of AWT components, you end up with a code that is difficult to maintain and is bug-prone. Using subclassing just to implement event handling code is cumbersome and violates object-oriented design principles (you should subclass only when you are extending the class in some functional or visual manner).

The JDK 1.0 event model does not scale up to applications with a large number of GUI components. The conditional statement in the first approach gets overly complicated and becomes a source of logical errors. (It is easy for a programmer to forget to handle an event within the conditional block.) The second approach is not scaleable due to the sheer number of derived classes that it produces. The Java AWT package itself cannot be scaled to add new event types without potentially breaking user applications in very unpredictable ways.

The 1.0 event model also suffers from a lack of performance because there is no event filtering—that is, events are always delivered to components whether or not the components are interested in them. The performance degradation is especially prominent for high-frequency event types, such as mouse moves or clicks. Furthermore, the conditional block in the first approach usually performs costly string comparisons in order to identify the method that should handle the event. These comparisons degrade the performance, particularly for high-frequency events, and are unwieldy to localize.

The JDK 1.0 event model has been completely revamped in JDK 1.1 in favor of a *delegation-based* model. This model addresses the short-comings of its predecessor and supports Java Beans and different propagation models, as described below.

The 1.0 model provides a framework to define an extensible set of low-level and semantic events, and it supports different delivery semantics. The delegation model separates the application code from the GUI code, and facilitates the creation of more robust, maintainable, and extensible event handling systems. The new model supports dynamic discovery of the events that a subsystem generates, as well as dynamic discovery of events that it can observe. It also allows for the registration of event listeners and dynamic manipulation of relationships between event sources and event listeners. The delegation model supports the visual builder tools, and it results in high-performance, scaleable, robust systems. In the rest of this section, we will introduce you to all of the aspects of this new event model.

 The new delegation-based event model in JDK 1.1 has been introduced to resolve the inherent problems with the JDK 1.0 model and support the Java Beans technology.

The JDK 1.1 Event-Related Objects

There are two different processes necessary to designing an event-driven system in JDK 1.1: relationship creation and event processing. You create a relationship between an *event source* and an *event observer* through an *event listener*, and you add component-specific code to an event observer to process events.

Registering an event listener with an event source creates this relationship. An object identifies itself as an event source by defining a pair of registration methods that conform to a specific design pattern and associate a listener object with an event type. An object takes the role of a listener by implementing a listener interface inherited from **java.util.EventListener**.

An event listener acts as a bridge between an object that generates events and an object that observes events. The relationship between an event source and an event listener is one-to-many, which means that there can be any number of listeners associated with a source. Similarly, there is a one-to-many relationship between a listener and an observer, although in practice you usually call only one observer from within a listener. Figure 7.1 graphs these relationships.

Registering event listeners with an event source creates a directed graph between an event source, event listeners, and event observers.

An event source generates event objects, which flow through listeners and *sink* in event observers (as determined by relationship graphs). An event object is a subclass of **java.util.EventObject** and has all the necessary information to recover the change of state that transpired in an event source. Event objects are *immutable*—an observer takes whatever action necessary to respond to an event, but it can neither alter the event nor recycle it back into the event system. This behavior is different from the JDK 1.0 event model, in which you can propagate the event upward in the chain of AWT components.

The life cycle of an event object begins in an event source, transits through an event listener, and ends in an event observer.

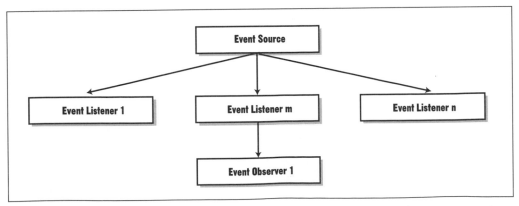

Figure 7.1 The relationships among an event source, event listeners, and an event observer.

You integrate your component-specific code with an observer. This code determines your component's response when an event occurs in another component. For example, if you are designing a fault-tolerant system, an observer subsystem might respond to a failure elsewhere by shutting down that subsystem and rerouting the internal messages through a redundant subsystem. The logic that performs this task should be in your observer class, cleanly separated from the classes that trigger events. Again, this characteristic is quite different than the 1.0 model, which essentially bundles up the event handling code with the GUI code.

The JDK 1.1 event model separates the code that sources an event, such as the GUI code, from the code that responds to an event.

In the JDK 1.1 event model, you need to explicitly express your interest in receiving events by registering your listeners with an event source. Because only the relevant objects receive events, this approach speeds up the overall performance of the system and creates a robust system that can be easily scaled up.

The 1.1 event model results in robust, high-performance, scaleable event-driven systems.

Event State Objects

An event state object represents a change in the state of an object and contains all the necessary information to identify the change. For example, the **PropertyChangeEvent** object can convey the change of value in a property because it holds the object whose property has changed, the name of the property, the old value, and the new value.

An event represents the old state of an object and a change that has occurred in that state, such as PropertyChangeEvent. An event also contains the object whose state has changed.

In JDK 1.1, events are no longer represented by the single **java.awt.Event** class with numeric IDs. The new event model defines the root **java.util.EventObject** event class and requires programmers to extend this class or any of its subclasses to create more specific event types. This approach is fundamentally different from that of the JDK 1.0 model because it uses a class to identify an event instead of a numeric ID. The **EventObject** class has one instance variable that keeps track of the object that has fired an event, as well as a constructor of the form **EventObject(Object)**.

The **java.awt.Event** class in JDK 1.0 is now superseded with **java.awt.AWTEvent**, which is extended from **java.util.EventObject** and is the parent class for all the windowing-related events. This class defines a number of constants, such as FOCUS_EVENT_MASK, KEY_EVENT_MASK, that are used to determine the event types that should be delivered to AWT components. These masks are automatically set when a component expresses its interest in an event through the process of registration. The **AWTEvent** class also defines an internal variable that keeps track of the ID of an event, which is used to identify an event within a small set of related events and is accessed via **AWTEvent.getId()**. You can create an object of this class through the **AWTEvent(Object, int)** constructor, where you need to provide the object that has generated the event and the event ID.

Because some event classes may represent more than one event type, however, they may contain an ID that identifies one member of a set of possible event types. **MouseEvent**, for instance, uses this approach to designate all the possible set of mouse-related events (mouse-drag, mouse-enter, mouse-exit, mouse-move, mouse-press, and mouse-release). In this case, you need to call **MouseEvent.getId()** and compare the returned value with the list of constant values defined in **MouseEvent** to determine the exact event type.

If you create beans or use the JDK 1.1 event model to design event-driven systems, you may need to define your own event types. If you find yourself in this situation, look over all the standard event types defined in the **java.awt.event** package to ensure that the event you need is not already defined there and to determine whether you can extend any of the standard classes. As a last resort, extend your new event type from **java.awt.AWTEvent** (if you are creating an AWT event) or **java.util.EventObject** (for non-AWT events). The code segment in Listing 7.1 shows the definition of a custom event of type **FailureEvent**.

The **FailureEvent** class represents a general failure event in FCM. This class identifies two types of system failure events: total and partial. A system cannot recover from a total failure; in such cases, it notifies any registered listeners and powers down. A system may continue operation if it fails partially. The class **Failure**, used in **FailureEvent**, contains more detailed information about a failure. You should observe that **FailureEvent** encapsulates these two event types by defining two constants and defining the internal variable **m_id**.

You should use the word "Event" to end the name of your event type. For example, if you are defining an event to represent a general failure in a system, name your event **FailureEvent**. *If you are defining a set of closely related events, you may want to bundle them up in one class and use a numeric ID to distinguish between the sub-events. Always remember to call the superclass constructor.*

Listing 7.1   Defining FailureEvent.

```java
import java.util.*;

/**
 * This class implements a very simple event object
 * that represents a module failure in a system.
 * The FailureEvent class defines two event types,
 * representing total and partial failures.
 */
public class FailureEvent extends EventObject
{
  private Failure m_failure;
  private int m_id; // event type id (total/partial)

  /**
   * Total failure event type.
   */
  public final static int TOTAL_FAILURE = 0;

  /**
   * Partial failure event type.
   */
  public final static int PARTIAL_FAILURE = 1;

  public
  FailureEvent(Module module, int id, Failure failure)
```

```
    {
      super(module);
      m_id = id;
      m_failure = failure;
    }

    public Failure getFailure()
    {
      return m_failure;
    }
}
```

Event state objects are immutable because an event captures a single change of state for an object. Of course, the object can go through more state changes, but these changes are captured by additional event objects.

Because events are immutable, you should not define any of their data members as **public**. You can expose these internal fields through getter accessor methods. Make sure that you adhere to the design patterns set forth for accessor methods in Chapter 6. There are circumstances, however, in which you must modify an event, for example, when translating view-relative coordinates when propagating a windowing event through a view hierarchy. In these cases, you should provide methods for your events that perform the appropriate modifications, instead of allowing a user to directly manipulate an event's internal states.

An event is immutable and does not usually change as it propagates from an event source to an event sink. (Note: the term "event sink" is interchangeable with "event observer." We will use both throughout this chapter, as they are both commonly used.)

Low-Level Vs. Semantic Events

AWT defines two types of events: low-level and semantic. A *low-level event* represents a low-level, uninterpreted user interaction with a visual component on the screen that corresponds to some input device. For example, **java.awt.event.KeyEvent** represents a raw, component-level keyboard event that a user has triggered by interacting with the keyboard input device. The JDK 1.1 AWT package currently defines nine such events, as shown in Figure 7.2.

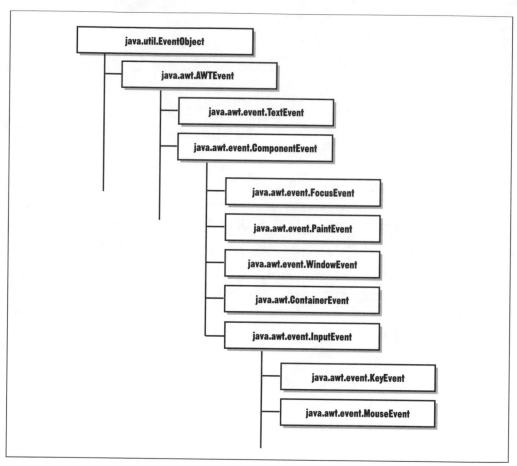

Figure 7.2 The hierarchy of low-level events defined in the JDK 1.1 AWT.

Semantic events are higher-level events that represent the intentions of a user when he or she interacts with a windowing component. These semantic events do not directly correspond to any specific component; they are higher-level events that may apply across a set of components that share a similar semantic model. For example, **java.awt.event.ActionEvent** is triggered by a button when it is pressed, by a list when one of its items is double-clicked, or by a menu when one of its items is selected. The AWT package in the JDK 1.1 identifies three semantic events, as depicted in Figure 7.3.

A semantic event represents the user's intention interacting with a bean, whereas a low-level event corresponds to a raw, uninterpreted interaction.

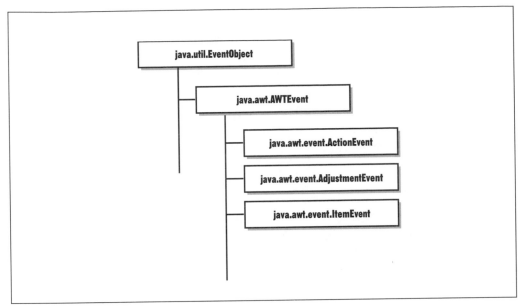

Figure 7.3 The hierarchy of semantic events defined in the JDK 1.1 AWT.

Event Listeners

Event listeners create relationships between event sources and event sinks (refer to Figure 7.1). They allow event state objects to flow from a source bean to a target bean. An event listener is essentially a callback object—a target bean creates a listener callback object and gives it to a source bean; the source calls back the listener when an event transpires that is significant to the target bean.

A listener encapsulates one or more related methods. For example, **java.awt.event.MouseListener** defines **mouseClicked()**, **mouseEntered()**, **mouseExited()**, **mousePressed()**, and **mouseReleased()**. The grouping of a number of methods under one listener object is useful for maintaining a balance between the number and the granularity of listener objects. All of the methods, however, must be conceptually related and have the same signature. All of the methods in **MouseListener**, for example, take one argument of **MouseEvent** type.

An event listener is a callback object and serves as a bridge between a source and a consumer of events. A listener may encapsulate a number of semantically related methods.

In general, you use interfaces in Java to implement a callback object in the following manner. First, you define an interface with one or more methods (recall that an interface merely identifies a method without actually implementing it). You then define a trigger class that takes an instance of the interface and, based on certain conditions, invokes a method of the interface. Finally, you create an implementation of the interface and pass an instance of it to the trigger class. You are now ready to apply the above procedure to create a very simple event-driven timer system.

Create an interface called **ICallback** that declares a **wakeup()** method, as shown in Listing 7.2. This interface has the **ICallback** type, and any class that implements this interface acquires this type and can be used wherever the interface can be used.

Listing 7.2   ICallback interface.

```
/**
 * This interface defines a callback method.
 */
public interface ICallback
{
  public void wakeup();
}
```

Define a **Timer** class that extends **java.lang.Thread**. The constructor of this class takes an object of **ICallback** type and assigns it to an internal data member; the **run()** method of **Timer** sleeps for one second and then calls back to the callback object by invoking **wakeup()**. The **Timer** class is presented in Listing 7.3.

Listing 7.3   The Timer trigger class.

```
/**
 * This class implements a very simple timer class.
 * The timer sleeps for 1 second and then invokes the
 * wakeup() method of the callback object.
 */
public class Timer extends java.lang.Thread
{
  ICallback m_cb;

  public Timer(ICallback cb)
  {
    m_cb = cb;
  }
```

```
    public void run()
    {
      while (true)
      {
        try
        {
          sleep(1000);
          m_cb.wakeup();
        }
        catch (java.lang.InterruptedException e)
        {
          System.out.println(e);
        }
      }
    }
  }
}
```

The **ICallback** and **Timer** objects conceptually represent general-purpose utility classes. You now need to provide some application-specific behavior by creating a class that implements **ICallback**. A simple such class, shown in Listing 7.4, prints a message when its **wakeup()** method is called.

Listing 7.4   CallbackImp implements ICallback.

```
/**
 * This class provides a simple implementation of
 * ICallback.
 * It defines the wakeup() method to print a message
 * on the screen.
 */
public class CallbackImp implements ICallback
{
  public void wakeup()
  {
    System.out.println("wakeup is called");
  }
}
```

Proceed to connect **CallbackImp** with **Timer** by simply creating an instance of **CallbackImp**, instantiating **Timer** with a reference to the **CallbackImp** instance, and starting the timer thread, as shown in Listing 7.5. Run the **Main** class; you will see the message "wakeup is called" printed on your screen approximately every one second.

Listing 7.5 Connecting CallbackImp and Timer.

```
/**
 * This class tests the timer.
 */
public class Main
{
  public static void main(String[] argv)
  {
    // Create an instance of the callback object.
    //
    CallbackImp cb = new CallbackImp();

    // Create the timer.
    //
    Timer timer = new Timer(cb);

    // Start the timer.
    //
    timer.start();
  }
}
```

The **ICallback** interface is important because it allows you to separate the code specific to your application (in this case, **CallbackImp**) cleanly from the rest of the event-driven system. You can also extend the logic of your application simply by defining another implementation of **ICallback** (such as **CallbackImp1**) and using it instead of or in addition to **CallbackImp**. Another advantage of **ICallback** is that it defines a common type for all classes that implement it—for example, **CallbackImp** and **CallbackImp1** can be used in conjunction with **Timer** without causing any compile-time errors.

The usage of an event listener and its relationship with an event source and an event observer parallel the above description of **ICallback**, **Timer**, and **CallbackImp**. Like **ICallback**, an event listener is a Java interface that is used to separate the application-specific logic from the rest of any event-driven system (such as the Java windowing system). It also allows the creation of many applications in the form of event observers that can seamlessly integrate with an existing event system. An event source has the role of **Timer**: it can maintain a list of listeners and invoke their callbacks when appropriate. There is only one subtle difference between **CallbackImp**, which acts as a listener, and a general event listener. **CallbackImp** processes and consumes the event, whereas a general listener usually delegates the event processing to an event observer by invoking a method of the observer.

An event listener allows the application-specific code to be localized in an event observer.

All event listeners are interfaces rooted at **java.util.EventListener**. You create your own listeners by extending this class or of any of its subclasses. Your listeners can identify one or more methods; in general, you should group the conceptually related methods within one listener to avoid a proliferation of listener classes.

By convention, the name of an event listener should end in "Listener". For example, the listener class name for FailureEvent event object is FailureListener.

Callback methods in listener interfaces should conform to a standard design pattern to facilitate the documentation of a system of events, programmatic introspection of callbacks, and automatic construction of generic event adapters (which are discussed in a later section). The general signature of the design pattern for callback methods is as follows (note that a callback method may throw exceptions):

```
void <eventOccurenceMethodName> (<EventStateObjectType> evt);
```

FCM, for example, defines **FailureListener** to handle events of type **FailureEvent**. This listener, shown in Listing 7.6, identifies two callback methods, **failureTotal**() and **failurePartial**(), each of which takes an argument of **FailureEvent** type. You should note that **FailureListener** provides two callbacks because **FailureEvent** encapsulates two types of events. Also note that **failurePartial**() may throw an **EContinueOperation** exception to indicate to a partially failed system that it should not power down. This exception is shown in Listing 7.7.

As a rule of thumb, you should define one callback method for each subevent that an event object identifies.

Listing 7.6 FailureListener listener.

```java
import java.util.*;

/**
 * This interface defines a simple listener with
 * two callback methods.
 * The method failureTotal() is called if there is
 * a total failure, while failurePartial() is invoked
 * if the failure is partial.
 *
 * Note: FailureListener defines one callback method
 *  for each event type in FailureEvent.
 */
public interface FailureListener extends EventListener
{
  public void failureTotal(FailureEvent evt);

  /**
   * This callback method may throw an
   * EContinueOperation exception to instruct a
   * partially failed system to continue operation.
   */
  public void failurePartial(FailureEvent evt)
  throws EContinueOperation;
}
```

Listing 7.7 EContinueOperation exception.

```java
/**
 * This exception is thrown to signal a failed
 * system that it should continue operation and
 * must not power down.
 */
public class EContinueOperation extends Exception
{
  public EContinueOperation()
  {
    super ();
  }
}
```

If you are defining an interface with a group of methods, you should name the methods accordingly. For instance, **MouseListener** starts the names of all of its callback methods with "mouse" (**mouseClicked()**, **mouseEntered()**, **mouseExited()**, and so on). Similarly, **FailureListener** names its callback methods **failureTotal()** and **failurePartial()**.

Low-Level Vs. Semantic Events

Similar to event state objects, AWT identifies two types of event listeners: low-level and semantic. A *low-level listener* corresponds to an uninterpreted user interaction with a visual component, while a *semantic listener* is a higher-level event that represents the intentions of a windowing component's user. For example, **java.awt.event.KeyListener** represents a low-level listener, whereas **java.awt.event.ActionListener** is a semantic one. The JDK 1.1 AWT package currently defines eight low-level and three semantic event listeners, as depicted in Figure 7.4 and Figure 7.5.

A semantic event listener is used in conjunction with a semantic event object, whereas a low-level listener is used with a low-level event object.

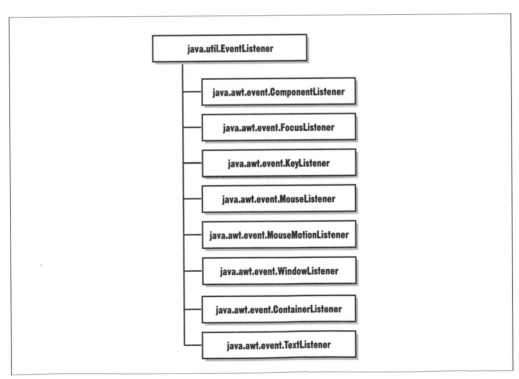

Figure 7.4   The hierarchy of low-level event listeners defined in the JDK 1.1 AWT.

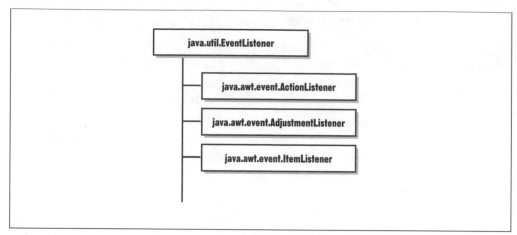

Figure 7.5 The hierarchy of semantic event listeners defined in the JDK 1.1 AWT.

Methods With Arbitrary Arguments

A callback method is usually required to take only one argument of **java.util.EventObject** type. Because an event is an object and can encapsulate an arbitrary number of data members, this restriction does not have any negative ramifications. There are cases, however, in which an event system needs to interface with another external event system that does not conform to this guideline (for example, this happens when bridging Java Beans events to other environments, such as ActiveX). In these cases, it is permissible to define callback methods that take one or more argument of any type, not just **EventObject**. These callbacks may throw exceptions and have the following general design pattern:

```
void <eventOccurenceMethodName> (...);
```

Visual builder tools should support both types of method signatures. In general, you should exercise restraint in defining callback methods with an arbitrary number of arguments.

You should almost always define callback methods that take only one argument of EventObject type.

Event Sources

An event source generates an event, which flows through a listener to reach and sink in an event observer. An event source fires an event usually as a response to some external stimulus, which causes its internal state to change. A button, for example, triggers an **ActionEvent** when it is pressed.

You can always determine the types of events that a bean triggers by looking for a pair of add/remove functions that take an **EventListener** as an argument in either the bean's documentation or its source code (these functions are explained in the next section). Similarly, a framework can examine a bean and deduce the events it fires. You should keep in mind that a component can fire low-level or/and semantic events. For example, **java.awt.Dialog** generates a low-level **WindowEvent** because it supports **addWindowListener(WindowListener)** and **removeWindow-Listener(WindowListener)**, and **java.awt.Checkbox** fires a semantic **ItemEvent** because it defines **addItemListener(ItemListener)** and **removeItemListener(ItemListener)**.

An event source must call back all of the appropriate listeners when it triggers an event; we will discuss the delivery of events to listeners in much more detail in a later section. A listener is considered appropriate if it has registered its interest in events of the same type as that generated by the event source, as described in the next section.

 An event source triggers an event state object when its internal state changes, usually as a result of some external stimulus.

Registration

When you design an event source, you must provide a way for an event observer to register and deregister its interest in receiving events from the source. For each event type, you need to decide whether you want to support the multicast or unicast registration semantic.

The *multicast semantic* allows an arbitrary number of listeners to be associated with an event type, whereas the *unicast semantic* permits only one listener to be registered with an event type.

Multicast

So far, all of the examples of event registration in this book have the multicast semantic. A multicast event admits one or more event listeners, and it invokes their callbacks when an event interesting to the listeners transpires. The multicast registration has the following design pattern:

```
public void add<ListenerType>(< ListenerType> lis);
public void remove<ListenerType>(< ListenerType> lis);
```

 You should always define your registration methods as multicast unless you have a reason to believe this semantic is inappropriate.

You should normally synchronize the above two methods to guard against races in multithreaded code. The Java Beans specification does not specify the behavior of a bean if you attempt to register the same event listener more than once with the same event source, to delete a listener more than once, or to delete a listener that is not registered. All of the above behavior is implementation dependent and cannot be predicted. Moreover, passing a **null** to the registration methods is illegal and may result in an **IllegalArgumentException** or a **NullPointerException**.

The **Module** event source in the FCM application supports a multicast registration for **FailureListener**, as shown in Listing 7.8. This class defines an internal data member of type **Vector**, which keeps track of all the listeners registered to receive event notifications when **Module** triggers an **FailureEvent**. **Module** implements two methods for registration and deregistration (**addFailureListener()** and **removeFailureListener**, respectively).

Listing 7.8   A multicast event registration.

```
// List of all listeners who are interested in the
// FailureEvent generated by this module.
//
private Vector m_failureLs;

/**
 * Informs the module that this FailureListener
 * is interested in FailureEvents.
 *
 * @param l the FailureListener
 */
public synchronized void
addFailureListener(FailureListener l)
```

```
{
  m_failureLs.addElement(l);
}


/**
 * Informs the module that this FailureListener
 * is no longer interested in FailureEvents.
 *
 * @param l the FailureListener
 */
public synchronized void
removeFailureListener(FailureListener l)
{
  m_failureLs.removeElement(l);
}
```

The multicast event registration allows any number of event listeners to be associated with an event source under the same event type.

Unicast

Although most events have a multicast semantic type, there might be cases where it is inappropriate or impractical to notify more than one listener when an event transpires. In such cases, you can use a unicast registration semantic, which permits only one listener to be associated with an event type. Any attempt to register a second listener for a unicast event fails. A unicast registration has the following naming convention:

```
public void add<ListenerType>(< ListenerType> lis)
throws java.util. TooManyListenersException;
public void remove<ListenerType>(< ListenerType> lis);
```

In the unicast semantic, the **add<ListenerType>** method may throw a **java.util.TooManyListenersException** if an attempt is made to associate more than one listener of the same type with an event source. As in the multicast model, the behavior of an event source is implementation dependent if you attempt to remove a listener that is not registered or pass a **null** argument to the registration methods.

The **Module** event source in FCM supports one unicast event—namely, **Failure1Event**. The internal variable **m_failure1L** (see Listing 7.9) holds only one **Failure1Listener**, as contrasted to **m_failureLs**, which has a **Vector** type. The **addFailure1Listener()** throws an exception if a listener has already registered for **Failure1Event**.

Listing 7.9 A unicast event registration.

```
// The listener who is interested in the
// Failure1Event generated by this module.
//
private Failure1Listener m_failure1L;

/**
 * Informs the module that this Failure1Listener
 * is interested in Failure1Events.
 *
 * Note: This is a unicast event.
 *
 * @param l the Failure1Listener
 */
public synchronized void
addFailure1Listener(Failure1Listener l)
throws TooManyListenersException
{
  if (m_failure1L != null)
  {
    throw new TooManyListenersException();
  }

  m_failure1L = l;
}

/**
 * Informs the module that this FailureListener
 * is not longer interested in Failure1Events.
 *
 * @param l the Failure1Listener
 */
public synchronized void
removeFailure1Listener(Failure1Listener l)
{
  m_failure1L = null;
}
```

The unicast event registration allows a maximum of one event listener to be associated with an event type in an event source.

Delivery

After you have identified the events that an event source fires and provided the registration methods for those events, you need to deliver triggered events to all of the appropriate listeners. Typically, you deliver an event to listeners by going through the list of event listeners that you have maintained through the registration methods and invoking the listeners' callbacks, passing them the triggered event as an argument.

This section explains in detail all of the important issues related to event delivery. We use the **Module** event source to illustrate the concepts. As shown in Listing 7.10, **Module** simulates the occurrences of events in its **run** method, which calls **simulateFailureEvents()** and **simulateFailure1Events()** to deliver the events.

Event delivery is the process of flowing a triggered event from an event source to an event observer through a listener.

Listing 7.10   Event triggering in Module.

```
/**
 * Runs the hardware module in a system.
 * To illustrate the processing of events,
 * this method simulates the generation of
 * FailureEvents and Failure1Events.
 */
public void run()
{
  int counter = 0;

  while (true)
  {
    try
    {
      sleep(1000);

      if ((counter % 4) == 0)
      {
        simulateFailureEvents(true);
      }
      else if ((counter % 2) == 0)
      {
        simulateFailureEvents(false);
      }
      else
```

```
      {
        simulateFailure1Events();
      }

      ++counter;
    }
    catch (java.lang.InterruptedException e)
    {
      System.out.println(e);
    }
  }
}
```

Multicast

For multicast events, you have to deliver the fired event to all of the
registered listeners. Listing 7.11 illustrates how **Module** delivers the
multicast **FailureEvent** to registered listeners, which are kept in
m_failureLs. We will dissect **simulateFailureEvents()** in the sections
that follow the section on unicast event delivery.

Listing 7.11   Multicast event delivery.

```
/**
   * Calls all the listeners that have registered to
   * receive FailureEvents.
   *
   * Note: This is a multicast delivery.
   *
   * @param type the specific type of FailureEvent
   *   true: total
   *   false: partial
   */
  private void simulateFailureEvents(boolean type)
  {
    Vector ls;

    // All the listeners who have expressed their
    // interest at the time the module triggers
    // an event should get notified.
    // You should clone the listeners in a
    // synchronized block to ensure that the list
    // of listeners does not change until all the
    // listeners are informed.
    //
    synchronized (this)
    {
```

```
      ls = (Vector) m_failureLs.clone();
    }

    // Create a failure event.
    //
    FailureEvent evt;
    Failure fail = new Failure();
    if (type) // total failure
    {
      evt = new FailureEvent(this,
                FailureEvent.TOTAL_FAILURE, fail);
    }
    else  // partial failure
    {
      evt = new FailureEvent(this,
                FailureEvent.PARTIAL_FAILURE, fail);
    }

    // Invoke all the callbacks.
    //
    for (int i = 0; i < ls.size(); i++)
    {
      FailureListener l;
      l = (FailureListener)ls.elementAt(i);

      if (type) // total failure
      {
        l.failureTotal(evt);
      }

      // Callback the partial failure.
      // Note that this callback throws an exception,
      //   which must be caught.
      else
      {
        try
        {
          l.failurePartial(evt);
        }
        catch (EContinueOperation e)
        {
          System.out.println(e);
        }
      }
    }
  }
```

Unicast

Because there is at most one listener associated with it, unicast event delivery is a more straightforward task than multicast delivery. When a unicast event is triggered, you need to determine whether there is a registered event listener for the event; if so, simply invoke the callback and pass the triggered event as an argument. Listing 7.12 shows you how **Module** delivers **Failure1Event**, which is a unicast event.

Listing 7.12 Unicast event delivery.

```
/**
   * Calls the listener that has registered to
   * receive Failure1Events.
   *
   * Note: This is a unicast delivery.
   */
  private void simulateFailure1Events()
  {
    if (m_failure1L != null)
    {
      Failure fail = new Failure();
      Failure1Event evt = new Failure1Event(this, fail);

      m_failure1L.failure1(evt);
    }
  }
}
```

Synchronous Delivery

The delivery of an event is synchronous with respect to an event source. When you call a listener's callback of an event observer, the call is executed in the same thread that is processing the triggered event in the event source, and the call does not return until the event is delivered to the event observer. Once the event is delivered, however, the event observer may process it asynchronously in a separate thread and return the control back to the event source.

 An event source delivers an event to a list of listeners sequentially using its own thread.

Concurrency Control

Although the event delivery is synchronous with respect to an event source, an event-driven system as a whole has an asynchronous nature and operates in a multithreaded environment. To understand this behavior better, suppose that while an event source is in the process of delivering events, an event observer attempts to register a listener with the source. The registration call issued by the observer is executed in the observer's thread, which is most likely different than the thread in the event source that is delivering the event. This situation can cause a race between the source and the observer. If the observer manages to register its listener before the source finishes the delivery process, it receives an event from the in-progress delivery; otherwise, it does not.

To prevent races and deadlocks, you should synchronize access to the data members that contain event listeners, either by synchronizing your registration methods or by using synchronized blocks within the registration methods. Furthermore, you should not use a synchronized method to fire listeners' callback methods; instead, you should use a synchronized block to clone the list of the listeners and then invoke the callbacks from within unsynchronized code. The **simulateFailureEvents()** method, shown back in Listing 7.11, is a good example of an event delivery method that conforms to the rules we have laid out.

*An event-driven system runs in a multithreaded environment and has an asynchronous nature. Such environments are subject to races and deadlocks. To reduce the risk of races and deadlocks, define your registration methods as **synchronized** and call event listeners from within unsynchronized code.*

Handling Exceptions

When invoked by an event source, an event observer may raise an exception to inform the source about some unanticipated situation that it encountered when handling the event. The event source may take whatever action necessary to remedy the exceptional situation. This remedial action, however, is completely governed by the source, and the observer cannot dictate it.

To raise an exception, an observer creates and throws an exception to an event source; this exception should contain all of the information about the situation that is needed for the source to perform appropriate corrective actions. The **simulateFailureEvents()** method in **Module**, for example, must catch and handle **EContinueOperation** when it calls back **failurePartial()**. The **EContinueOperation** exception instructs

Module to continue operation despite its partial failure and must contain whatever information is necessary for **Module** to resume its operation.

An event source must catch and handle all the exceptions raised when it calls listeners. The handling of exceptions is completely determined by the event source.

Order Of Delivery

The Java Beans specification does not mandate any correlation between the order of listener registration and the order of event delivery for multicast events. An event source is free to deliver an event to a number of registered listeners in the order they were registered, in the opposite order, or in a random order. The **Module** event source in the FCM application, for example, delivers the events to listeners in the same order that they were registered (refer back to Listing 7.11).

You should not write event handling code that relies on a particular delivery order. If you need to control the event delivery to your listeners, register only one listener and then chain the other listeners through the registered listener. This technique allows you to have complete control over the order of event delivery to your listeners.

Java Beans does not specify the order of event delivery to event listeners. It permits event sources to define their own delivery-order semantics.

Updating Event Listeners During Delivery

The Java Beans specification does not define the handling of races when an event delivery is in progress and another thread concurrently updates the listeners in the delivery list. An event source may elect to use the updated list, whereas another may choose to make a copy of the listeners at the moment an event is triggered and deliver the event to only those listeners. The **simulateFailureEvents()** method in **Module**, for instance, clones the list of listeners in a synchronized block to ensure the delivery of an event to all of the listeners registered when the event occurred.

Even though Java Beans does not mandate it, we strongly urge you to copy the list of listeners before you proceed with the event delivery. Otherwise, the behavior of your bean is subject to race conditions.

Event Observers

An event observer is the part of an event-driven system that reacts to events triggered in an event source. The behavior of an observer when it receives an event is completely application specific. If you are creating an AWT application, for example, AWT components are already predefined for you as event sources, and your application deals with registering predefined listeners and responding to the events generated by AWT. In this example, you are designing only the event observer and the GUI code of the application, and you do not have any control over the event sources or the events they generate.

CmdModule is the event observer in the FCM application. As shown in Listing 7.13, this class implements listeners for the events defined by **Module** and uses them to receive failure events from the modules of a system. The **CmdModule** observer simply prints events of the **FailureEvent** type to the screen and raises an exception when it receives an event of the type **Failure1Event**. Obviously, a more sophisticated version of **CmdModule** would have to incorporate more application-logic code in order to control the modules of a system.

You should cleanly separate the GUI code of your application from the event handling code, which resides in your event observer.

Listing 7.13   The CmdModule event observer.

```
import java.util.*;

/**
 * This class defines the command module of a system.
 * Its function is to monitor the system and respond
 * to the failures that occur in different modules.
 * In a real-world application, this command module
 * would take a failed subsystem out of the system
 * and re-route the system through a redundant module.
 * Our simple implementation, however, only prints
```

```
 * the failures that it receives.
 */
public class CmdModule
{
  public static void main(String[] argv)
  {
    CmdModule cmd = new CmdModule();
    Module mod = new Module();

    // Register a FailureListener with the module.
    //
    FailureListenerImp l;
    l = new FailureListenerImp(cmd);
    mod.addFailureListener(l);

    // Register a Failure1Listener with the module.
    // Note: This is a unicast event, and you must
    // handle the TooManyListenersException.
    //
    Failure1ListenerImp l1;
    l1 = new Failure1ListenerImp(cmd);

    try
    {
      mod.addFailure1Listener(l1);
    }
    catch (TooManyListenersException e)
    {
      System.out.println(e);
    }

    // Start the module.
    //
    mod.start();
  }

  public void failureTotal(FailureEvent evt)
  {
    System.out.println(evt);
  }

  public void failurePartial(FailureEvent evt)
  throws EContinueOperation
  {
    System.out.println(evt);

    throw new EContinueOperation();
  }
```

```
  public void failure1(Failure1Event evt)
  {
    System.out.println(evt);
  }
}

class FailureListenerImp implements FailureListener
{
  CmdModule m_cmd;

  FailureListenerImp(CmdModule cmd)
  {
    m_cmd = cmd;
  }

  public void failureTotal(FailureEvent evt)
  {
    m_cmd.failureTotal(evt);
  }

  public void failurePartial(FailureEvent evt)
  throws EContinueOperation
  {
    m_cmd.failurePartial(evt);
  }
}

class Failure1ListenerImp implements Failure1Listener
{
  CmdModule m_cmd;

  Failure1ListenerImp(CmdModule cmd)
  {
    m_cmd = cmd;
  }

  public void failure1(Failure1Event evt)
  {
    m_cmd.failure1(evt);
  }
}
```

You should compile and run the FCM application. The following shows the output of this program:

```
e:\coriolis\cdrom\chap7\failure>java CmdModule
FailureEvent[source=Thread[Thread-1,5,main]]
Failure1Event[source=Thread[Thread-1,5,main]]
FailureEvent[source=Thread[Thread-1,5,main]]
```

```
EContinueOperation
Failure1Event[source=Thread[Thread-1,5,main]]
FailureEvent[source=Thread[Thread-1,5,main]]
Failure1Event[source=Thread[Thread-1,5,main]]
FailureEvent[source=Thread[Thread-1,5,main]]
EContinueOperation
```

An event observer contains application-specific event handling logic that responds to events triggered in an event source.

Event Adapters

Because some of the AWT event listeners define more than one callback, when you create one of these listener classes, you have to implement all of the callback methods—even the ones that you are not interested in. For example, **WindowListener** (which listens on window-related events) identifies **windowClosed()**, **windowClosing()**, **windowDeiconified()**, **windowIconified()**, and **windowOpened()**. Even if you are interested only in the closing of a window, you must provide an implementation of all the above methods, not just **windowClosing()**.

To remedy this situation, JDK 1.1 provides seven standard adapters for AWT, shown in Figure 7.6. The methods in these adapter classes are all empty; the adapter classes are provided solely as an easier way to create listeners by extending them and overriding only the methods of interest. For example, instead of implementing the **WindowListener** interface, you can simply extend **WindowAdapter** and override **windowClosing()**, if that is the method you are interested in.

JDK 1.1 does not provide any default adapters for the semantic listeners, because each of those identifies only a single method; as a result, an adapter does not provide any convenience.

The notion of adapters can be generalized to any object that is placed between an event source and a listener to enforce a policy or provide supplementary functionality. The standard adapters packaged with JDK 1.1 provide a small amount of functionality by allowing you to implement only those methods of a listener that you are interested in. In a previous section, we showed you a chaining technique to control the

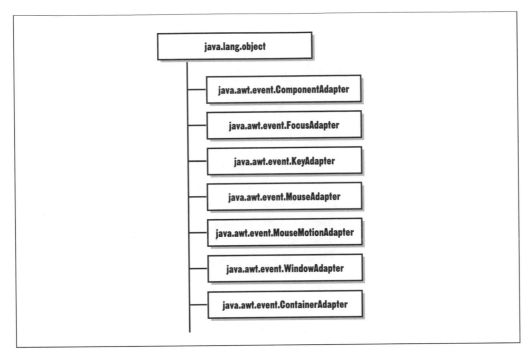

Figure 7.6 JDK 1.1 event adapters.

order of the event delivery to your listeners through one listener. This listener can be viewed as enforcing a policy on a set of listeners. You can use adapters to achieve a wide range of behaviors, such as implementing event queues for listeners, filtering events before they reach listeners, or demultiplexing multiple event sources into a single event listener.

An event adapter is interposed between an event source and an event listener to provide additional functionality or enforce a policy. An adapter essentially de-couples incoming event notifications from a listener.

Demultiplexing Adapters

When you use a listener to receive events from multiple event sources, you may want to target different methods on your event observer depending on the source of a particular event. To do this, of course, you will need to determine the source that actually generated a delivered event. Because an event always carries the source object that has triggered it, you may be able to make this determination based on the source information carried by the event. In some cases, however, this approach is impractical (for example, when possible event sources are instances of the same class).

Another approach is to use demultiplexing adapters, which can invoke different methods of a target event observer depending on the source of an event. You have already seen an example of such adapters in the HelloWorld applet in Chapter 5, which is shown again in Listing 7.14 for your convenience. This applet needs to invoke either the **on()** or **off()** method of the HelloDisplay bean, depending on whether the uses has clicked the "on" or "off" **PushButton**. Because these two buttons are instances of the same class, HelloDisplay uses two adapters, **OnButtonListener** and **OffButtonListener**, to accomplish the calling of different methods when a user presses a button. As you can see in Listing 7.14, these adapters are coded to call different methods on their target objects.

Listing 7.14   Demultiplexing adapters in the HelloWorld applet.

```
import java.awt.*;
import java.awt.event.*;

import mybeans.pushbutton.*;
import mybeans.hellodisplay.*;

/**
 * This class assembles three beans into an applet:
 * a display bean, an "on" button, and an "off" button.
 * The beans are hooked up so that the pushing of the
 * "on" button causes the message "Hello World" to
 * appear in the display bean. The "off" button turns
 * the display off.
 */
public class HelloWorld extends java.applet.Applet
{
  HelloDisplay hellodisp;

  public void init()
  {
    setLayout(new FlowLayout());

    // Add the display.
    //
    hellodisp = new HelloDisplay();
    add(hellodisp);
```

```
    // Add the "on" button.
    //
    PushButton btnOn = new PushButton("on");
    btnOn.addActionListener(new OnButtonListener());
    add(btnOn);

    // Add the "off" button.
    //
    PushButton btnOff = new PushButton("off");
    btnOff.addActionListener(new OffButtonListener());
    add(btnOff);
}


/**
 * This class calls the "on" method of the display
 * bean.
 */
class OnButtonListener implements ActionListener
{
  public void actionPerformed(ActionEvent eve)
  {
    hellodisp.on(eve);
  }
}


/*
 * This class calls the "off" method of the display
 * bean.
 */
class OffButtonListener implements ActionListener
{
  public void actionPerformed(ActionEvent eve)
  {
    hellodisp.off(eve);
  }
}
}
```

*Even though the above adapters are interposed directly
between an event source and an observer (rather than
between a source and a listener), they are still considered
to be demultiplexing adapters.*

One drawback of simple demultiplexing adapters (such as the one presented in Listing 7.14) is that they can result in a proliferation of adapters if there are a large number of different event targets, because a different adapter class is required for each source-target hook-up. For such cases, you can automatically synthesize adapter classes that exploit the Java introspection APIs to map incoming events from multiple event sources into specific methods. This technique is accomplished by using the **invoke()** method of **java.lang.reflect.Method** class. This approach, however, is only suitable for frameworks and should not be used in manually generated code, as it bypasses the compile-time type checks of Java compilers and can cause fatal runtime errors.

Security Issues

The Java Virtual Machine (JVM) severely restricts untrusted applets by preventing them from accessing local files or performing any other operation that might otherwise compromise the security of the host machine. JVM concludes that an applet is untrusted by scanning backwards through the stack of the current thread and checking to determine if any stack frame belongs to an untrusted applet. Because an event source fires an event object synchronously within its thread, an event callback is as trustworthy as the event source that has triggered it. An untrusted applet, therefore, cannot breach the sandbox security model in Java by firing bogus events.

Event adapters that might be installed on the local disk, however, must not subvert the mechanism of checking the stack frame by allowing an event firing to look more trustworthy than the applet that has fired it. Failure to do so will allow a downloaded, untrusted applet to use a locally installed adapter and bypass the Java security model. The standard event adapters in the JDK 1.1 are simple utility classes supplied to make it easier to implement event listeners; these do not pose any security issues.

Conclusion

In this chapter, we presented an overview of the JDK 1.0 event model and cited its shortcomings (specifically, a lack of scaleability and performance). We then introduced you to the JDK 1.1 delegation-based event model and explained how this model results in a clean separation of an application's code into the GUI and event handling code. We discussed in detail the life cycle of an event state object—its creation in an event source, passage through an event listener, and consumption in an event observer.

We designed and implemented a simple timer example to introduce you to the underlying elements of an event-driven system. We used the ideas in this example to implement a more rigorous event system, the Failure Command Module (FCM) application. We purposely did not use AWT in FCM to emphasize that the delegation-based event model in JDK 1.1 is a general-purpose model that can be applied to a wide range of applications, not just programs with front end GUIs. We used FCM to illustrate many concepts, such as low-level and semantic events, multicast and unicast registration, and event delivery.

By now, you know in detail the fundamentals of Java Beans: properties and events. What you don't know yet, however, is how to extend an AWT component and perform event handling in your subclass. Extended AWT widgets suffer from some of the shortcomings of the JDK 1.0 event model, and they result in complicated, error-prone logic code and a proliferation of classes. Therefore, you should subclass an AWT class only when you need to enhance an AWT class with a special look or behavior. You will learn much more about event handling in an extended AWT class in the next chapter.

Further Readings

Web Resources

http://www.javasoft.com/products/JDK/1.1/docs/guide/awt/index.html

Chapter 8

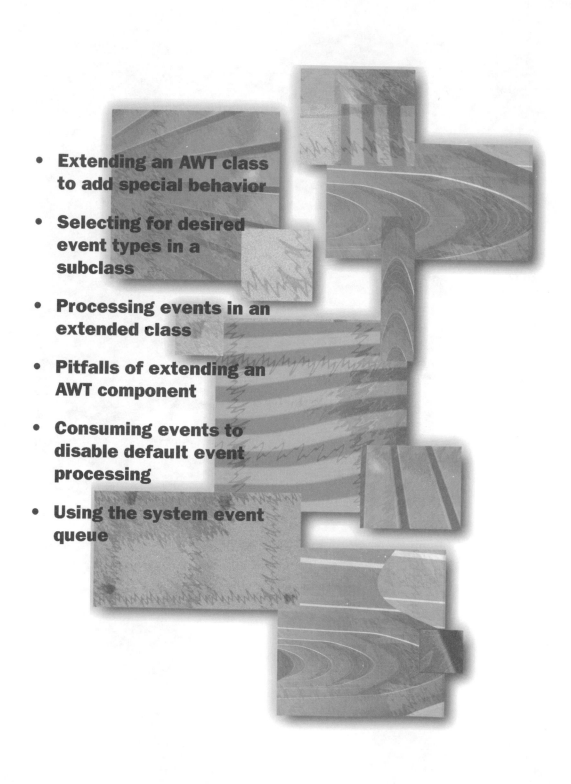

- **Extending an AWT class to add special behavior**

- **Selecting for desired event types in a subclass**

- **Processing events in an extended class**

- **Pitfalls of extending an AWT component**

- **Consuming events to disable default event processing**

- **Using the system event queue**

Chapter 8

Events In Extended AWT Components

You should use the delegation-based event modeling techniques discussed in Chapter 7 for typical event-driven applications. Some situations, however, require you to enhance the look or functionality of an AWT component, or to create windowing-related beans. As a result, you may have to subclass an AWT component, integrating your event handling or GUI code within the subclass.

In this chapter, we'll show you how to extend an AWT class, enable the delivery of events to your subclass, and process the delivered events. We will discuss in detail how the Java windowing system dispatches events to components, as well as the mechanisms a component uses to intercept and process these events. We will also teach you how to consume an event to prevent a component from performing its normal event processing. Finally, we will introduce you to the Java system event queue and provide a description of its methods.

Event Handling In An Extended Component

Extending an AWT component consists of two tasks: event processing and event selection. You may process all of the events in one single method, or use multiple processing methods. Unlike its predecessor, the JDK 1.1 event model does not deliver events to a component unless the component has expressed its interest in those events. A subclassed AWT class, therefore, must inform its parent class about the types of events in which it is interested. We will discuss the details of event handling in an AWT subclass in the following sections.

An extended class needs to select the event types it wishes to receive and to process the delivered events.

Event Processing

There are two ways to handle events when you extend an AWT component. The first approach is to override **processEvent(AWTEvent)**, which is a **protected** method and returns **void**, in your subclass. Because all of the events targeted at a component are first funneled through this method, a subclass that overrides this method will intercept all of the events occurring in its containment hierarchy from the Java windowing system. This approach is very similar to the JDK 1.0 event model, which funnels all of the events through the **handleEvent()** method.

If you override the **processEvent()** method in your extended class, though, you will receive *all* of the events occurring in the containment hierarchy—not just the event types that you are interested in. To remedy this problem, the JDK 1.1 event model provisions a series of methods, which are at the event-type level, with the following signature:

```
protected void process<EventType>(<EventType>)
```

Every standard AWT component defines all of the relevant methods of the above form, depending on the component's functionality. By default, the **processEvent()** method invokes all the proper **process<EventType> (<EventType>)** methods; these, in turn, invoke all of the registered listeners.

The processEvent() method intercepts all events, whereas process<EventType>() receives specific event types. The processEvent() method invokes all appropriate process<EventType>() methods.

The **java.awt.Button**, for example, implements **processEvent(AWTEvent)** and **processActionEvent(ActionEvent)**. The **processEvent()** method simply calls **processActionEvent()** if its argument is of the **ActionEvent** type; **processActionEvent()** invokes the callbacks of all the registered listeners. Extending **Button** gives you the choice of overriding either **processEvent()** or **processActionEvent()** in your subclass. If you redefine **processEvent()**, you will receive a great number of event types that are generated by the Java windowing system, such as mouse events and key events. If you override **processActionEvent()**, however, you will only receive events of the **ActionEvent** type.

Because **Button** supports one event of the **ActionEvent** type, it defines **processActionEvent()** only, and the **processEvent()** method contains only one call to this event-type processing method. An AWT component that generates more than one event type implements a corresponding number of event-type processing methods. For example, because the **java.awt.List** component generates events of the **ActionEvent** and **ItemEvent** types, it defines the following methods:

```
protected void processActionEvent(ActionEvent e)
protected void processItemEvent(ItemEvent e)
```

Override process<EventType>() in your subclass unless this method is not defined by your parent classes.

EVENT DISPATCHING

Here's how an AWT component interacts with the Java windowing system to receive and handle events. AWT events are posted through the **dispatchEvent()** method defined in the **java.awt.Component** (a segment of this method, taken from the JDK 1.1 beta 3 release, is shown in Listing 8.1). The first **if** statement in **dispatchEvent()** performs event delivery for the JDK 1.1 event model; the Boolean **newEventsOnly** variable has the value of **true**, for example, when you register a listener to receive events from a component. If an extended class of **Component** has expressed its interest in receiving events, **eventEnabled()** returns **true**, and **processEvent()** is called for further event processing. (Event enabling will be discussed in the next section.)

Listing 8.1 The dispatchEvent() method in Component.

```
/**
    * Dispatches an event to this component or one of its
    * sub components.
    * @param e the event
    */
void dispatchEvent(AWTEvent e) {

// skipping …

/*
 * 2. Deliver event for normal processing
 */
if (newEventsOnly) {
    // Filtering needs to really be moved to happen at a lower
    // level in order to get maximum performance gain;  it is
    // here temporarily to ensure the API spec is honored.
    //
    if (eventEnabled(e)) {
        processEvent(e);
    }

// skipping …
}
```

*The Java windowing system uses the **dispatchEvent**() method to route events to components.*

The **processEvent()** method in **Component** calls all of the event-type processing functions that correspond to the supported event types in **Component** (**processFocusEvent()**, **processMouseMotionEvent()**, and so on). Listing 8.2 shows **processEvent**, and Listing 8.3 displays **processMouseMotionEvent()**, one of the event-type processing routines; these listings are taken from the JDK 1.1 source code. As you can see in Listing 8.3, **processMouseMotionEvent()** simply calls all of the registered listeners.

Listing 8.2   The processEvent() method in Component.

```
/**
 * Processes events occurring on this component.  By default
 * this method will call the appropriate processXXXEvent
 * method for the class of event.
 * @see #processComponentEvent
 * @see #processFocusEvent
 * @see #processKeyEvent
 * @see #processMouseEvent
 * @see #processMouseMotionEvent
 * @param e the event
 */
protected void processEvent(AWTEvent e) {

    //System.err.println("Component.processNewEvent:" + e);
    if (e instanceof FocusEvent) {
        processFocusEvent((FocusEvent)e);

    } else if (e instanceof MouseEvent) {
        switch(e.getId()) {
          case MouseEvent.MOUSE_PRESSED:
          case MouseEvent.MOUSE_RELEASED:
          case MouseEvent.MOUSE_CLICKED:
          case MouseEvent.MOUSE_ENTERED:
          case MouseEvent.MOUSE_EXITED:
            processMouseEvent((MouseEvent)e);
            break;
          case MouseEvent.MOUSE_MOVED:
          case MouseEvent.MOUSE_DRAGGED:
            processMouseMotionEvent((MouseEvent)e);
            break;
        }

    } else if (e instanceof KeyEvent) {
        processKeyEvent((KeyEvent)e);
```

```
        } else if (e instanceof ComponentEvent) {
            processComponentEvent((ComponentEvent)e);
        }
    }
```

Listing 8.3 The process MouseMotionEvent() method in Component.

```
/**
 * Processes mouse motion events occurring on this component
 * by dispatching them to any registered MouseMotionListener
 * objects.
 * NOTE: This method will not be called unless mouse motion
 * events are enabled for this component; this happens when
 * one of the following occurs:
 * a) A MouseMotionListener object is registered via
 * addMouseMotionListener()
 * b) Mouse Motion events are enabled via enableEvents()
 * @param e the mouse motion event
 */
protected void processMouseMotionEvent(MouseEvent e) {
    if (mouseMotionListener != null) {
        int id = e.getId();
        switch(id) {
          case MouseEvent.MOUSE_MOVED:
            mouseMotionListener.mouseMoved(e);
            break;
          case MouseEvent.MOUSE_DRAGGED:
            mouseMotionListener.mouseDragged(e);
            break;
        }
    }
}
```

Now, here's how **java.awt.Button**, which is an extended class of **Component**, performs event handling. **Button** triggers one event of the **ActionEvent** type, and it overrides **processEvent()** to carry out the actions necessary to handle this event type. This method checks the type of its event argument, and it calls **processActionEvent()** if the argument has the **ActionEvent** type. In order to give other components further up in its containment hierarchy a chance to do their event handling chores, **processEvent()** must call its superclass **processEvent()** for the event types that it does not handle. (Note that this method need not call the superclass method when the event type is **ActionEvent**, because **Component** is not interested in this event type and would ignore it.) The **processActionEvent()** in **Button** invokes the registered listeners. These two methods are shown in Listing 8.4.

Listing 8.4   Event handling in Button.

```
/**
 * Processes events on this button. If the event is an
 * ActionEvent, it invokes the processActionEvent
 * method, else it invokes its superclass'
 * processEvent.
 * @param e the event
 */
protected void processEvent(AWTEvent e) {
        if (e instanceof ActionEvent) {
            processActionEvent((ActionEvent)e);
            return;
        }
    super.processEvent(e);
}


/**
 * Processes action events occurring on this button by
 * dispatching them to any registered ActionListener objects.
 * NOTE: This method will not be called unless action events
 * are enabled for this component; this happens when one of the
 * following occurs:
 * a) An ActionListener object is registered via
 * addActionListener()
 * b) Action events are enabled via enableEvents()
 * @see Component#enableEvents
 * @param e the action event
 */
protected void processActionEvent(ActionEvent e) {
        if (actionListener != null) {
            actionListener.actionPerformed(e);
        }
}
```

*You have to call the superclass event processing method whenever you override that method in your extended class. The **Button** component, for example, calls its superclass method in the overridden **processEvent()** method.*

Event Selection

One of the shortcomings of the JDK 1.0 event model is the performance degradation caused by delivering events to components that were not interested in receiving them. The JDK 1.1 event model addresses this issue by providing a mechanism for an AWT component to explicitly designate the set of event types in which it is interested. Because the Java windowing system does not deliver events to a component that has not requested them, the overall performance of the event system is drastically improved.

An AWT component expresses its interest in receiving windowing events either implicitly (by having a registered listener) or explicitly (by enabling the delivery of events). In Chapter 7, we explained how to register listeners with an event source. When a listener is registered to receive events from an AWT component, the Java windowing system starts to deliver all the appropriate events to the component, which will subsequently deliver them to the listener.

We have presented a segment of the **eventEnabled()** method in **java.awt.Component** in Listing 8.5. As noted in the previous section, **dispatchEvent()** calls this method to determine whether it should do any kind of processing on an event. As you can see in Listing 8.5, **eventEnabled()** returns **true** if **Component** has a registered listener, or if the appropriate event masks are set by an extended component.

Listing 8.5   The eventEnabled() method in Component.

```
boolean eventEnabled(AWTEvent e) {
    switch(e.id) {
      case ComponentEvent.COMPONENT_MOVED:
      case ComponentEvent.COMPONENT_RESIZED:
      case ComponentEvent.COMPONENT_SHOWN:
      case ComponentEvent.COMPONENT_HIDDEN:
        if ((eventMask & AWTEvent.COMPONENT_EVENT_MASK) != 0 ||
            componentListener != null) {
            return true;
        }
        break;

        // skipping ...
    }
    return false;
}
```

Extending an AWT component requires you to select the specific types of events the component is to receive. To do this, call the following method from within your extended component:

```
protected final void enableEvents(long eventsToEnable)
```

The argument to this method is a bitwise mask of the event types you wish to enable. The event masks are defined in **java.awt.AWTEvent**. Note that changing this mask does not affect the delivery of events to listeners; it only controls the delivery to an extended component. Listing 8.6 shows the source code of this method. You can call **disableEvents()** to stop delivery of certain events to your extended component.

Listing 8.6   The enableEvents() method in Component.

```
/**
    * Enables the events defined by the specified event mask
    * parameter to be delivered to this component.  Event types
    * are automatically enabled when a listener for that type
    * is added to the component, therefore this method only
    * needs to be invoked by subclasses of a component which
    * desire to have the specified event types delivered to
    * processEvent regardless of whether a listener is
    * registered.
    * @param eventsToEnable the event mask defining the event
    * types
    */
   protected final void enableEvents(long eventsToEnable) {
       eventMask |= eventsToEnable;
       newEventsOnly = true;

  // if this is a lightweight component, enable mouse events
  // in the native container.
  if (peer instanceof java.awt.peer.LightweightPeer) {
     parent.proxyEnableEvents(eventMask);
  }
}
```

Putting The Pieces Together

How do you extend an AWT component and integrate your own specialized functionality or GUI in the subclass? Suppose that you need to change the visual representation of **java.awt.TextField** to display certain graphics when **TextField** has the mouse focus. Because this truly enhances the behavior of **TextField**, subclass this class and create an extended **TextField1** class, as shown in Listing 8.7. Call **enableEvents()** to explicitly ask the Java windowing system to deliver events of the **FocusEvent** type in your extended class. **TextField1** calls this method in its constructor, passing it **FOCUS_EVENT_MASK** as an argument to designate the desired event type.

Now redefine the **processFocusEvent()** method and add the special event handling logic code for your subclass. **TextField1**, for example, simply sets the value of the **m_haveFocus** data member and calls **repaint()** to render the special graphics. You must call the superclass **process-FocusEvent()** method when you redefine it in order to give **TextField** (and its chain of superclasses) a chance to dispatch events to its listeners. Finally, add the required graphics to the **paint()** method, which is invoked as a result of calling **repaint()**.

Listing 8.7   TextField1 extends TextField.

```
import java.awt.*;
import java.awt.event.*;

/**
 * This class illustrates how to implement an extended
 * AWT class.
 * TextField1 adds some specialized GUI look to
 * TextField when it receives the focus.
 */
public class TextField1 extends TextField
{
    boolean m_haveFocus = false;

    public TextField1()
    {
      super();

      // Enable the focus events.
      //
      enableEvents(AWTEvent.FOCUS_EVENT_MASK);
    }

    /**
     * Process the focus events.
     * This method causes the paint() method
     * to be called if this component has the
     * focus.
     */
```

```
  protected void processFocusEvent(FocusEvent evt)
  {
    switch(evt.getId())
    {
      case FocusEvent.FOCUS_GAINED:
      m_haveFocus = true;
      break;

      case FocusEvent.FOCUS_LOST:
      m_haveFocus = false;
      break;
    }

    repaint();

    // Give the superclass a chance to dispatch to
    // its listeners.
    //
    super.processFocusEvent(evt);
  }

  /**
   * Give this extended class some specialized
   * visual representation when it has the focus.
   */
  public void paint(Graphics g)
  {
    if (m_haveFocus)
    {
      // Render special focus feedback...
    }
  }
}
```

The code presented in Listing 8.7 suffers from some of the shortcomings of the JDK 1.0 event model. You had to explicitly enable the event delivery, provide error-prone code in **processFocusEvent()** to filter for events, and remember to call the superclass **processFocusEvent()**. As an alternative to using the above approach, simply have your component subclass implement the particular listener interface for the events it wishes to receive and then register itself as a listener. Listing 8.8 presents **TextField2**, which is similar to **TextField1** in behavior but avoids some of its drawbacks. Note that the **TextField2** source code is more modular and easier to understand.

*Use the alternative approach if your extended class is simple.
For more complex subclasses, you may want to use the first
approach, which is more flexible but more prone to errors.*

Listing 8.8   TextField2 implements FocusListener.

```java
import java.awt.*;
import java.awt.event.*;

/**
 * This class illustrates how to add some specialized
 * GUI look to TextField without explicitly enabling
 * the focus events and overriding processFocusEvent.
 *
 * Note: For simplicity, this class also acts as
 *   a listener.
 */
public class TextField2 extends TextField
implements FocusListener
{
    boolean m_haveFocus = false;

    public TextField2()
    {
      super();

      // Register this class as a listener for
      // focus events.
      // Note: Registering a listener with TextField
      // enables the events to be delivered to it.
      //
      addFocusListener(this);
    }

    public void focusGained(FocusEvent evt)
    {
      m_haveFocus = true;
      repaint();
    }

    public void focusLost(FocusEvent e)
    {
      m_haveFocus = false;
      repaint();
    }
```

```
/**
 * Give this extended class some specialized
 * visual representation when it has the focus.
 */
public void paint(Graphics g)
{
  if (m_haveFocus)
  {
    // Render special focus feedback...
  }
}
}
```

Consuming Events

Consuming an input event prevents an event source from performing its normal processing of that event. The event source, however, will continue to deliver the event to all of its registered listeners. For example, you can consume a mouse-pressed event (which is a subtype of **MouseEvent**) to prevent a **Button** from getting activated. This behavior might be useful if you are implementing a container and wish to allow users to press on a **Button** to move it without activating it.

The explicit consumption of an event is supported by the following two methods in **java.awt.event.InputEvent** (which is the root event class for all the component-level input events, such as **KeyEvent** and **MouseEvent**):

```
public void consume()
public boolean isConsumed()
```

 Consuming an event alerts an event source that the default processing of the event is not desirable. The source, however, will continue to dispatch the event to its registered listeners.

The Event Queue

The JDK 1.1 introduces a system event queue class, a platform-independent class that queues events both from the underlying peer classes and from trusted application classes. The **java.awt.EventQueue** class represents the system event queue; there can be only one **EventQueue** for a Java system.

The JDK 1.1 windowing system posts all events generated by components to this queue before they are dispatched to their intended components. The system event queue then dispatches the events in its queue in a separate thread to the target components. The EventQueue has the following important methods:

```
public static EventQueue getEventQueue()
public synchronized void postEvent(AWTEvent e)
public synchronized AWTEvent getNextEvent()
public synchronized AWTEvent peekEvent()
```

The **getEventQueue()** method returns the system event queue (note that this method is static, because there is only one event queue in a system). The **postEvent()** method inserts an event into the queue, whereas **getNextEvent()** extracts an event from the queue and deletes it. Finally, **peekEvent()** retrieves an event without removing it from the queue.

Because it is a security breach to allow untrusted applets to manipulate the system event queue unconditionally, the **getEventQueue()** method is checked by the **SecurityManager** class to prevent an untrusted applet from accessing the event queue. In some cases, however, an applet may need to peek in the queue (for example, for compressing the mouse events in the queue). The **Applet** class therefore provides appropriate methods for viewing the event queue, with the restriction that an applet only observes the events generated by components within its own containment hierarchy.

The JDK 1.1 event system supports a system queue that orders all of the events generated in a running Java system. Events are subsequently dispatched from this queue to their intended components. There is only one instance of this queue in a system, and a trusted program can freely access and manipulate the queue.

Conclusion

In this chapter we introduced you to event handling in an extended AWT component. We emphasized that you should not attempt to subclass an AWT class unless you truly need to extend the functionality of the component or modify its visual presentation. We outlined the steps that must be performed in order for the extended component to select and process desired event types. We also discussed the procedure for consuming an event, as well as how to access and manipulate the system event queue.

The state of a bean might change when a developer assembles the bean into an application, or when an end user interacts with the bean. You should save the state of your bean to a persistent medium when a user changes its value in order to make it available for future invocations of the bean instance. For example, if an end user changes the foreground color of your bean, you should keep track of the new value in a file. In Chapter 9, we discuss the details of how to achieve persistence in your beans.

Chapter

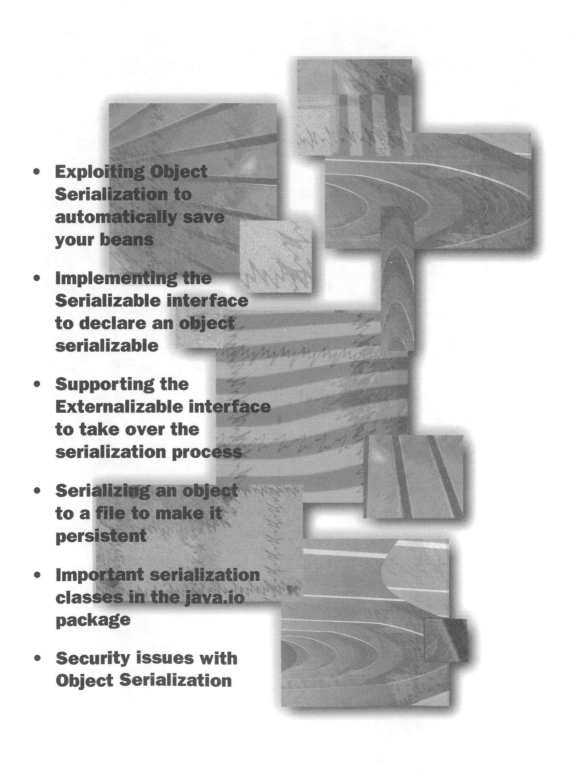

- **Exploiting Object Serialization to automatically save your beans**

- **Implementing the Serializable interface to declare an object serializable**

- **Supporting the Externalizable interface to take over the serialization process**

- **Serializing an object to a file to make it persistent**

- **Important serialization classes in the java.io package**

- **Security issues with Object Serialization**

Chapter 9

Object Serialization And Bean Persistence

The requirements on bean persistence are twofold. First, a bean that allows a user to change its properties must be able to store its internal states effortlessly in a persistent medium, such as a file or a database. In the event of a system or application crash, a persistent bean can then perform crash recovery by restoring its states to the values of its last invocation. Second, persistence must provide a flexible way for a bean to be used within other storage architectures. For example, a bean that is used as an Excel spreadsheet within a Word document must be able to store its data in a manner consistent with Microsoft's Structured Storage.

Java Beans leverages Object Serialization to support persistence. Introduced in JDK 1.1, Object Serialization provides a general mechanism for an object to serialize its data to a stream and to reconstruct itself from a stream. This quite elaborate process is able to correctly serialize an object that has references to other objects, handles shared objects that must be serialized only once, and manages object versioning.

In this chapter, we will introduce you to the fundamentals of Object Serialization and use numerous examples to show in detail how an object is serialized and deserialized. We will also demonstrate how an object can override the default serialization behavior and assume responsibility for storing and recovering its state. In addition, we will examine the security pitfalls in Object Serialization.

A Simple Persistent Bean

Before we delve into the details of Object Serialization, we will offer a very simple example of persistence in Java Beans. This demonstration involves instantiating a bean in the BeanBox framework, changing its "name" property, storing away the bean in a file, and then reloading the bean from the file. The bean maintains its "name" property across different invocations by serializing its state to a file. The objectives of this demonstration are to present the "big picture" right from the start and to reveal how easy it is to make a bean persistent.

Listing 9.1 presents PersistBean, which exports one property called **name** through a pair of **getName()** and **setName()** accessor methods. Bring up the BeanBox framework and instantiate PersistBean. Notice that the visual representation of this bean consists of a rectangle and the string "bean", which is the default **name**. Use the PropertySheet editor to change the value of **name** from "bean" to "mybean", and then store the bean into a file by using the File|Save menu, as shown in Figure 9.1. Clear the BeanBox container and proceed to restore PersistBean to its last saved state via File|Load. You should notice that the stored PersistBean displays "mybean" instead of "bean," indicating that it has retained its internal state across multiple invocations.

Listing 9.1 The PersistBean source code.

```
package mybeans.persistbean;

import java.awt.*;
import java.beans.*;
```

```java
/**
 * This simple bean illustrates the idea behind
 * persistent beans. PersistBean has only one property
 * called "name".
 */
public class PersistBean extends Canvas
{
  // The "name" property.
  // This property is stored away when the bean is
  // serialized.
  //
  private String m_name;

  public PersistBean()
  {
    m_name = "bean";

    setSize(new Dimension(80, 105));
  }

  // Draws a rectangle and displays the value of
  // the "name" property.
  //
  public void paint(Graphics g)
  {
    g.drawRect(0, 0, 75, 100);
    g.drawString(m_name, 15, 15);
  }

  public String getName()
  {
    return m_name;
  }

  public void setName(String name)
  {
    m_name = name;
  }
}
```

The interesting point about the above demonstration is that PersistBean serializes its state without implementing a single line of code. In this chapter, you will learn how BeanBox stored away PersistBean, what to do if you have sensitive data that must not be written out, and the mechanism for overriding the default serialization behavior in Java, among other useful tips.

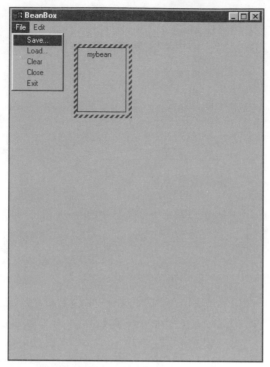

Figure 9.1   Saving PersistBean to a file.

Overview Of Object Serialization

Serialization is the process of *flattening* an object into a series (sequence) of bytes. The *byte stream* can be saved in a persistent medium (hard disk, floppy disk, or tape) in order to reconstruct the object later, or it can be sent to another process for reconstruction. The latter case provides a mechanism for transferring objects to different machines. Deserialization is the process of converting (or *inflating*) a stream of bytes into an appropriate object.

A hierarchical object is flattened into a byte stream through serialization, and it is inflated (reconstructed or restored) from a byte stream via deserialization. The byte stream can be saved in a file, or it can be sent to another process.

As noted earlier, serialization is an elaborate process. It must store away enough information about the serialized object's type to allow the object type to be determined during reconstruction. In addition, it must save all of the appropriate objects that are reachable from a root object. It should provide a common way to serialize any object, and yet it must allow for an object to override the default mechanism and define its own external format. Serialization must also address the issues of security and versioning.

JDK 1.0 did not support automatic serialization of objects. Instead, the programmer had to augment every class that needed to be serialized with two methods—one to flatten the class and the other one to inflate it. JDK 1.1 provides native language support for Object Serialization by automatically serializing and deserializing an object; a programmer needs to write serialization code only if the provided default behavior is insufficient.

The HelloWorld Example

In this section we demonstrate the **HelloWorld** class (presented in Listing 9.2), which writes a **String** object and an integer to a file and then recovers them by reading from the file. We explain only the highlights of Object Serialization with this example; the details will be covered in the remainder of this chapter.

HelloWorld exploits **ObjectOutputStream** to serialize the "Hello World" string and the version number of the class to an output stream. Because the output stream is bound to a file, the serialized objects are stored in a file, which is subsequently opened as an input stream. HelloWorld uses **ObjectInputStream** to reconstruct the **String** object and its version from the input stream.

The **ObjectOutputStream** class defines **writeObject()** to serialize an arbitrary object and a distinct method (**writeInt()** or **writeShort()**, for example) to serialize each primitive data type (**byte, short, int, long, float**, and **double**) into a byte stream. The **writeObject()** method recursively traverses all the references within a root object and serializes them; any object that is referenced more once is serialized only once to preserve the hierarchy of the class.

The **ObjectInputStream** class is the counterpart of **ObjectOutputStream**; it provides all the necessary methods to deserialize objects and primitive data types from a byte stream. The **readObject()** method, the most important one defined in this class, is used to recover an object from a stream. Note that this method returns an instance of **Object** class—you must downcast the return value into an appropriate, more specialized class.

 *In Java, arrays and strings are considered to be objects; therefore, they are handled by **writeObject()** and **readObject()**.*

Listing 9.2   The HelloWorld source code.

```java
import java.io.*;

/**
 * This class illustrates how to serialize objects
 * into a file and reconstruct them from the file.
 */
public class HelloWorld
{
  public static void main(String argv[])
  {
    try
    {
      // Open a file and serialize objects to it.
      //
      FileOutputStream fos;
      ObjectOutputStream oos;
      String hw = "Hello World";
      int version = 1;

      fos = new FileOutputStream("t.tmp"); //open file
      oos = new ObjectOutputStream(fos);
      oos.writeObject(hw);  // write string
      oos.writeInt(version);  // write integer
      oos.flush();
      fos.close();

      // Open a file and deserialize objects from it.
      //
      FileInputStream fis;
      ObjectInputStream ois;

      fis = new FileInputStream("t.tmp");
      ois = new ObjectInputStream(fis);
      String s = (String)ois.readObject(); // read
      int i = ois.readInt();
      fis.close();
```

```
System.out.println(s + " version: " + i);
      }
    catch (IOException e)
    {
      System.out.println(e);
    }
    catch (ClassNotFoundException e)
    {
      System.out.println(e);
    }
  }
}
```

Object Graphs

In object-oriented programming, an object usually contains references to other objects in addition to primitive data types. The top-level object is referred to as the *root object*, and the contained objects are called *referenced objects*. (A referenced object itself can be a root object, having references to other objects.) An object that is flat and does not refer to any other object is termed a *leaf object*; such an object can contain only primitive data types.

An *object graph* represents the hierarchy of a root object and all of its referenced objects. A referenced object in an object graph may be *reachable* from more than one path starting at the root object, creating *cycles* in the graph. Cycles are formed in a *cyclical graph* because an object is referenced more than once in the hierarchy of a root object.

Figure 9.2 represents the object graph of a root object **A**, which contains one object of type **B** and one object of type **C**. Each of these contained objects share the same reference to an object of type **D**. (Note that **B** and **C** share the same instance of **D**, as opposed to each having its own distinct instance.) As Figure 9.2 illustrates, **D** is reachable from **A** via two distinct paths: one going through **B** and the other going through **C**. These two paths form a cycle in this graph.

A (Java) object and all of its referenced objects form a hierarchy, which is represented by a graph.

Listing 9.3 presents the source code that results in the cyclical object graph shown in Figure 9.2. All of the classes defined in this sample

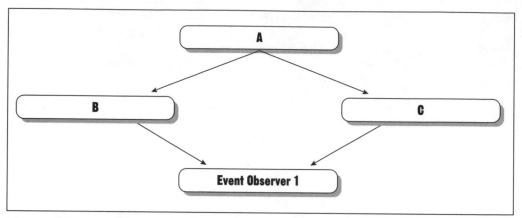

Figure 9.2   A cyclical graph.

code implement the **Serializable** interface to signal to the Java Virtual Machine (JVM) their willingness to be serialized (this interface is covered in detail in a later section). The class **A** defines a reference to class **B** and a reference to class **C**; each of these referenced classes contain a reference to class **D**. The cycle in Figure 9.2 is created because **A** creates an instance of **D** and passes it to each of the constructors for **B** and **C**.

Listing 9.3   The source code for the object graph in Figure 9.2.

```
import java.io.*;

/**
 * This class demonstrates object serialization
 * for a cyclical object graph.
 * Object A contains objects B and C, each of
 * which contains the same object D.
 */
public class A
implements Serializable
{
  B m_b;
  C m_c;

  public A()
  {
    D d = new D();
    m_b = new B(d);
    m_c = new C(d);
  }
```

```java
  public static void main(String[] argv)
  {
    try
    {
      A a = new A();

      // Serialize A into a file.
      //
      FileOutputStream fos;
  ObjectOutputStream oos;
      fos = new FileOutputStream("t.tmp");
      oos = new ObjectOutputStream(fos);
      oos.writeObject(a);
      oos.flush();
      fos.close();

      // Deserialize A from a file.
      //
      FileInputStream fis;
      ObjectInputStream ois;
      fis = new FileInputStream("t.tmp");
      ois = new ObjectInputStream(fis);
      A a1 = (A) ois.readObject();
      fis.close();

      System.out.println("A: " + a1);
      System.out.println("B: " + a1.m_b);
      System.out.println("C: " + a1.m_c);
      System.out.println("D[B]: " + a1.m_b.m_d);
      System.out.println("D[C]: " + a1.m_c.m_d);
    }
    catch (IOException e)
    {
      System.out.println(e);
    }
    catch (ClassNotFoundException e)
    {
      System.out.println(e);
    }
  }
}

class B
implements Serializable
{
  D m_d;
```

```
  B(D d)
  {
    m_d = d;
  }
}

class C
implements Serializable
{
  D m_d;

  C(D d)
  {
    m_d = d;
  }
}

class D
implements Serializable
{
}
```

Object Serialization in JDK 1.1 handles the serialization of an object graph by serializing the root object and all of its reachable referenced objects into a byte stream. If an object is reachable from more than one path in the graph, Object Serialization serializes the object only once (using the already created reference when the object is reached again from a different path). Deserialization of the byte stream restores the object graph by recreating the root object and all of its referenced objects; cycles are handled by creating a multiply-referenced object once and sharing its reference with other objects.

 Object Serialization saves a root object and all of its reachable objects into a stream of bytes, and it correctly restores the root object and its referenced objects from the stream.

The sample code presented in Listing 9.3 illustrates the flattening and inflating of the object shown in Figure 9.2. The **main**() method calls **writeObject**() to serialize the root object **A** and all the other objects contained in it into a stream. This method then invokes **readObject**() to deserialize the stream and prints the references of the reconstructed objects. The following is the output of the program—note that the object **D,**

which is reachable from both **B** and **C**, has been created only once, and its reference (**1cc7f1**) is shared by them.

```
e:\coriolis\cdrom\chap9\objgraph>java A
A: A@1cc7d6
B: B@1cc7e7
C: C@1cc802
D[B]: D@1cc7f1
D[C]: D@1cc7f1
```

When you write an object into a stream, all of the objects referenced by it are automatically written to the stream as well.

The Serializable Interface

A class implements the **Serializable** interface to declare its willingness to be serialized. A container or an application can then use the Object Serialization techniques in JDK 1.1 to save and restore the state of a serializable class. The **Serializable** interface is defined in the JDK 1.1 as follows (note that this interface provides only a semantic type—it does not define any methods or constants):

```
package java.io;
public interface Serializable {};
```

*A class implements the **Serializable** interface to permit its internal states to be written and read as a sequence of bytes.*

Object Serialization in JDK 1.1 is capable of dynamically determining the data members of a class and serializing them into a stream of bytes. By default, Object Serialization serializes all the **public**, **protected**, or **private** data members of a class, except for the **static** members. A **static** data member has the same value for all the instances of a class (as opposed to a non-static member, which can have a different value for each instance). Object Serialization does not serialize the data members that are marked by the **transient** keyword; the values of **transient** members do not persist when an object goes through serialization and deserialization.

The default behavior of Object Serialization saves the states of all the data members of a class except for **static** or **transient** members.

Protecting Sensitive Data

Serializing the data members of a class may compromise the security of sensitive data. For example, suppose you have defined a merchandising class for electronic commerce that contains a data member to keep track of a customer's credit card number. Serializing this data member will write the credit card number to a stream, which can potentially be examined by a rogue application designed to inspect a stream and recover these numbers.

There are two ways to protect the sensitive data within a class. First, you can designate all of the sensitive members as **transient**. As we have already noted, Object Serialization, by default, does not serialize such data fields. Because a subclass can override this default behavior and leak important information, you should define sensitive data members as **private transient** to preclude subclasses from accessing them. If a **transient** variable needs to retain its value when an application shuts down, you can save its value in a more secure medium, such as a database. Second, a sensitive class may choose not to implement the **Serializable** interface at all, thus eliminating any potential security risks.

Serializing Object Graphs

We have already explained how Object Serialization traverses an object graph and serializes all the reachable objects. If an object reachable from a root object does not implement **Serializable,** Object Serialization throws the **NotSerializableException** and identifies the class of the non-serializable object. The GraphNotSer application in the CD-ROM illustrates a simple object graph where one of the objects, **B**, does not implement the **Serializable** interface. The following is the output of the JVM when trying to serialize this graph:

```
e:\coriolis\cdrom\chap9\graphnotser>java GraphNotSer
java.io.NotSerializableException: B
```

Custom Serialization

There are cases in which you might need to override the default behavior of Object Serialization and take control of the serialization and deserialization process. Custom serialization allows you to serialize classes that require special handling, such as writing extra data to an output stream or bypassing the storage of some data members. You must define the following methods in a class in order to take charge of the serialization process (note that the class must also implement the **Serializable** interface):

```
private void writeObject(java.io.ObjectOutputStream out)
throws IOException;
private void readObject(java.io.ObjectInputStream in)
throws IOException, ClassNotFoundException;
```

*You must define the above two methods as **private** and declare all of the thrown exceptions.*

The **writeObject()** method writes the required state of an object to **ObjectOutputStream**, which is passed to **writeObject()** as an argument. As we will discuss later, this class contains all the necessary methods for writing objects and primitive data types. Note that this method does not need to serialize the states of its superclasses or subclasses, because Object Serialization automatically performs this task. You can always invoke the default serialization behavior from inside **writeObject()** by calling the **defaultWriteObject()** method defined in **ObjectOutputStream**.

The **readObject()** method is responsible for reversing the serialization process and restoring the data members of an object. All of the "write" methods handled inside **writeObject()** must be matched with a corresponding "read" method. The **readObject()** method is passed an argument of **ObjectInputStream** type, which contains methods to read an object or any primitive data type from an input stream. You can always invoke **ObjectInputStream.DefaultReadObject()** inside **readObject()** in order to revert back to the default deserialization mechanism.

*A class that requires special handling during the serialization and deserialization process can implement the **writeObject()** and **readObject()** methods. These methods should not concern themselves with storing and recovering the state of the superclass if the latter implements the **Serializable** interface.*

Listing 9.4 presents a simple application of custom serialization. The class **B**, which extends **A**, defines the **writeObject()** and **readObject()** methods in order to take over the serialization process. Three arguments are required to construct an object of type **B**: a **String**, an **int**, and a **short**. The **short** argument is passed to the superclass **A**, whereas the **String** and **int** arguments are kept inside **B**. The **writeObject()** method saves the value of the **String** data member only; the **int** member is not stored. Note that **writeObject()** does not attempt to save the **short** member of class **A**, because this class itself implements the **Serializable** interface and is subject to the default serialization behavior. The **readObject()** method simply reads one **String** object from the input stream and assigns it to the appropriate data member.

The **main()** routine of this application constructs an instance of class **B**, serializes it into a stream, recovers the instance, and then prints the data members of the deserialized instance. Note that **main()** here differs slightly from the **main()** routine of Listing 9.3 in order to show you how to serialize a class without necessarily writing it to a (persistent) file. The **main()** routine of Listing 9.4 exploits the **ByteArrayOutputStream** class to provide an in-memory output stream for serialized objects; this stream can be sent through a network connection to another machine, or it can later be saved to the hard disk as a file.

The output produced by this application is shown below. Note that the original value of the **int** argument supplied to the constructor of class **B** has been lost because **B** did not store its **int** data member in **writeObject()**.

```
e:\coriolis\cdrom\chap9\custser>java CustomSer
writeObject()
readObject()
The values are: 0 1
```

Listing 9.4   Custom serialization.

```
import java.io.*;

/**
 * This class serializes an object, which performs
 * custom serialization, into a stream of
 * bytes and then reconstructs the object from the
 * stream.
 */
public class CustomSer
{
  public static void main(String[] argv)
  {
```

```java
    try
    {
      B b = new B("The values are: ", 9, (short) 1);

      // Serialize B into a stream of bytes.
      //
      ByteArrayOutputStream bos;
      ObjectOutputStream oos;
      bos = new ByteArrayOutputStream();
      oos = new ObjectOutputStream(bos);
      oos.writeObject(b);
      oos.flush();

      // Deserialize B from a stream of bytes.
      //
      ByteArrayInputStream bis;
      ObjectInputStream ois;
      byte[] data = bos.toByteArray();
      bis = new ByteArrayInputStream(data);
      ois = new ObjectInputStream(bis);
      B b1 = (B) ois.readObject();

      String s = b1.getStr() + b1.getInt() + " " +
                    b1.getShort();
      System.out.println(s);
    }
    catch (IOException e)
    {
      System.out.println(e);
    }
    catch (ClassNotFoundException e)
    {
      System.out.println(e);
    }
  }
}

class A
implements Serializable
{
  short m_ver;

  A(short ver)
  {
    m_ver = ver;
  }
```

```java
  short getShort()
  {
    return m_ver;
  }
}


/**
 * This class performs custom Object Serialization
 * by providing the readObject() and writeObject()
 * methods.
 *
 * Note: You don't need to save/restore the state
 *  of the superclass A. Object Serialization
 *  automatically serializes all the superclasses.
 *
 */
class B extends A
implements Serializable
{
  String m_s;
  int m_i;

  B(String s, int i, short sh)
  {
    super(sh);

    m_s = s;
    m_i = i;
  }

  public String getStr()
  {
    return m_s;
  }

  public int getInt()
  {
    return m_i;
  }

  // The method restores only the value of the string.
  //
  private void readObject(ObjectInputStream stream)
  throws IOException, ClassNotFoundException
  {
    System.out.println("readObject()");
    m_s = (String) stream.readObject();
  }
```

```
// This method saves only the value of its string
// member. The integer field is not stored.
//
private void writeObject(ObjectOutputStream stream)
throws IOException
{
  System.out.println("writeObject()");
  stream.writeObject(m_s);
}
}
```

Non-Serializable Superclasses

A class that implements the **Serializable** interface acquires the **Serializable** type, which is passed down to all of its subclasses. Object Serialization provides default behavior to serialize a class and all of its serializable superclasses. The application presented in Listing 9.4 demonstrates the serialization of a class whose superclass is also serializable.

You may encounter situations where a class needs to be serialized, but its superclass is not serializable. Because Object Serialization is not capable of serializing the state of a not-serializable class, the extended class may assume the responsibility of saving and restoring the state of the superclass's **public** and **protected** fields. This responsibility may be assumed only if the superclass has an accessible *no-arg constructor* (a constructor that does not take any arguments) to initialize its state. An attempt to serialize a class whose superclass is not serializable and does not have a no-arg constructor will cause an error, which will be detected by the JVM at runtime.

You can utilize the **writeObject()** method (described in the previous section) inside an extended class to store the appropriate data members of a non-serializable superclass. These members can be accessed if they are **public** or **protected**, or if the superclass has provided access methods for them.

During deserialization, the fields of a non-serializable class are first initialized using its no-arg constructor. All fields that have been written out within the **writeObject()** method of an extended class must be read back in a corresponding **readObject()** method (which is also defined in the extended class) and assigned to the data members of the superclass or the extended class accordingly. Note that an extended class may define **writeObject()** and **readObject()** only if it wishes to store the state of its superclass. Otherwise, the no-arg constructor defined by the superclass is used to initialize the state. You may want to refer to the sample program of Listing 9.4 to understand how to perform custom serialization.

An extended class whose superclass is not serializable can still be serialized if the superclass provides a no-arg constructor. A subclass may assume the responsibility of serializing the state of its superclass if the no-arg constructor does not provide suitable initial values.

The Externalizable Interface

A class can implement the **Externalizable** interface in order to have complete control over the format and contents of the data written to an output stream. Object Serialization saves only the name of an externalizable object; it is the responsibility of the object to save and restore its contents and the state of its superclass. This **Externalizable** interface, which extends **Serializable**, is defined below.

*Object Serialization does not serialize the state of the super-class of an **Externalizable** class even if the superclass has implemented the **Serializable** interface.*

```
package java.io;

public interface Externalizable extends Serializable
{
  public void writeExternal(ObjectOutput out)
  throws IOException;

  public void readExternal(ObjectInput in)
  throws IOException, java.lang.ClassNotFoundException;
}
```

Object Serialization uses the following procedure to serialize an object. First, the object is tested to determine if it supports the **Externalizable** interface. If so, its **writeExternal()** method is called to store the object, and **readExternal()** is invoked to recover it. If the object does not support **Externalizable** but does implement **Serializable**, then either the

writeObject() and **readObject()** methods are invoked (if the object has defined them) or default serialization is employed. Finally, if the object does not support any of the above two interfaces, an exception is thrown.

Because the **writeExternal()** method is **public**, a rogue program can invoke it on an externalizable object and then examine the generated output stream in order to gain access to sensitive information. Similarly, the program can use the **readExternal()** method to force the object into a state that might compromise its integrity. An object, therefore, must not expose any sensitive information within these two methods. A sensitive class may elect not to support this interface at all in order to eliminate any risk to its security

*An object can support the **Externalizable** interface in order to gain full control over the storing and recovery of its data and its superclass's data.*

Serialization And Deserialization Inside Containers

Although an object can either leverage the default serialization behavior or define its own in order to serialize its state, it usually does not know when it should serialize its data or what type of an output stream it should use. For example, if the object is within an application, it may use a **FileOutputStream**, whereas an object inside an untrusted applet cannot serialize its data to a local file. Furthermore, a program usually consists of many independent objects and relationships between them; serializing the state of a program involves saving the states of all the objects and their relationships. An object by itself cannot oversee the overall serialization of a program.

Only the container (an applet, an application, or a Java Beans container) of a set of objects possesses the necessary information to manage the serialization process as a whole. In addition to providing default serialization behavior for objects, Object Serialization also provides a set of classes for containers to facilitate obtaining a "snapshot" of the state of a program. These classes can essentially be divided into two groups: one for serializing data to output streams and the other for deserializing data from input streams. Detailed coverage of all of the methods in these classes is beyond the scope of this book; for more information, refer to the Java documentation that is shipped as a part of JDK 1.1.

This rest of this section covers the important classes and interfaces that are used to support the serialization of data to output streams and deserialization of data from input streams.

The DataOutput Interface

DataOutput is an interface defined to describe streams that can write out data in a machine-independent format. Such streams can be sent to machines with different hardware architectures (which may have different internal representations for integral and floating-point data) and be correctly deserialized. This interface identifies all of the methods needed to write out primitive data types, such as **writeBoolean()**, **writeInt()**, and **writeDouble()**. The **DataOutput** interface is defined as follows:

```
public interface DataOutput
{
  // Methods to write primitive data types.
  //
  void writeBoolean(boolean v) throws IOException;
  void writeInt(int v) throws IOException;
  void writeDouble(double v) throws IOException;

// ...
}
```

The ObjectOutput Interface

This interface extends the **DataOutput** interface to support writing of objects. Note that in Java arrays are considered to be objects and, therefore, can be written out by a class that implements this interface. The **ObjectOutput** interface is defined as follows:

```
public interface ObjectOutput extends DataOutput
{
    /**
     * Write an object to the underlying storage or stream.  The
     * class that implements this interface defines how the
     * object is written.
     *
     * @exception IOException Any of the usual Input/Output
     * related exceptions.
     */
```

```
    public void writeObject(Object obj)
    throws IOException;

    // ...
}
```

The **writeObject()** method is the most notable method defined in the **ObjectOutput** interface. This interface also defines **close()**, which must be called to release any resources associated with a stream.

The ObjectOutputStream Class

This class is responsible for providing most of the functionality of Object Serialization. You already have seen many examples of the usage of this class in this chapter. **ObjectOutputStream** implements the **ObjectOutput** interface, which identifies all of the methods needed to write primitive data types and objects to a stream. Listing 9.5 presents the methods defined in this class.

Listing 9.5   The ObjectOutputStream methods.

```
package java.io;

public class ObjectOutputStream
extends OutputStream
implements ObjectOutput, ObjectStreamConstants
{
  public ObjectOutputStream(OutputStream out)
  throws IOException;

  public final void writeObject(Object obj)
  throws IOException;

  public final void defaultWriteObject()
  throws IOException, NotActiveException;

  public void reset() throws IOException;

  protected void annotateClass(Class cl) throws IOException;

  protected Object replaceObject(Object obj) throws IOException;

  protected final boolean enableReplaceObject(boolean enable)
  throws SecurityException;

  protected void writeStreamHeader() throws IOException;
```

```
public void write(int data) throws IOException;

public void write(byte b[]) throws IOException;

public void write(byte b[], int off, int len)
throws IOException;

public void flush() throws IOException;

public void drain() throws IOException;

public void close() throws IOException;

public void writeBoolean(boolean data) throws IOException;

public void writeByte(int data) throws IOException;

public void writeShort(int data)  throws IOException;

public void writeChar(int data)  throws IOException;

public void writeInt(int data)  throws IOException;

public void writeLong(long data)  throws IOException;

public void writeFloat(float data) throws IOException;

public void writeDouble(double data) throws IOException;

public void writeBytes(String data) throws IOException;

public void writeChars(String data) throws IOException;

public void writeUTF(String data) throws IOException;
}
```

The DataInput Interface

This interface describes streams that can read input data in a machine-independent format. **DataInput** identifies methods for reading all primitive data types, such as **readBoolean()**, **readInt()**, and **readDouble()**. The **DataInput** interface is defined as follows:

```
public interface DataInput
{
  // Methods to read primitive data types.
  //
```

```
boolean readBoolean() throws IOException;
int readInt() throws IOException;
double readDouble() throws IOException;

// ...
}
```

The ObjectInput Interface

This interface extends **DataInput** to support the reading of objects from
an input stream. The **readObject()** method is the most important method
identified by this interface, which is defined below.

```
public interface ObjectInput extends DataInput
{
    /**
     * Read and return an object. The class that implements this
     * interface defines where the object is "read" from.
     *
     * @exception java.lang.ClassNotFoundException If the class
     * of a serialized object cannot be found.
     * @exception IOException If any of the usual Input/Output
     * related exceptions occur.
     */
    public Object readObject()
    throws ClassNotFoundException, IOException;

    // ...
}
```

The ObjectInputStream Class

This class implements the **ObjectInput** interface, which defines all of
the methods needed to read primitive data types and objects from a
stream. We have already presented some examples in this chapter that
illustrate the use of this class. Listing 9.6 shows the methods supported
by this class.

Listing 9.6 The ObjectInputStream methods.

```
package java.io;

public class ObjectInputStream
extends InputStream
implements ObjectInput, ObjectStreamConstants
{
    public ObjectInputStream(InputStream in)
    throws StreamCorruptedException, IOException;
```

```
public final Object readObject()
throws OptionalDataException,
  ClassNotFoundException, IOException;

public final void defaultReadObject()
throws IOException, ClassNotFoundException,
  NotActiveException;

public synchronized void registerValidation(
  ObjectInputValidation obj, int prio)
throws NotActiveException, InvalidObjectException;

protected Class resolveClass(ObjectStreamClass v)
throws IOException, ClassNotFoundException;

protected Object resolveObject(Object obj)
throws IOException;

protected final boolean enableResolveObject(
  boolean enable)
throws SecurityException;

protected void readStreamHeader()
throws IOException, StreamCorruptedException;

public int read() throws IOException;

public int read(byte[] data, int offset, int length)
throws IOException

public int available() throws IOException;

public void close() throws IOException;

public boolean readBoolean() throws IOException;

public byte readByte() throws IOException;

public int readUnsignedByte()  throws IOException;

public short readShort()  throws IOException;

public int readUnsignedShort() throws IOException;

public char readChar()  throws IOException;

public int readInt()  throws IOException;
```

```
public long readLong()  throws IOException;

public float readFloat() throws IOException;

public double readDouble() throws IOException;

public void readFully(byte[] data)
throws IOException;

public void readFully(byte[] data, int offset, int size)
throws IOException;

public int skipBytes(int len) throws IOException;

public String readLine() throws IOException;

public String readUTF() throws IOException;
}
```

Bean Persistence Guidelines

In this section we offer a set of guidelines that you should follow when you design beans:

- The **java.awt.Component** class implements the **Serializable** interface. If a bean extends this class or any of its subclasses, it automatically becomes a **Serializable** bean.

- If a bean does not extend a **Serializable** class, it must explicitly implement the **Serializable** interface. Otherwise, the bean cannot be serialized by containers. Note in particular that a bean, which does not specify a superclass, inherits from the **Object** class, which is not **Serializable**.

- All classes used by a **Serializable** bean, and reachable from it, must also be **Serializable**.

- A bean should store away the values of all of its exported properties in addition to any internal states that might be useful during its reconstruction. The default behavior of Object Serialization serializes all the data members of an object except for those marked with the **transient** keyword. If you override the default behavior, however, you are responsible for correctly serializing the state of the bean.

- Containers are responsible for maintaining the interconnections between beans during serialization and deserialization. A bean, therefore, should not save away references to external beans or containers. Instead, it should declare such references as **transient**.

- Event adapters should typically define their internal states as **transient**.

Conclusion

This chapter introduced you to the principles of Object Serialization. You learned about the **Serializable** interface, which a class implements to allow its state to be saved. You also found out about the default serialization mechanism in JDK 1.1, as well as how to override this mechanism and provide custom serialization for your classes. You can use Object Serialization to serialize an object to a persistent medium, such as a file on a hard disk, in order to make the object persistent.

In the next chapter, we will introduce introspection within JDK 1.1 and explain how a Java Beans framework analyzes beans. We will also demonstrate how to provide explicit information about beans.

Further Readings
Web Resources

http://www.javasoft.com/products/JDK/1.1/docs/guide/serialization/

Chapter 10

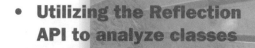

- **Utilizing the Reflection API to analyze classes**

- **The new java.lang.reflect package in JDK 1.1**

- **Using the Class class to create new instances of the reflection classes**

- **Exploiting the Field class to gain access to the data members of a class**

- **Employing the Method class to examine the member methods of a class**

- **Building the Inspector application to report on the members of a class**

- **Security considerations with the Core Reflection API**

Chapter 10

The Core Reflection API

When we covered properties and events in the previous chapters, we frequently touched on the subjects of reflection and introspection. We explained that a Java Beans container introspects on a bean's methods to deduce its properties and generated events. For each property, the container can conclude whether it is bound, constrained, multicast, or unicast. When connecting an event of a source bean to a target bean, the container uses introspection to generate and present to a user the list of all methods of the target bean that can be invoked when the event is fired. Object Serialization also leverages the Core Reflection API to determine which data members of an object must be stored or recovered during serialization and deserialization.

In this chapter, we will formalize these concepts by discussing the Java Core Reflection API and details about some of the more important classes in the java.lang.reflect package. We will show you how to write code that reflects on an object and prints out all of its data members, methods, and constructors. As always, a section is dedicated to security issues you need to consider when using the Reflection API.

More thorough coverage of the Reflection API, however, is beyond the scope of this book. For added information, you should refer to the "Further Readings" section at the end of this chapter, or to reference documentation about the Java programming language.

Overview Of Java Core Reflection

The Java Core Reflection API consists of a handful of classes in the java.lang.reflect package and some enhancements made to the **Class** class. The java.lang package also is extended in several ways. First, two new classes, **Byte** and **Short**, are added in order to act as class wrappers for **byte** and **short** primitive data types. Second, the **Void** class is included to hold a reference to the **Class** object representing the primitive **void** type. Third, each of the eight class wrappers for the primitive data types (**byte**, **short**, **int**, **long**, **float**, **double**, **boolean**, and **char**) now includes a reference to a **Class** object that represents its corresponding primitive type at runtime.

The Reflection API supports two sets of applications—lightweight and heavyweight—with varying degrees of complexity. *Lightweight* applications need to discover the **public** fields, methods, and constructors of a target object based on its runtime class. Java Beans and object inspectors are examples of applications in this category.

Sophisticated, or *heavyweight,* applications require runtime access to the implementation of a class at the same level as provided by a class file in order to gain access to all the **public, protected**, default (package), and **private** fields, methods, and constructors of a target object. Development tools such as debuggers, interpreters, object inspectors, class browsers, and runtime services such as Object Serialization all fall into this category.

In addition to providing access to members of an object, the Reflection API supports the creation of class instances and array objects, modifying the fields of objects and classes, and invoking methods on objects and classes.

The JDK 1.1 beta 3 release of the java.lang.reflect package contains six classes and one interface: **Field**, **Method**, **Constructor**, **Modifier**, **Array**, **InvocationTargetException**, and **Member**. The **Member** interface provides identifying information about a single data member,

member function, or a constructor; it also prescribes a number of abstract methods that **Field**, **Method**, or **Constructor** classes must implement.

The **InvocationTargetException** class is a checked exception that is thrown when a method or constructor is improperly invoked through the Reflection API. The **Array** class, which is **final** and cannot be instantiated, provides **static** methods to dynamically create, get, and set Java arrays. The **Modifier** class defines **static** methods and constants to decode class and member access modifiers, such as **abstract**, **final**, **interface**, **native**, **private**, **protected**, **public**, **static**, **synchronized**, **transient**, and **volatile**. The Reflection API uses integer values to represent each distinct combination of access modifiers. For instance, the combination of the **public final** access modifiers has some preassigned integer value. You can use the methods in **Modifier**, such as **isFinal(int)** or **isPublic(int)**, to find out whether an integer-encoded value of access modifiers includes a desired access modifier.

The **Field**, **Method**, **Constructor** classes are final and can be instantiated only by the Java Virtual Machine (JVM). Their instances can access the members of their corresponding underlying objects, get and set field values, invoke methods on objects and classes, and instantiate new classes. These classes and the **Class** class are discussed later in this chapter.

The Java Core Reflection API provides a secure mechanism for a program to analyze the data members, methods, and constructors of a target bean. The Reflection API also enables the creation of new instances of other classes or the invocation of methods on existing objects.

The Inspector Application

In this chapter, we develop the Inspector application, which can inspect the data members, methods, and constructors of an object and print them out. This application is an example of the aforementioned lightweight programs, which require access to all of the publicly defined members of a class. The Inspector example also sheds light on the manner in which a Java Beans container might use the Reflection API in order to analyze a bean and deduce its properties and events. This application contains good examples of how to use the methods provided by the **Class**, **Field**, **Method**, and **Constructor** classes.

Listing 10.1 presents a portion of the **Inspector** class, which provides a constructor and three methods: **printFields()**, **printMethods()**, and **printConstructors()**. The constructor simply accepts one argument (which contains a reference to the object under inspection) and assigns it to an internal field. Note that the details of the three "print" methods provided by this class are omitted from Listing 10.1; these methods will be shown in later sections.

Listing 10.1   The Inspector class.

```java
import java.lang.reflect.*;

/**
 * This class illustrates how to use the
 * Core Reflection API to reflect on an object and
 * print its members.
 */
public class Inspector
{
  Object m_obj;

  public Inspector(Object obj)
  {
    m_obj = obj;
  }

  public void printFields()
  {
    // code...
  }

  public void printMethods()
  {
    // code...
  }

  public void printConstructors()
  {
    // code...
  }
}
```

We have also implemented a straightforward program that acts as a command interpreter for the **Inspector** class. Shown in Listing 10.2, this program reads one line from the standard input and invokes the appropriate method of **Inspector**. The interpreter currently is hard-coded to inspect on an instance of the class **B**; a more elaborate version of the interpreter should allow a user to specify the class to be inspected.

Listing 10.2   The command interpreter.

```java
import java.io.*;

/**
 * This class provides a command interpreter for the
 * Inspector class.
 *
 * Note: This class currently inspects on
 * class B only.
 */
public class Main
{
  public static void main(String argv[])
  {
    B b = new B();
    Inspector insp = new Inspector(b);

    InputStreamReader isr;
    isr = new InputStreamReader(System.in);
    BufferedReader br = new BufferedReader(isr);

    while (true)
    {
      try
      {
        String input = br.readLine();

        if (input.equals("print fields"))
        {
          insp.printFields();
          System.out.print("> ");
        }
        else if (input.equals("print methods"))
        {
          insp.printMethods();
          System.out.print("> ");
        }
        else if (input.equals("print constructors"))
        {
          insp.printConstructors();
          System.out.print("> ");
        }
```

```
        else if (input.equals(""))
        {
          System.out.print("> ");
        }
        else if (input.equals("exit"))
        {
          br.close(); // close the reader
          System.exit(0);
        }
        else
        {
          System.out.print("Supported commands are ");
          System.out.println("[print fields] " +
            "[print methods] [print constructors] ");
          System.out.print("> ");
        }
      }
      catch (IOException e)
      {
        System.out.println(e);
      }
    }
  }
}
```

The **B** class is designed to contain data members with different access modifiers in order to provide a better demonstration of the Reflection API. Because this class extends the class **A** and implements the interface **Intf**, it includes members that are inherited from **A** and **Intf**. Listings 10.3, 10.4, and 10.5 present **B**, **A**, and **Intf**, respectively.

Listing 10.3   B provides sample input.

```
/**
 * This class provides input for the Inspector class.
 * It extends the class A and implements the Intf
 * interface.
 */
public class B extends A
implements Intf
{
  public C m_c;
  protected double m_double;
  private float m_float;
  short m_short;
  public static byte m_static;
```

```
  // Initialize some of the data fields.
  //
  public B()
  {
    m_double = 3.14;
    m_float = (float) 1.14;
    m_short = 1997;
  }

  public int bar()
  {
    return 0;
  }

  public static void foobar(C c)
  {
  }
}
```

Listing 10.4   A serves as the superclass of B.

```
/**
 * This class provides input for the Inspector class.
 */
public class A
{
  public int m_integer;

  public A()
  {
    m_integer = 2000;
  }

  public void foo(int i)
  {
  }
}
```

Listing 10.5   Interface Intf is implemented by B.

```
/**
 * This class provides input for the Inspector class.
 */
public interface Intf
{
  public final long LONG = 1000;

  public int bar();
}
```

The java.lang.Class Class

The **Class** class provides runtime information for Java classes, interfaces, arrays, primitive types, and the keyword **void**. Because **Class** does not define any public constructors, user programs cannot create instances of this class. The JVM automatically constructs **Class** objects as it loads classes from the local file system or from the network.

You can utilize this class to create new class instances at runtime; determine whether a **Class** object represents an array, primitive, or interface type; obtain the fully qualified name of the class of an object; and so on. As enhanced in the JDK 1.1 to support the Reflection API, **Class** now includes methods to retrieve the fields, methods, and constructors of a **Class** object. You should refer to the JDK 1.1 reference guide for a complete description of this class. The methods used in **Inspector** are described as follows:

```
package java.lang;
public final class Class extends Object
implements Serializable
{
  public Field[] getFields() throws SecurityException;
  public Method[] getMethods() throws SecurityException;
  public Constructor[] getConstructors() throws
SecurityException;
  // …
}
```

The **getFields()** method returns an array of **Field** objects containing all of the accessible **public** fields (data members) of a class and all of its superclasses, or an interface and all of its superinterfaces. If the class or interface has no accessible **public** fields, or if it represents an array type or a primitive type, the returned array has a length of 0.

The **getMethods()** method returns an array of **Method** objects, which contain all of the **public** member methods of a class or an interface and those defined by its superclasses and superinterfaces. The returned array has a length of 0 if the class or interface has no **public** methods. Similarly, **getConstructors()** returns an array of **Constructor** objects that reflect all of the **public** constructors of a class. This method returns an array of length 0 if the class has no **public** constructors. (Note that **getConstructors()** does not include the constructors of the superclasses of a class.) All of the above methods throw a **SecurityException** if reflecting on a class violates the security policy of the running JVM.

 *Although the **Class** class belongs in the java.lang.reflect package, it is kept in the java.lang package for backward compatibility with JDK 1.0.*

The java.lang.reflect.Field Class

The **Field** class provides information about a single instance or **static** field (data member) of a class or an interface. You can use the methods of this class to obtain the type of a field, get its value, or set a new value for it. You cannot directly create new instances of the **Field** class— only JVM may construct such objects. Instead, you receive **Field** instances through the **getField()**, **getFields()**, **getDeclaredField()**, and **getDeclaredFields()** methods of the **Class** class. The definition of **Field** and some of its member methods are shown below:

```
package java.lang.reflect;
public final class Field extends Object
implements Member
{
  public Class getDeclaringClass();
  public String getName();
  public int getModifiers();
  public Class getType();
  public String toString();
  public Object get(Object obj)
  throws NullPointerException,
    IllegalArgumentException,  IllegalAccessException;
  public void set(Object obj, Object value)
  throws NullPointerException,
    IllegalArgumentException, IllegalAccessException;
  // ...
}
```

The **getDeclaringClass()** returns the class that has declared the underlying field object. The **getName()** method obtains the name of a field, whereas **getType()** returns its type. The **getModifiers()** method provides information about the access modifiers of a field, which is encoded in an integer value. The **get()** method can be used to retrieve the value of a field, while **set()** changes this value. Note that data-widening conversions may occur during **get()** or **set()** operations, whereas data-narrowing conversions throw an **IllegalArgumentException**.

Listing 10.6 presents the **printFields()** method of the **Inspector** class, which exercises some of the above methods. Note that this method calls the **getClass()** method to obtain the **Class** object of the entity under reflection, then invokes **getFields()** on the **Class** object to gain access to all the **public** data members.

Listing 10.6   The printFields() method of Inspector.

```
public class Inspector
{
  // ...

  // Print all the fields (data members) of a class
  // to the standard output.
  //
  public void printFields()
  {
    try
    {
      Class cl = m_obj.getClass();
      Field[] fields = cl.getFields();

      for(int i = 0; i < fields.length; ++i)
      {
        // Retrieve info about the field.
        //
        Field field = fields[i];
        String name = field.getName();
        Class clDecl = field.getDeclaringClass();
        int modf = field.getModifiers();
        Class clType = field.getType();
        String string = field.toString();
        Object obj = field.get(m_obj);  // field value

        // Print the info.
        //
        System.out.println("Name: " + name);
        System.out.println("clDecl: " + clDecl);
        System.out.println("modf: " + modf);
        System.out.println("clType: " + clType);
        System.out.println("string: " + string);
        System.out.println("obj: " + obj);
```

```
          System.out.println("\n");
        }
      }
      catch (SecurityException e)
      {
        System.out.println(e);
      }
      catch (NullPointerException e)
      {
        System.out.println(e);
      }
      catch (IllegalArgumentException e)
      {
        System.out.println(e);
      }
      catch (IllegalAccessException e)
      {
        System.out.println(e);
      }
    }

    // ...
}
```

Proceed to run the **Main** class in the Inspector application and invoke **printFields**() to get a listing of all of the fields of **B**, which are returned by **Class.getFields**(). As expected, **printFields**() reports all of the **public** data members of **B**, including the ones inherited from the **A** class and the **Intf** interface. The output of this method is shown below:

```
E:\coriolis\cdrom\Chap10\inspector>java Main
> print fields
Name: LONG
clDecl: interface Intf
modf: 25
clType: long
string: public static final long Intf.LONG
obj: 1000

Name: m_integer
clDecl: class A
modf: 1
clType: int
string: public int A.m_integer
obj: 2000
```

```
Name: m_c
clDecl: class B
modf: 1
clType: class C
string: public C B.m_c
obj: null

Name: m_static
clDecl: class B
modf: 9
clType: byte
string: public static byte B.m_static
obj: 0

>
```

*The **Field** class provides access to all the data members of an object. The methods of this class can be used to obtain information about a data member, retrieve its value, or change its value to a different one.*

The java.lang.reflect.Method Class

The **Method** class provides information about a single **static** or instance method of a class or an interface. You can utilize **Method** to obtain the name of member method, get its return type, find out about its parameters, invoke it on an object, and so on. You cannot directly create new instances of this class; instead, you obtain **Method** objects through the **getMethod()**, **getMethods()**, **getDeclaredMethod()**, and **getDeclaredMethods()** methods of the **Class** class. The **Method** class and some of its methods are defined as follows:

```
package java.lang.reflect;
public final class Method extends Object
implements Member
{
  public Class getDeclaringClass();
  public String getName();
  public int getModifiers();
  public Class getReturnType();
  public Class[] getParameterTypes();
  public Class[] getExceptionTypes();
  public String toString();
  public Object invoke(Object obj, Object[] args)
```

```
    throws NullPointerException,
      IllegalArgumentException,   IllegalAccessException,
      InvocationTargetException;
    // ...
}
```

The **getReturnType()** method fetches the return type of a method, and **getParameterTypes()** returns information about a method's arguments. The **getExceptionTypes()** method obtains the list of all exceptions that are thrown by a method. **Invoke()** allows an object to call a method on another object and pass an arbitrary number of arguments to the method call.

Listing 10.7 shows the **printMethods()** method of the **Inspector** class, which demonstrates the use of the above methods. Note that **printMethods()** employs **Class.getMethods()** to receive references to all of the **public** member methods of a class, as well as those inherited from superclasses and superinterfaces. Because all classes in Java inherit from the **Object** class, which defines a large number of methods, **printMethods()** uses an **if** statement in order to filter out all such methods.

Listing 10.7   The printMethods() method of Inspector.

```
public class Inspector
{
   // ...

   // Print the list of methods of a class to
   // the standard output.
   //
   // Note: The superclass methods are not printed.
   //
   public void printMethods()
   {
     try
     {
       Class cl = m_obj.getClass();
       Method[] methods = cl.getMethods();

       for(int i = 0; i < methods.length; ++i)
       {
         // Retrieve info about the methods.
         //
         Method method = methods[i];
```

```
        Class clDecl = method.getDeclaringClass();
        String name = method.getName();
        int modf = method.getModifiers();
        Class clRetType = method. getReturnType();
        Class[] params = method.getParameterTypes();
        Class[] excepts = method.getExceptionTypes();
        String string = method.toString();

        // Print.
        // Omit the superclass methods.
        // Note: The "params" and "excepts" are array
        //   types and require a looping construct to
        //   print their values.
        //
        String superClass = "class java.lang.Object";
        if(!(clDecl.toString()).equals(superClass))
        {
          System.out.println("Name: " + name);
          System.out.println("clDecl: " + clDecl);
          System.out.println("modf: " + modf);
          System.out.println("clRetType: " + clRetType);
          System.out.println("params: " + params);
          System.out.println("excepts: " + excepts);
          System.out.println("string: " + string);
          System.out.println("\n");
        }
      }
    }
  }
  catch (SecurityException e)
  {
    System.out.println(e);
  }
}

  // ...
}
```

You can run **printMethods()** to obtain a listing of all the methods defined in **B**, its superclass **A**, and its superinterface **Intf**. The output of this method is as follows:

```
E:\coriolis\cdrom\Chap10\inspector>java Main
> print methods
Name: foobar
clDecl: class B
modf: 9
clRetType: void
params: [Ljava.lang.Class;@1cc68c
```

```
excepts: [Ljava.lang.Class;@1cc68b
string: public static void B.foobar(C)

Name: foo
clDecl: class A
modf: 1
clRetType: void
params: [Ljava.lang.Class;@1cc867
excepts: [Ljava.lang.Class;@1cc64d
string: public void A.foo(int)

Name: bar
clDecl: class B
modf: 1
clRetType: int
params: [Ljava.lang.Class;@1cc642
excepts: [Ljava.lang.Class;@1cc647
string: public int B.bar()

>
```

*The **Method** class provides access to all of the member methods of an object. The methods of this class can be exploited to receive information about a method, its return type, its arguments, and the exceptions thrown, as well as to invoke it on another object.*

The java.lang.reflect.Constructor Class

The **Constructor** class provides access to a single constructor of a class. **Constructor** can be used to create and initialize a new instance of any instantiable class. You can exploit the methods defined in this class to obtain the name of a constructor, determine its parameters, create new instances with it, and so on. As with **Field** and **Method**, you cannot directly create new instances of **Constructor**; you must use the **getConstructor()**, **getConstructors()**, **getDeclaredConstructor()**, and **getDeclaredConstructors()** methods of the **Class** class to receive **Constructor** objects. The **Constructor** class and some of its methods are defined as follows:

```
package java.lang.reflect;
public final class Constructor extends Object
implements Member
{
```

```
    public Class getDeclaringClass();
    public String getName();
    public int getModifiers();
    public Class[] getParameterTypes();
    public Class[] getExceptionTypes();
    public String toString();
    public Object newInstance(Object initargs[])
    throws InstantiationException,
      IllegalArgumentException,  IllegalAccessException,
      InvocationTargetException
    // ...
}
```

The methods provided by the **Constructor** class are very similar to those of **Method**. Because constructors do not have a return type, **Constructor** does not have a method to obtain the return type of a constructor. This class provides the **newInstance()** method, which can be used to create new instances of a class.

Listing 10.8 shows the **printConstructors()** method of the **Inspector** class. This method uses **Class.getConstructors()** to obtain all of the **public** constructors of a class. Note that **getConstructors()** does not include the constructors of the superclasses.

Listing 10.8   The printConstructors() method of Inspector.

```
public class Inspector
{
  // ...

  // Print the list of constructors of a class to
  // the standard output.
  //
  public void printConstructors()
  {
    try
    {
      Class cl = m_obj.getClass();
      Constructor[] xtors = cl.getConstructors();

      for(int i = 0; i < xtors.length; ++i)
      {
        Constructor xtor = xtors[i];
```

```
          // Retrieve info about the constructors.
          //
          Class clDecl = xtor.getDeclaringClass();
          String name = xtor.getName();
          int modf = xtor.getModifiers();
          Class[] params = xtor.getParameterTypes();
          Class[] excepts = xtor.getExceptionTypes();
          String string = xtor.toString();

          // Print.
          // Note: The "params" and "excepts" are array
          //   types and require a looping construct to
          //   print their values.
          //
          System.out.println("Name: " + name);
          System.out.println("clDecl: " + clDecl);
          System.out.println("modf: " + modf);
          System.out.println("params: " + params);
          System.out.println("excepts: " + excepts);
          System.out.println("string: " + string);
          System.out.println("\n");
        }
      }
    catch (SecurityException e)
    {
      System.out.println(e);
    }
  }

  // ...
}
```

Run the **printConstructors()** method of **Inspector** to obtain the list of all of the constructors defined in **B**, as shown in the following:

```
e:\coriolis\cdrom\chap10\inspector>java Main
> print constructors
Name: B
clDecl: class B
modf: 1
params: [Ljava.lang.Class;@1cc650
excepts: [Ljava.lang.Class;@1cc655
string: public B()

>
```

*The **Constructor** class provides access to all of the constructors of an object. This class can be used to obtain the name of a constructor, its arguments, and the exceptions it throws, as well as to create new instances of a class.*

Security Considerations

Security measures must be taken to ensure that malicious code does not exploit the Core Reflection API to gain unauthorized access to privileged members of a class. The Java Security model uses a two-step approach to thwart such attacks. First, the reflection classes (**Field**, **Method**, and **Constructor**) are designed to prevent a user from instantiating them directly—all requests for new instances of these classes must be funneled through the **Class** class. This class delegates the task of granting or denying reflection access to the **SecurityManager** class, which enforces the overall security policy of the JVM.

Second, once access is granted, standard access control checks are performed to ensure that a program does not use an instance of a reflection class to get or set the value of a privileged field, or to invoke a restricted method or constructor. All such attempts cause the **IllegalAccessException** to be thrown.

A look at some of the actual JDK 1.1 source code may help you understand this two-step process. Shown below are two methods, taken from the **Class** class, that create an instance of **Field**. The **getField()** method calls **checkMemberAccess()** to check whether the caller can be given access to the desired data member. Note that the argument to **checkMemberAccess()** is **Member.PUBLIC**, which designates that the caller is only requesting access to the **public** fields of the class. The **getDeclaredField()** method also calls **checkMemberAccess()**, which is passed **Member.DECLARED** to request access to all of the declared fields of the class (**public**, **protected**, **private**, and default).

```
// The getField() method defined in Class.
//
public Field getField(String name)
throws NoSuchFieldException, SecurityException
{
  checkMemberAccess(Member.PUBLIC);
  return getField0(name, Member.PUBLIC);
}
```

```
// The getDeclaredField() method defined in Class.
//
public Field getDeclaredField(String name)
throws NoSuchFieldException, SecurityException
{
  checkMemberAccess(Member.DECLARED);
  return getFieldO(name, Member.DECLARED);
}
```

The **checkMemberAccess()** method is defined in **Class** as shown below. This method obtains the **SecurityManager** of the JVM and delegates the task of access authorization to it via the **SecurityManager.checkMember-Access()** method. Note that the parameters for this method are the name of the class (which is to be reflected on) and the level of the access requested.

```
/*
 * Check if client is allowed to access members.  If access is
 * denied, throw a SecurityException.
 *
 * <p>Default policy: allow all clients access with normal Java
 * access control.
 */
private void checkMemberAccess(int which)
{
  SecurityManager s = System.getSecurityManager();
  if (s != null)
  {
    s.checkMemberAccess(this, which);
  }
}
```

Finally, the **get()** method of the **Field** class is shown below. This method ensures that the caller is not attempting to retrieve the value of an access-restricted field. Note that **get()** is a **native** method and does not have an underlying Java implementation. Only the **get()** and **set()** methods and their derivatives (**getBoolean()**, **setBoolean()**, and so forth) check for **IllegalAccessException** access violations. Other methods, such as **getType()** and **getName()**, do not perform any access-control checks beyond the initial phase.

```
/**
 * If this Field object enforces Java language access
 * control, and the underlying field is inaccessible,
 * the method throws an IllegalAccessException.
```

```
 * ...
 */
public native Object get(Object obj)
throws IllegalArgumentException,
  IllegalAccessException;
```

 *The Java Security Model uses the **SecurityManager** class to ensure that the usage of the Core Reflection API conforms to the security policies of the JVM.*

Conclusion

In this chapter, we demonstrated that the JVM provides a considerable amount of dynamic runtime information about classes. We also explained how to use the Core Reflection API to tap into this information to analyze a class and identify its data members, member methods, and constructors. In addition, we explored how to use the Reflection API to retrieve or change the value of a data member, invoke a member method, or create new instances of a class, as well as the security issues involved when using this API.

In the next chapter, we will refocus our attention on Java Beans and demonstrate how a container utilizes the Reflection API and design patterns to discover implicit information about a bean. We will then show you how to provide explicit information about your beans instead of, or in addition to, any implicit information.

Further Readings
Web Resources

http://www.javasoft.com/products/JDK/1.1/docs/guide/reflection/

Chapter 11

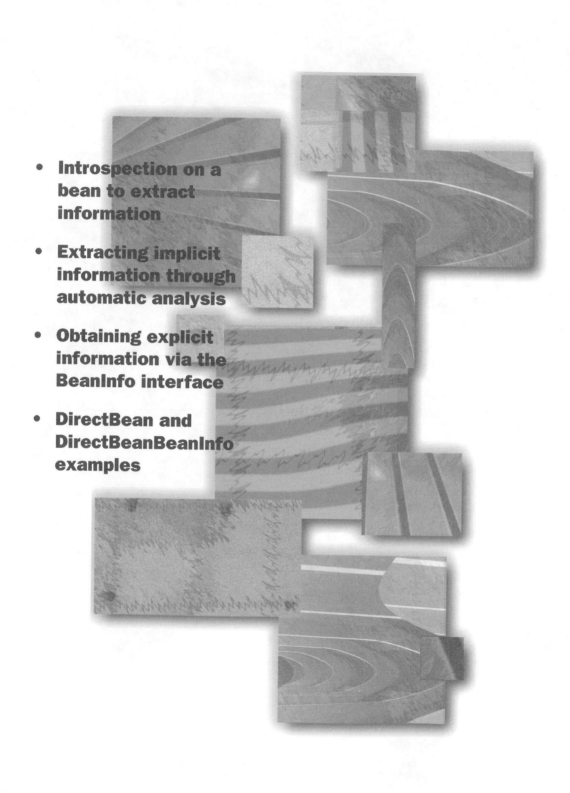

- Introspection on a bean to extract information

- Extracting implicit information through automatic analysis

- Obtaining explicit information via the BeanInfo interface

- DirectBean and DirectBeanBeanInfo examples

Chapter 11

Providing Explicit Bean Information

A framework *introspects* on a bean in order to determine its properties, events, and methods. Java Beans identifies two ways for a bean to provide this information to a framework: automatic analysis using the Core Reflection API and explicit information provided through a **BeanInfo** class.

Automatic analysis is suitable for simple beans. In this approach, a framework applies the Reflection API (which we covered at length in Chapter 10) to obtain information about the methods of a bean and uses the Java Beans standard design patterns to deduce the bean's properties, events, and methods. The Java Beans specification delineates the design patterns that a bean should follow to allow for its automatic analysis—for instance, a bean should provide a pair of **getX()** and **setX()** accessor methods for a property called **x**. Because we have already explained the Java Beans design patterns in the context of properties and events (discussed in Chapters 6 and 7, respectively), we will not discuss them further here.

More complex beans, however, need to provide more information than one can obtain through automatic analysis. A bean, for example, may need to provide localized display names for its programmatic property names, or it may want to supply a short description for each event. For such circumstances, a bean can offer a class that provides this added information. This class must implement the **BeanInfo** interface, and its name must be that of the bean it describes followed by the suffix "BeanInfo". For instance, the name of the class that provides explicit information for a bean called **MyBean** must be **MyBeanBeanInfo**.

Most often, the explicit information furnished by a **BeanInfo** class is used in conjunction with the implicit information obtained by automatic analysis. In this case, a bean supplies a **BeanInfo** class to provide only the information that may not be captured by automatic analysis, and it also adheres to the standard design patterns to allow a framework to extract the remaining implicit information through automatic deduction.

In this chapter, we will show you how to provide explicit information about your beans through a step-by-step analysis of **DirectBeanBeanInfo** (which is the **BeanInfo** class for **DirectBean**). We will also cover all of the relevant classes in the java.beans package that are used in the **DirectBeanBeanInfo** example.

The DirectBean Bean

In this section we will cover **DirectBean** and discuss its properties, events, and methods. **DirectBean** provides a very simple visual representation: it draws a rectangle and lists the names of all of its properties and their corresponding values. Figure 11.1 shows the **DirectBean** GUI in the BeanBox framework, and Listing 11.1 presents its header comment.

Listing 11.1   The DirectBean header comment.

```
package mybeans.directbean;

import java.awt.*;
import java.awt.event.*;
import java.util.*;
import java.beans.*;
```

```
/**
 * DirectBean defines a number of properties, events,
 * and methods that are used to illustrate the use of
 * the BeanInfo interface.
 *
 * This bean defines 7 properties, including
 * single-valued, multi-valued, constrained,
 * read/write, read-only, and write-only.
 * One of the defined properties, "hiddenProp",
 * is not exported through the DirectBeanBeanInfo
 * class.
 *
 * DirectBean fires two events: ActionEvent and
 * and PropertyChangeEvent. The ActionEvent is fired
 * via a custom-made timer class at regular
 * intervals, which is exposed as the property.
 * The PropertyChangeEvent is fired to support
 * the constrained property "rateProp".
 *
 * DirectBean also defines two methods: reportEvent()
 * and ignore(). The reportEvent() method simply
 * takes an argument of EventObject type and assigns
 * it to an internal variable whose value is printed
 * out by the bean. The ignore() method, which is not
 * exposed through the DirectBeanBeanInfo, does not
 * perform any actions.
 *
 */
public class DirectBean extends Canvas
{
  // ...
}
```

Properties

As shown in Listing 11.2, **DirectBean** defines an assortment of properties in order to illustrate how a **BeanInfo** class can be used to export different types of properties. The **m_stdProp** data member has two standard accessor methods, **getStdProp()** and **setStdProp()**, which follow the standard naming conventions. A framework can analyze the names of these two methods and infer that **DirectBean** has a property named **stdProp**; the same name appears in the PropertySheet editor in Figure 11.1.

The internal variable **m_unstdProp** has a pair of accessors that do not conform to the standard design patterns. Although **m_unstdProp** cannot

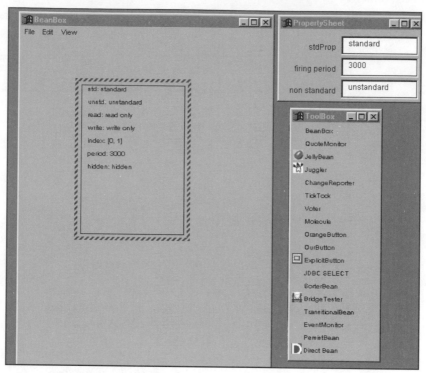

Figure 11.1 **DirectBean** instantiated in BeanBox.

be deduced through automatic analysis, BeanBox has found out about it and shown its value "unstandard" under the name "non standard". We will explain later how we have accomplished this via **DirectBeanBeanInfo**.

DirectBean also defines a read-only, a write-only, and an indexed property. We will show you how **DirectBeanBeanInfo** explicitly exports these properties; in the BDK 1.0 release, however, BeanBox is not capable of displaying them in the PropertySheet editor.

The data member **m_rateProp** is used to control the firing rate of **ActionEvent** events; this rate is discussed in the next section. Even though this property has a standard pair of accessor methods—namely, **getRateProp()** and **setRateProp()**—the display name of **m_rateProp** in PropertySheet is "firing period," which is very different than what would have been obtained through automatic analysis. (Note that **m_rateProp** is a constrained property.) Finally, **DirectBean** defines a property called **hiddenProp**, which is not identified by BeanBox because it is not exported in the **DirectBeanBeanInfo** class.

Listing 11.2   Properties defined in DirectBean.

```
public class DirectBean extends Canvas
{
  // "stdProp" is a single-valued read/write property
  // with standard getStdProp() and setStdProp()
  // access methods.
  //
  private String m_stdProp = "standard";

  // "unstdProp" is a single-valued read/write
  // property with unsdtProp() and unstdProp(String)
  // getter/setter methods, which do not follow
  // the Java Beans standard design patterns.
  //
  private String m_unstdProp = "unstandard";

  // "readProp" is a single-valued read-only property.
  //
  private String m_readProp = "read only";

  // "writeProp" is a single-valued write-only property.
  //
  private String m_writeProp = "write only";

  // "indexProp" is an indexed read/write property.
  //
  private String[] m_indexProp = {"0", "1"};

  // "rateProp" is a single-valued, read/write,
  // constrained property.
  private int m_rateProp = 3000;

  // "hiddenProp" is not exported in the BeanInfo.
  //
  private String m_hiddenProp = "hidden";

  // ...
}
```

Events

DirectBean fires two events: **ActionEvent** and **PropertyChangeEvent**. **ActionEvent** is fired at regular intervals by a timer; this interval can be changed through the "firing period" property. You can observe this event if you connect one instance of **DirectBean** to the **stopJuggling()** method of the **Juggler** bean and another instance to its **startJuggling**() method. (Note that you may need to adjust the "firing period" properties.) The **addActionListener**() and **removeActionListener**() implement the registration and deregistration methods for this event, as presented in Listing 11.3. The other two methods in this listing, **addVetoableChangeListener**() and **removeVetoableChangeListener**(), support the constrained "firing period" property.

Figure 11.2 shows the events of **DirectBean** as identified by BeanBox. First, as the figure illustrates, BeanBox has listed only these two events— it has not included the events inherited from the superclasses of **DirectBean**. Second, **BeanBox** uses the display name "Action Event" instead of "actionPerformed," which would have been derived from automatic analysis. We will shortly list the piece code in **DirectBean** that accounts for the above behavior.

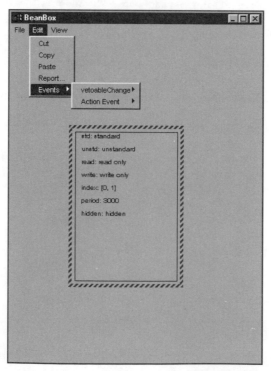

Figure 11.2 The events of **DirectBean** as identified by BeanBox.

Listing 11.3 Events fired by DirectBean.

```java
public class DirectBean extends Canvas
{
  // ...

  /**
   * A bean calls all the registered
   * VetoableChangeListeners' propertyChange callback
   * methods before the value of a constrained property
   * is changed.
   *
   * Use addVetoableChangeListener() to register
   * your listener and removeVetoableChangeListener()
   * to deregister a listener.
   *
   * Note: the Java Beans specification does not
   * require VetoableChangeListeners to run in any
   * particular order.
   * Note: These listeners are global to all
   * constrained properties. You cannot use a
   * listener registered in this manner to listen on
   * a change of value in a specific property.
   *
   * @see # removeVetoableChangeListener
   * @param l the VetoableChangeListener
   */
  public void
  addVetoableChangeListener(VetoableChangeListener l)
  {
    m_vcsGlob.addVetoableChangeListener(l);
  }

  /**
   * Deregister this VetoableChangeListener.
   * This call is harmless if VetoableChangeListener
   * isn't on the list.
   *
   * @see # addVetoableChangeListener
   * @param l the VetoableChangeListener
   */
  public void
  removeVetoableChangeListener(
    VetoableChangeListener l)
  {
    m_vcsGlob.removeVetoableChangeListener(l);
  }
```

```
// Methods to support ActionEvent.
//
public synchronized void
addActionListener(ActionListener lis)
{
  m_actionLs.addElement(lis);
}

public synchronized void
removeActionListener(ActionListener lis)
{
  m_actionLs.removeElement(lis);
}

// ...
}
```

Methods

As shown in Listing 11.4, **DirectBean** implements two methods: **reportEvent()** and **ignore()**. You can hook up a source bean that fires events to the **reportEvent()** method of **DirectBean**; when the source bean fires an event, **DirectBean** displays the name of the event. The other method, **ignore()**, is provided to illustrate how methods are exposed in the **BeanInfo** class.

Listing 11.4 Methods implemented in DirectBean.

```
public class DirectBean extends Canvas
{
  // ...

  /**
   * Report an event received from other beans.
   */
  public void reportEvent(EventObject evt)
  {
    m_receivedEvent = evt;
    repaint();
  }

  // This method is a no op.
  //
  public void ignore(EventObject evt)
  {
  }

  // ...
}
```

The DirectBeanBeanInfo Class

As noted earlier, the **BeanInfo** class for **DirectBean** must be called **DirectBeanBeanInfo**. This class provides explicit information about **DirectBean**, including its icon, properties, events, and methods. Listing 11.5 presents the definition of **DirectBeanBeanInfo**.

Listing 11.5   DirectBeanBeanInfo definition.

```
package mybeans.directbean;

import java.awt.*;
import java.awt.event.*;
import java.lang.reflect.*;
import java.util.*;
import java.beans.*;

/**
 * This class provides explicit information about
 * DirectBean instead of, and in addition to, the
 * information obtained by automatic analysis and
 * design patterns.
 */
public class DirectBeanBeanInfo extends SimpleBeanInfo
{
  // ...
}
```

DirectBeanBeanInfo is packaged in mybeans.directbean, which is the same package used for **DirectBean**. It subclasses **SimpleBeanInfo**, a class that implements the **BeanInfo** interface and provides no-op methods, which do not perform any actions. These two classes are discussed in the following sections.

The BeanInfo Interface

A class that provides explicit information about a bean must implement the **BeanInfo** interface or extend a class that implements it. This interface identifies all of the methods that a framework needs in order to introspect on a bean.

When you provide a class that implements this interface, however, you do not need to code all of its methods. You may implement only the methods that are suitable for your beans and program the remaining methods to return **null**, thus instructing the framework to perform automatic analysis to obtain any missing information. We will explain this technique in the next section. The **BeanInfo** interface is defined in Listing 11.6.

Listing 11.6 The BeanInfo interface.

```
package java.beans;
public interface BeanInfo
{
  BeanDescriptor getBeanDescriptor();
  EventSetDescriptor[] getEventSetDescriptors();
  int getDefaultEventIndex();
  PropertyDescriptor[] getPropertyDescriptors();
  int getDefaultPropertyIndex();
  MethodDescriptor[] getMethodDescriptors();
  BeanInfo[] getAdditionalBeanInfo();
  Image getIcon(int iconKind);
  final static int ICON_COLOR_16x16 = 1;
  final static int ICON_COLOR_32x32 = 2;
  final static int ICON_MONO_16x16 = 3;
  final static int ICON_MONO_32x32 = 4;
}
```

The **getBeanDescriptor**() method creates a **BeanDescriptor**, which provides overall information about a bean (such as its customizer class and display name). A return value of **null** indicates that this information should be obtained by automatic analysis. The **getEventSetDescriptors**(), **getPropertyDescriptors**(), and **getMethodDescriptors**() methods return references to the event, property, and method descriptor classes, respectively. The **getDefaultEventIndex**() and **getDefaultPropertyIndex**() methods determine the most common event and property for a bean. You can specify an arbitrary number of other **BeanInfo** classes that provide additional information about the current bean via the **getAdditionalBeanInfo**() method. Finally, **getIcon**() returns an icon for the bean, which might be used as a graphical representation of the bean in a palette.

The SimpleBeanInfo Class

This utility class implements the **BeanInfo** interface and provides no-op methods, which return **null**. You can selectively override these methods to provide suitable explicit information about your beans. The remaining no-op methods instruct the framework to apply low-level introspection and design patterns to analyze the beans automatically.

Identifying The Icons

You can override the **getIcon**() method to specify the different icons associated with your bean. Icon images typically are in the GIF format, although Java Beans may support other formats in future. The **BeanInfo** interface defines constant values to identify four types of icons: **ICON_COLOR_16x16**, **ICON_COLOR_32x32**, **ICON_MONO_16x16**, and **ICON_MONO_32x32**. Listing 11.7 shows the overridden **getIcon**() method in **DirectBeanBeanInfo**.

Listing 11.7   The getIcon() method.

```
public class DirectBeanBeanInfo extends SimpleBeanInfo
{
  /**
   * Returns the icon associated with this bean.
   * The icon is used in the container's palette.
   */
  public Image getIcon(int iconKind)
  {
    Image img = null;

    if (iconKind == BeanInfo.ICON_COLOR_16x16)
    {
      img = loadImage("DirectBeanIconColor16.gif");
    }
    else if (iconKind == BeanInfo.ICON_COLOR_32x32)
    {
      // load 32x32 image...
    }
    else if (iconKind == BeanInfo.ICON_MONO_16x16)
    {
      // load 16x16 mono image...
      // note: you can return the 16x16 color icon
    }
    else if (iconKind == BeanInfo.ICON_MONO_32x32)
    {
      // load 32x32 mono image...
      // note: you can return the 32x32 color icon
    }

    return img;
  }

  // ...
}
```

tip

If you are providing only one icon, you should support **ICON_COLOR_32x32.** *Your icons should have a transparent background in order to be rendered onto an existing background.*

Exporting The Properties

Listing 11.8 presents the **getPropertyDescriptors**() method of the **DirectBeanBeanInfo** class. This method creates and returns an array of **PropertyDescriptor** objects, each of which describes a particular exported property. We will discuss the **PropertyDescriptor** class at length a bit later.

Note that although **DirectBean** does define a property called **hiddenProp**, this property is not visible to frameworks because **getPropertyDescriptors**() does not expose it. You can also use this method to define display names for properties or to designate them as bound or constrained.

Listing 11.8   The getPropertyDescriptors() method.

```
public class DirectBeanBeanInfo extends SimpleBeanInfo
{
  // ...

  /**
   * Returns the descriptors for all the properties
   * exported by this bean.
   *
   * Note: This method overrides the implicit, deduced
   *   properties obtained by applying the standard
   *   design patterns unless you return null.
   */
  public PropertyDescriptor[] getPropertyDescriptors()
  {
    PropertyDescriptor[] props = null;

    try
    {
      PropertyDescriptor std;
      std = new PropertyDescriptor("stdProp",
              DirectBean.class);
```

```java
        PropertyDescriptor unstd;
        unstd = new PropertyDescriptor("non standard",
                    DirectBean.class,
                    "unstdProp",
                    "unstdProp");

        PropertyDescriptor read;
        read = new PropertyDescriptor("read only",
                    DirectBean.class,
                    "getReadProp",
                    null);

        PropertyDescriptor write;
        write = new PropertyDescriptor("write only",
                    DirectBean.class,
                    null,
                    "setWriteProp");

        IndexedPropertyDescriptor index;
        index = new IndexedPropertyDescriptor("indexProp",
                    DirectBean.class);

        PropertyDescriptor period;
        period = new PropertyDescriptor("period",
                    DirectBean.class,
                    "getRateProp",
                    "setRateProp");
        period.setBound(false);
        period.setConstrained(true);
        period.setDisplayName("firing period");

        props = new PropertyDescriptor[6];
        props[0] = std;
        props[1] = unstd;
        props[2] = read;
        props[3] = write;
        props[4] = index;
        props[5] = period;
    }
    catch (IntrospectionException e)
    {
        System.out.println(e);
    }

    return props;
}
```

```
/**
 * Returns the index of the most commonly used
 * property.
 */
public int getDefaultPropertyIndex()
{
  return 1; // non-standard property
}

// ...
}
```

The FeatureDescriptor Class

The **FeatureDescriptor** class is the common superclass for the
EventSetDescriptor, **IndexedPropertyDescriptor**, **MethodDescriptor**,
ParameterDescriptor, and **PropertyDescriptor** classes. This class
provides methods to set and retrieve a feature's short description, display
name, and programmatic name. It also supports an extension mechanism
to associate arbitrary name/value pairs with a design feature. Listing
11.9 shows the methods supplied by **FeatureDescriptor**.

Listing 11.9   The FeatureDescriptor methods.

```
package java.beans;
public class FeatureDescriptor
{
  public String getName();
  public void setName(String name) ;
  public String getDisplayName();
  public void setDisplayName(String displayName) ;
  public boolean isExpert();
  public void setExpert(boolean expert);
  public boolean isHidden();
  public void setHidden(boolean hidden);
  public String getShortDescription();
  public void setShortDescription(String text);
  public void setValue(String attributeName, Object value);
  public Object getValue(String attributeName);
  public java.util.Enumeration attributeNames() ;
}
```

The PropertyDescriptor Class

This class extends **FeatureDescriptor** to provide information more
specific to properties, such a property's accessor method names, type,

and editor class. You can also use this class to specify whether a property is bound or constrained. Listing 11.10 presents the definition of this class.

Listing 11.10   The PropertyDescriptor class.

```
package java.beans;

import java.lang.reflect.*;

public class PropertyDescriptor extends FeatureDescriptor
{
  public PropertyDescriptor(String propertyName,
    Class beanClass)
    throws IntrospectionException;
  public PropertyDescriptor(String propertyName,
    Class beanClass,
    String getterName, String setterName)
    throws IntrospectionException;
  public PropertyDescriptor(String propertyName,
    Method getter, Method setter)
    throws IntrospectionException;
  public Class getPropertyType();
  public Method getReadMethod();
  public Method getWriteMethod() ;
  public boolean isBound();
  public void setBound(boolean bound) ;
  public boolean isConstrained() ;
  public void setConstrained(boolean constrained) ;
  public void setPropertyEditorClass(Class propertyEditorClass);
  public Class getPropertyEditorClass() ;
}
```

*You should use **IndexedPropertyDescriptor** class, which is a subclass of **PropertyDescriptor**, to describe the indexed properties of your beans.*

Specifying The Events

DirectBeanBeanInfo explicitly describes the events generated by **DirectBean** in its **getEventSetDescriptors()** method, which is presented in Listing 11.11. This method exposes two events identified by the **ActionListener** and **VetoableChangeListener** listeners; these events in turn are packed into an array of **EventSetDescriptor** objects. Note

that Listing 11.11 also shows the **getDefaultEventIndex**() method,
which returns the index of the most common event fired by **DirectBean**.

Listing 11.11   The getEventSetDescriptors() method.

```
public class DirectBeanBeanInfo extends SimpleBeanInfo
{
  // ...

  /**
   * Returns the descriptors for all the events
   * fired by this bean.
   *
   * Note: This method overrides the implicit, deduced
   *   events obtained by applying the standard
   *   design patterns unless you return null.
   */
  public EventSetDescriptor[] getEventSetDescriptors()
  {
    EventSetDescriptor[] events = null;

    try
    {
      EventSetDescriptor action;
      action = new EventSetDescriptor(DirectBean.class,
                    "actionPerformed",
                    ActionListener.class,
                     "actionPerformed");
      action.setDisplayName("Action Event");


      EventSetDescriptor veto;
      veto = new EventSetDescriptor(DirectBean.class,
                    "vetoableChange",
                    VetoableChangeListener.class,
                    "vetoableChange");

      events = new EventSetDescriptor[2];
      events[0] = action;
      events[1] = veto;
    }
    catch (IntrospectionException e)
    {
      System.out.println(e);
    }
```

```
    return events;
  }


  /**
   * Returns the index of the most commonly used
   * event.
   */
  public int getDefaultEventIndex()
  {
    return 0; // actionPerformed
  }

  // ...
}
```

 *The **getEventSetDescriptors**() method should also include all of the events that support your bound or constrained properties.*

The EventSetDescriptor Class

As shown in Listing 11.12, **EventSetDescriptor** extends **Feature-Descriptor** to describe a group of events fired by a bean. This class provides a handful of constructors to initialize its instances; the one that you need to use varies, depending how closely you have followed the standard design patters. In the **getEventSetDescriptors**() method of **DirectBeanBeanInfo**, for example, we have used the first constructor, which is the simplest of all. This constructor is suitable when an event listener has only a single argument and can be registered/ deregistered via the appropriately named add/remove methods.

Listing 11.12   The EventSetDescriptor class.

```
package java.beans;

import java.lang.reflect.*;

public class EventSetDescriptor extends FeatureDescriptor
{
  public EventSetDescriptor(Class sourceClass,
    String eventSetName, Class listenerType,
    String listenerMethodName)
    throws IntrospectionException;
```

```
public EventSetDescriptor(Class sourceClass,
  String eventSetName, Class listenerType,
  String listenerMethodNames[],
  String addListenerMethodName,
  String removeListenerMethodName)
  throws IntrospectionException;
public EventSetDescriptor(String eventSetName,
  Class listenerType, Method listenerMethods[],
  Method addListenerMethod,
  Method removeListenerMethod)
  throws IntrospectionException;
public EventSetDescriptor(String eventSetName,
  Class listenerType,
  MethodDescriptor listenerMethodDescriptors[],
  Method addListenerMethod,
  Method removeListenerMethod)
  throws IntrospectionException;
public Class getListenerType();
public Method[] getListenerMethods();
public MethodDescriptor[] getListenerMethodDescriptors();
public Method getAddListenerMethod();
public Method getRemoveListenerMethod();
public void setUnicast(boolean unicast);
public boolean isUnicast();
public void setInDefaultEventSet(boolean inDefaultEventSet);
public boolean isInDefaultEventSet();
}
```

 *Note that because **EventSetDescriptor** is a subclass of **FeatureDescriptor**, you can use the superclass's methods to describe your events.*

Determining The Methods

DirectBeanBeanInfo overrides **getMethodDescriptors**() in order to expose the **reportEvent**() method of **DirectBean**. As shown in Listing 11.13, the **getMethodDescriptors**() method uses the **java.lang.reflect.Method** class (covered in Chapter 10) to initialize an array of **MethodDescriptor** objects. This array is used during the introspection phase to determine the methods supported by a bean. Because the **ignore**() method of **DirectBean** is not included in the **MethodDescriptor** array, frameworks will not detect the presence of this method in **DirectBean**.

Listing 11.13   The EventSetDescriptor() method.

```
public class DirectBeanBeanInfo extends SimpleBeanInfo
{
  // ...

  /**
   * Returns the descriptors for all the methods
   * supported by this bean.
   *
   * Note: This method overrides the implicit, deduced
   *   methods obtained by applying the standard
   *   design patterns unless you return null.
   */
  public MethodDescriptor[] getMethodDescriptors()
  {
    MethodDescriptor[] methods = null;

    // List only the reportEvent method.
    //
    try
    {
      Class args[] = {EventObject.class};
      Method method = null;
      method = DirectBean.class.getMethod
                  ("reportEvent", args);

      methods = new MethodDescriptor[1];
      methods[0] = new MethodDescriptor(method);
    }
    catch (Exception e)
    {
      System.out.println(e);
    }

    return methods;
  }

  // ...
}
```

The MethodDescriptor Class

This class defines only a few methods for instance creation and parameter description. Refer to Listing 11.14 for a listing of these methods.

Listing 11.14 The MethodDescriptor class.

```
package java.beans;

import java.lang.reflect.*;

public class MethodDescriptor extends FeatureDescriptor
{
  public MethodDescriptor(Method method) ;
  public MethodDescriptor(Method method,
    ParameterDescriptor parameterDescriptors[]);
  public Method getMethod();
  public ParameterDescriptor[] getParameterDescriptors();
}
```

Providing Overall Information About Beans

The **DirectBeanBeanInfo** class redefines **getBeanDescriptor()** to supply a display name for **DirectBean**. You can also use this method to specify the name of the customizer class for your beans. The **getBeanDescriptor()** method is shown in Listing 11.15.

Listing 11.15 The getBeanDescriptor() method.

```
public class DirectBeanBeanInfo extends SimpleBeanInfo
{
  // ...

  public BeanDescriptor getBeanDescriptor()
  {
    BeanDescriptor desc;
    desc = new BeanDescriptor(DirectBean.class);

    desc.setDisplayName("Direct Bean");

    String s = "This bean provides explicit info";
    desc.setShortDescription(s);

    return desc;
  }
}
```

The BeanDescriptor Class

BeanDescriptor provides overall information about a bean, such as its display name and its customizer class. A return value of **null** indicates

that this information should be obtained by automatic analysis. The
BeanDescriptor class is presented in Listing 11.16.

Listing 11.16   BeanDescriptor provides overall information.

```
package java.beans;

public class BeanDescriptor extends FeatureDescriptor
{
  public BeanDescriptor(Class beanClass);
  public BeanDescriptor(Class beanClass,
    Class customizerClass);
  public Class getBeanClass();
  public Class getCustomizerClass();
}
```

The Introspector Class

The **Introspector** class provides a standard way for Java Beans frameworks to learn about a bean's properties, events, and methods. The **getBean-
Info**() method of this class analyzes a bean's class and all of its
superclasses to obtain either explicit or implicit information, which is
returned as a **BeanInfo** object. After calling this method on a bean, you
can use the methods available in **BeanInfo** to query about that bean's
properties, events, and methods. We already have covered the methods
of **BeanInfo** in the previous section; the **Introspector** class is presented
in Listing 11.17.

Listing 11.17   The Introspector class.

```
package java.beans;

import java.lang.reflect.*;

public class Introspector
{
  public static BeanInfo getBeanInfo(Class beanClass)
    throws IntrospectionException;
  public static BeanInfo getBeanInfo(Class beanClass,
    Class stopClass)
    throws IntrospectionException;
  public static String decapitalize(String name);
  public static String[] getBeanInfoSearchPath();
  public static void setBeanInfoSearchPath(String path[]);
}
```

*If you are a bean implementor or application developer, you normally do not need to be concerned with the **Introspector** class unless you are developing a framework as an analysis tool for beans.*

Conclusion

In this chapter, we explained how to provide explicit information about your beans. Such information can be used in conjunction with the information obtained through automatic analysis. The **DirectBean** and **DirectBeanBeanInfo** examples demonstrated many of the techniques that you can use to expose the properties, events, and methods of your beans.

Chapter 12 will introduce you to the last major topic in this book: property editors and customizers. Property sheet editors are adequate for customizing simple beans. For more complex beans, however, you will need to provide special classes to configure your beans.

- **Providing custom property editors**

- **Implementing the PropertyEditor interface**

- **Supporting the getAsText() and setAsText() methods of PropertyEditor**

- **Creating editors with custom GUI using paintValue() and getCustomEditor()**

12

Custom Property Editors

In the previous chapters, we frequently have used properties to capture the states of beans. Properties can be as simple as primitive data types, or they can be instances of arbitrary complex classes. A Java Beans framework provides a property sheet editor to view or modify these properties.

In order to display their values in its property sheet editor, however, a framework must provide a specific editor for each property type. For example, release 1.0 of the BeanBox framework supplies editors for all the primitive data types, as well as for the **Color**, **Font**, and **String** classes.

All of the properties used in the preceding chapters have a corresponding property editor in BeanBox. Because you probably will be using complex properties in your beans, though, you need to know how to provide custom editors for them.

Java Beans provides a rather elaborate mechanism for bean implementers to supply custom property editors. We will provide an overview of this mechanism and then discuss the **CustBean** bean in detail, which supplies three custom editors with varying degrees of complexity. The first editor supports a property limited to a fixed number of values, similar to the **enum** data types in C or C++ languages. The second editor uses the **getAsText()** and **setAsText()** methods of the **PropertyEditor** interface to manipulate a property as a text. The third custom editor provides its own graphical user interface (GUI) to view and modify a property.

Overview Of Custom Property Editors

A custom property editor collaborates with a Java Beans framework to display or edit the value of a property. This collaboration is imperative because the property actually resides as an instance in a bean and must be handed off to its editor in order to be viewed or edited. Any changes made to the value of the property must be transmitted back to the bean via the corresponding **set()** method of the property.

Java Beans frameworks manage these interactions by requiring all property editors to implement the **PropertyEditor** interface. Through this interface, an editor establishes a procedure to display or edit a property and defines methods to receive it from the framework and return it in a modified form. Java Beans supplies a class, called **PropertyEditorSupport**, that provides a default implementation of **PropertyEditor**. Often, you may be able to extend this class and redefine only the methods you need instead of implementing all the methods of **PropertyEditor**; the first property editor example that we will discuss uses this approach. Java Beans also provides the **PropertyEditorManager** class, which is used to locate a property editor for a given property type.

The PropertyEditor Interface

All custom property editors must implement the **PropertyEditor** interface in order to be integrated seamlessly with a framework. This interface, shown in Listing 12.1, identifies methods to exchange property objects between a framework and an editor, set and get properties as text, display properties in a custom GUI, and register/deregister **PropertyChangeListener** listeners.

Listing 12.1   The PropertyEditor interface.

```
package java.beans;

public interface PropertyEditor
{
  void setValue(Object value);
  Object getValue();
  boolean isPaintable();
  void paintValue(java.awt.Graphics gfx,
    java.awt.Rectangle box);
  String getJavaInitializationString();
  String getAsText();
  void setAsText(String text)
    throws java.lang.IllegalArgumentException;
  String[] getTags();
  java.awt.Component getCustomEditor();
  boolean supportsCustomEditor();
  void addPropertyChangeListener(
    PropertyChangeListener listener);
  void removePropertyChangeListener(
    PropertyChangeListener listener);
}
```

The **setValue()** method sets the property to be edited, while **getValue()** retrieves its value. The **paintValue()** method paints a GUI representation of the value of a property into a given area of the screen, usually inside the main property sheet editor of the framework. (Note that the custom editor is responsible for doing its own clipping in order to fit itself into the bounding box provided as the argument to **paintValue()**.) The **isPaintable()** method determines whether a custom editor has implemented **paintValue()**. To obtain a fragment of Java code to initialize a variable with the current value of a property, **getJavaInitializationString()** is called.

The **getAsText()** method returns a property value as a human-readable string, which can be modified and converted back to an instance of the property through **setAsText()**. If a property can only assume values within a finite set of known strings, **getTags()** can be used to return the enumerated values as an array.

A custom property editor may choose to provide a **Component** object that displays and edits its corresponding properties. In this case, the editor must return **Component** from the **getCustomEditor()** method and return **true** from **supportsCustomEditor()**. Note that the framework might embed the **Component** object within its own property sheet editor or create an individual dialog box for it.

The **addPropertyChangeListener**() and **removePropertyChange-Listener**() methods provide standard registration and deregistration procedures. When a property is modified inside a property editor, the editor should fire a **PropertyChangeEvent** on all registered listeners, specifying "" as the property name and **null** for the old and new values.

A custom property editor does not need to support every feature of the **PropertyEditor** interface. Instead, it can support only the **setValue**() method and a no-arg constructor, plus any of the features listed below. Other combinations are possible, but these choices (each of which is covered by an example in this chapter) are the most typical ones:

- **getAsText**() and **setAsText**()

- **getAsText**(), **setAsText**(), and **getTags**()

- **paintValue**() and **getCustomEditor**()

*The **PropertyEditor** interface provides a mechanism to integrate custom property editors into a framework. This general-purpose interface allows the integration of editors with different levels of complexity. Custom editors usually support only a subset of the **PropertyEditor** interface.*

The PropertyEditorSupport Class

This class provides a very simple implementation of the **PropertyEditor** interface that serves mostly to support **String** properties. It supplies adequate implementations of **getValue**(), **setValue**(), **getAsText**(), and **setAsText**(), which sets the value of **String** properties only. The **addPropertyChangeListener**() and **removePropertyChange-Listener**() methods also have full-fledged implementations; all of the other methods are no-ops, return **null**, or return **false**.

An example using this support class is shown in Listing 12.5, which appears later in this chapter.

*Typically, instead of implementing the **PropertyEditor** interface, you should extend the **PropertyEditorSupport** class and redefine only the methods that do not meet your needs.*

The PropertyEditorManager Class

This class locates a custom property editor for a property by using a search algorithm. First, it determines whether any custom editors have been explicitly registered for the class of the property using its **registerEditor()** method. Second, if no explicit editor is found, it attempts to locate a suitable editor by adding "Editor" to the full qualified class name of the property. Third, it adds "Editor" to the unqualified class name and searches the **CLASSPATH** for a match.

*As a bean implementer or a bean application developer, you don't need to concern yourself with **PropertyEditorManager**. Frameworks have the responsibility of finding suitable custom editors for your properties.*

The CustBean Bean

CustBean provides a good example of a bean with custom property editors of varying degrees of complexity. Figure 12.1 shows **CustBean** instantiated in the BeanBox container, and Listing 12.2 presents its source code.

Listing 12.2   The CustBean source code.

```
package mybeans.custbean;

import java.awt.*;

/**
 * This class illustrates the use of custom property
 * editors. It provides three properties, each of
 * which has an editor with a varying degree of
 * complexity.
 */
public class CustBean extends Canvas
{
  // This property has an editor that
  // displays a list of three items to choose from.
  //
```

```
String m_enum = "one|two|three";

// The editor for this property uses the property
// sheet editor to modify the property.
//
PropType1 m_type1A = new PropType1(12, "A string");

// This property comes with an editor that provides
// its own user interface (dialog box) to edit
// the property. Note that the type of this property
// is the same as the above property. The editors,
// however, are different.
//
PropType1 m_type1B = new PropType1(12, "B string");

public CustBean()
{
    setSize(new Dimension(200, 150));
}

// Draws a rectangle and displays the values of
// all the properties.
//
public void paint(Graphics g)
{
    g.drawRect(5, 5, 190, 140);
    g.drawString("enum: " + m_enum, 15, 15);
    g.drawString("PropType1[A][int]: " + m_type1A.getInt(),
        15, 35);
    g.drawString("PropType1[A][string]: " +
        m_type1A.getString(), 15, 55);
    g.drawString("PropType1[B][int]: " + m_type1B.getInt(),
        15, 75);
    g.drawString("PropType1[B][string]: " +
        m_type1B.getString(), 15, 95);
}

public String getEnum()
{
    return m_enum;
}

public void setEnum(String enum)
{
    m_enum = enum;
}
```

```
public PropType1 getType1A()
{
  return m_type1A;
}

public void setType1A(PropType1 type1)
{
  m_type1A = type1;
}

public PropType1 getType1B()
{
  return m_type1B;
}

public void setType1B(PropType1 type1)
{
  m_type1B = type1;
}
}
```

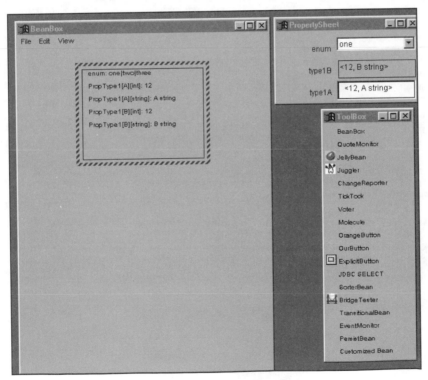

Figure 12.1 CustBean instantiated in BeanBox.

CustBean defines one property of **String** type and two properties of **PropType1** type. The **String** property **m_enum** is intended to have a value of 1, 2, or 3. Figure 12.2 shows the custom editor for this property.

The editor only allows the user to choose from the above values, thereby ensuring that **m_enum** will never have a value outside the allowable set. This custom editor is based on the **getAsText()**, **setAsText()**, and **getTags()** methods of the **PropertyEditor** interface. Note that the default editor that BeanBox provides for **String** properties is not used for **m_enum** because **CustBean** specifically registers the custom editor in **CustBeanBeanInfo**.

In general, many custom property editors may be able to edit a property of a given type. In such cases, the bean can designate the desired editor in its corresponding **BeanInfo** *class.*

The property **m_type1A** is of type **PropType1**. Unless **CustBean** defines a custom editor for **PropType1**, BeanBox won't be able to edit or even display properties of this type.

Figure 12.3 shows the custom editor for **m_type1A**, which is based on the **getAsText()** and **setAsText()** methods of the **PropertyEditor** interface. Note that this property is shown as the last field in the PropertySheet editor, and its value has already been modified from its default value (refer back to Figure 12.1).

A property editor that uses **getAsText()** *and* **setAsText()** *must be able to convert the value of the property into a string and be prepared to parse a string and reconstruct the property. If the string cannot be parsed, the editor should throw* **java.lang.IllegalArgumentException**. *This approach, therefore, is suitable for rather simple properties.*

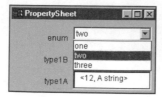

Figure 12.2   The custom property editor for **m_enum**.

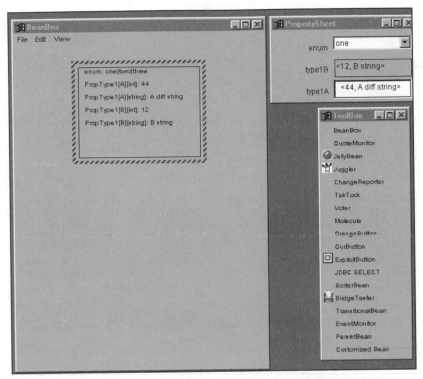

Figure 12.3   The custom property editor for **m_ type1A**.

CustBean defines another property of **PropType1** type called **m_type1B**. This property, however, uses a more complex editor to display and modify its values. This custom editor, shown in Figure 12.4, supports the **paintValue()** and **getCustomEditor()** methods of **PropertyEditor** in order to provide its own GUI. The **getCustomEditor()** creates the **Component** that is used in the dialog box of Figure 12.4, whereas **paintValue()** renders the value of the property in the PropertySheet editor of BeanBox. BeanBox will automatically pop up a dialog box when a user clicks in the "type1B" field of the PropertySheet editor.

*An editor that supports the **paintValue()** and **getCustomEditor()** methods provides the most flexible user interface. All non-trivial properties should have custom editors that support these two methods.*

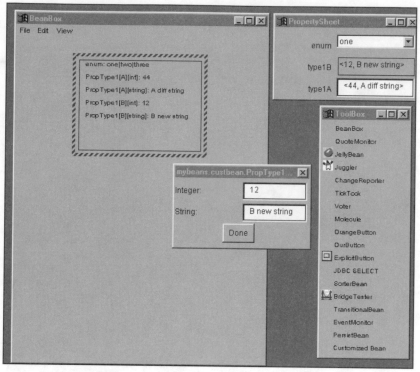

Figure 12.4   The custom property editor for **m_ type1B**.

The PropType1 Class

The **PropType1** property used in **CustBean** is a simple class with two data members, as shown in Listing 12.3.

Listing 12.3   The PropType1 class.

```
package mybeans.custbean;

/**
 * This class illustrates the use of property editors.
 * It defines a property class with one integer and
 * one string data member.
 */
public class PropType1
{
  private int m_i;
  private String m_str;

  public PropType1()
  {
```

```
    this(0, "");
  }

  public PropType1(int i, String str)
  {
    m_i = i;
    m_str = str;
  }

  public int getInt()
  {
    return m_i;
  }

  public String getString()
  {
    return m_str;
  }
}
```

The CustBeanBeanInfo Class

The **CustBeanBeanInfo** class defines all three properties of **CustBean**
and specifies their custom property editors through calls to
setPropertyEditorClass(), as shown in Listing 12.4.

Listing 12.4   The CustBeanBeanInfo source code.

```
package mybeans.custbean;

import java.beans.*;

/**
 * This class provides explicit information about
 * CustBean instead of, and in addition to, the
 * information obtained by automatic analysis and
 * design patterns.
 */
public class CustBeanBeanInfo extends SimpleBeanInfo
{
  public BeanDescriptor getBeanDescriptor()
  {
    BeanDescriptor desc;
    desc = new BeanDescriptor(CustBean.class);

    desc.setDisplayName("Customized Bean");

    String s = "This bean illustrates custom editors";
    desc.setShortDescription(s);
```

```java
      return desc;
    }



    /**
     * Returns the descriptors for all the properties
     * exported by this bean.
     *
     * Note: This method overrides the implicit, deduced
     *  properties obtained by applying the standard
     *  design patterns unless you return null.
     */
    public PropertyDescriptor[] getPropertyDescriptors()
    {
      PropertyDescriptor[] props = null;

      try
      {
        PropertyDescriptor enum;
        enum = new PropertyDescriptor("enum",
                   CustBean.class);
        enum.setPropertyEditorClass(EnumEditor.class);

        PropertyDescriptor type1A;
        type1A = new PropertyDescriptor("type1A",
                   CustBean.class);
        type1A.setPropertyEditorClass(PropType1EditorA.class);


        PropertyDescriptor type1B;
        type1B = new PropertyDescriptor("type1B",
                   CustBean.class);
        type1B.setPropertyEditorClass(PropType1EditorB.class);

        props = new PropertyDescriptor[3];
        props[0] = enum;
        props[1] = type1A;
        props[2] = type1B;
      }
      catch (IntrospectionException e)
      {
        System.out.println(e);
      }

      return props;
    }
}
```

The EnumEditor Custom Editor

The **EnumEditor** editor extends the **PropertyEditorSupport** class and overrides its **getTags()** method, as shown in Listing 12.5. The **getTags()** method simply creates an array of strings, each corresponding to a legal value of the property. Because **PropertyEditorSupport** already provides implementations for **getValue()** and **setValue()** (as noted earlier), **EnumEditor** needs only to redefine **getTags()**.

Listing 12.5 The EnumEditor custom editor.

```
package mybeans.custbean;

/**
 * Special property editor for enum data member.
 * This editor presents a list of three items.
 */
public class EnumEditor
extends java.beans.PropertyEditorSupport
{
  public String[] getTags()
  {
    String tags[] = {
      "one",
      "two",
      "three"};

    return tags;
  }
}
```

The PropType1EditorA Custom Editor

PropType1EditorA implements the **PropertyEditor** interface and provides a custom editor based on the **getAsText()** and **setAsText()** methods. The **getAsText()** method is straightforward—it formats the property into a string of the form "<i, s>", where "i" is the integer and "s" is the string data member of the property. The string returned by **getAsText()** is used by BeanBox to display a textual representation of the property in the PropertySheet editor (refer to Figure 12.3).

The **setAsText()** method is more complex. This method should parse a string—which should have the form "<i, s>"—back into the data members of the property. It also must cope with badly formatted strings and throw an exception of **IllegalArgumentException** type if the string cannot be parsed. Note that **setAsText()** does not modify the property; rather, it creates a new instance of **PropType1** with the new values and treats the instance as the new property being edited. Also note that **setAsText()** calls the **firePropertyChange()** method of **Property-ChangeSupport** after the string is parsed successfully.

The source code of **PropType1EditorA** is presented in Listing 12.6. We have included print statements in methods so that you can easily trace the methods as they are called by BeanBox.

Listing 12.6   The PropType1EditorA editor.

```
package mybeans.custbean;

import java.awt.*;
import java.awt.event.*;
import java.beans.*;

/**
 * This class serves as the property editor
 * for properties of PropType1.
 *
 * This editor supports the setAsText() and
 * getAsText() methods.
 */
public class PropType1EditorA extends Panel
implements PropertyEditor
{
  private PropType1 m_type1;  // property being edited
  private PropertyChangeSupport m_pcs =
          new PropertyChangeSupport(this);

  public PropType1EditorA()
  {
    System.out.println("PropType1EditorA()...");
  }


  // Set the property being edited.
  //
  public void setValue(Object obj)
  {
    m_type1 = (PropType1) obj;
    m_pcs.firePropertyChange("", null, null);
  }
```

```java
// Return the property being edited.
//
public Object getValue()
{
  System.out.println("getValue()...");

  return m_type1;
}


// Set the property by parsing "s" and
// retrieving the data members.
// The format of "s" should be "<i, s>",
// where "i" represents the integer and "s" represents
// the string data members of PropType1.
//
// Note: You should not modify the existing
//   property. Rather, you should create a new
//   instance of PropType1 with the new values.
//
// Note: More error checking should be performed
//   on "s".
//
public void setAsText(String s)
throws java.lang.IllegalArgumentException
{
  System.out.println("setAsText()...");

  int mark = s.indexOf(',');

  if (mark < 0 || // invalid string
      s.charAt(0) != '<' ||
      s.charAt(s.length()-1) != '>')
  {
    throw new IllegalArgumentException(s);
  }

  try
  {
    int i = Integer.parseInt(s.substring(1, mark));
    String str = s.substring(mark+2, s.length()-1);
    PropType1 type1 = new PropType1(i, str);

    m_type1 = type1;
    m_pcs.firePropertyChange("", null, null);
  }
  catch (NumberFormatException e)
  {
```

```java
          throw new IllegalArgumentException(e.toString());
    }
}

// Parse PropType1 into a string with
// the format: "<i, s>".
//
public String getAsText()
{
    System.out.println("getAsText()...");

    String s = "<" + m_type1.getInt() + ", " +
               m_type1.getString() + ">";
    return s;
}


public void
addPropertyChangeListener(PropertyChangeListener l)
{
    m_pcs.addPropertyChangeListener(l);
}

public void removePropertyChangeListener(
    PropertyChangeListener l)
{
    m_pcs.removePropertyChangeListener(l);
}


public boolean isPaintable()
{
    System.out.println("isPaintable()...");

    return false;
}

public void paintValue(Graphics gfx, Rectangle box)
{
}

public Component getCustomEditor()
{
    System.out.println("getCustomEditor()...");

    return null;
}
```

```java
public boolean supportsCustomEditor()
{
  System.out.println("supportsCustomEditor()...");

  return false;
}

public String[] getTags()
{
  System.out.println("getTags()...");

  return null;
}

public String getJavaInitializationString()
{
  System.out.println(
    "getJavaInitializationString()...");

  return null;
}

public Dimension preferredSize()
{
  return new Dimension(200, 60);
}
}
```

The PropType1EditorB Custom Editor

PropType1EditorB provides a more sophisticated property editor for **PropType1** properties. As shown in Listing 12.7, this editor supports the **paintValue()** and **getCustomEditor()** methods. The constructor of **PropType1EditorB** creates a **Component** consisting of two **TextField** objects, each handling a data member of **PropType1**. Note that the editor itself implements the **TextListener** listener in order to receive callbacks from the **TextField** objects.

The **paintValue()** method is not overly complex. It simply paints a visual representation of the property into the bounding box provided as its argument. This method uses the same format ("<i, s>") to paint the property. The bounding box is usually an area inside the BeanBox's PropertySheet editor, as shown in Figure 12.4.

The **textValueChanged()** method, which is called back when the value of a field changes inside the text fields, is responsible for obtaining the new value of the modified data member and updating the property. Like the **setAsText()** method in **PropType1EditorA**, this method does not modify the property under editing; instead, it replaces the modified property with a new instance of **PropType1**.

Listing 12.7   The PropType1EditorB custom editor.

```
package mybeans.custbean;

import java.awt.*;
import java.awt.event.*;
import java.beans.*;

/**
 * This class serves as the property editor
 * for properties of PropType1. It creates two
 * text fields to allow data members of PropType1
 * to be modified.
 * Remember that this property has an integer
 * and a string data member.
 *
 * This editor supports the paintValue() and
 * getCustomEditor() methods.
 *
 * NOTE: This class implements TextListener in order
 *       to receive events from TextField components.
 *       An alternative approach would be to use
 *       adapter classes instead.
 */
public class PropType1EditorB extends Panel
implements PropertyEditor, TextListener
{
  private PropType1 m_type1; // property being edited
  private TextField m_tfInt; // text field for int
  private TextField m_tfStr; // text field for string
  private PropertyChangeSupport m_pcs =
          new PropertyChangeSupport(this);

  public PropType1EditorB()
  {
    System.out.println("PropType1EditorB()...");

    setLayout(new GridLayout(2,2,5,5));
```

```java
// Create a textfield to edit the integer member.
//
m_tfInt = new TextField("", 5);
m_tfInt.addTextListener(this);
Label lblInt = new Label("Integer: ");

// Create a textfield to edit the string member.
//
m_tfStr = new TextField("", 14);
m_tfStr.addTextListener(this);
Label lblStr = new Label("String: ");

// Add the components to the panel.
//
add(lblInt);
add(m_tfInt);
add(lblStr);
add(m_tfStr);

setSize(200, 60);
}


// Set the property being edited.
//
public void setValue(Object obj)
{
  System.out.println("setValue()...");

  m_type1 = (PropType1) obj;

  m_tfInt.setText("" + m_type1.getInt());
  m_tfStr.setText(m_type1.getString());

  m_pcs.firePropertyChange("", null, null);
}

// Return the property being edited.
//
public Object getValue()
{
  System.out.println("getValue()...");

  return m_type1;
}
```

```java
public boolean isPaintable()
{
   System.out.println("isPaintable()...");

   return true;
}


// This method paints the value of this property
// into the PropertySheet editor.
//
// Note: This method must ensure that it won't
//   paint outside the bounding box.
//
public void paintValue(Graphics gfx, Rectangle box)
{
   System.out.println("paintValue()...");

   String s = "<" + m_type1.getInt() + ", " +
              m_type1.getString() + ">";
   gfx.drawRect(box.x, box.y, box.width-3, box.height-3);
   gfx.drawString(s, box.x+2, box.y+ box.height/2);
}


public Component getCustomEditor()
{
   System.out.println("getCustomEditor()...");

   return this;
}

public boolean supportsCustomEditor()
{
   System.out.println("supportsCustomEditor()...");

   return true;
}


// This method gets called by either of the
// two text fields when the user changes the value
// of the fields.
// When a value changes, this method creates
// a new instance of PropType1 and replaces the
// current value being edited with it.
//
// Note: You must not change the value of the
//   property being modified. You should replace
//   it with a new instance.
//
```

```
public void textValueChanged(TextEvent te)
{
  TextField tf = (TextField) te.getSource();

  PropType1 type1;
  if (tf == m_tfInt)
  {
    int newInt;
    try
    {
      newInt = Integer.parseInt(tf.getText());
    }
    catch (NumberFormatException e)
    {
      newInt = m_type1.getInt();
      m_tfInt.setText("" + newInt);
    }

    type1 = new PropType1(newInt, m_type1.getString());
  }
  else  // tf == m_tfStr
  {
    type1 = new PropType1(m_type1.getInt(), tf.getText());
  }

  m_type1 = type1;
  m_pcs.firePropertyChange("", null, null);
}


public void
addPropertyChangeListener(PropertyChangeListener l)
{
  m_pcs.addPropertyChangeListener(l);
}

public void removePropertyChangeListener(
  PropertyChangeListener l)
{
  m_pcs.removePropertyChangeListener(l);
}


public void setAsText(String s)
throws java.lang.IllegalArgumentException
{
  System.out.println("setAsText()...");
}
```

```
public String getAsText()
{
  System.out.println("getAsText()...");

  return null;
}

public String[] getTags()
{
  System.out.println("getTags()...");

  return null;
}

public String getJavaInitializationString()
{
  System.out.println(
    "getJavaInitializationString()...");

  return null;
}

public Dimension preferredSize()
{
  return new Dimension(200, 60);
}
}
```

Conclusion

In this chapter, we demonstrated how to provide custom editors for properties. We explained the **PropertyEditor** interface and its methods, and we provided detailed examples of custom property editors with varying degrees of complexity.

Your journey of learning about Java Beans is now complete. We have analyzed all of the fundamentals of Java Beans, examined all of the classes in the java.beans package, and walked through many examples. Part III of this book presents some "super beans," which are much more complex that the beans we have presented so far. You should be able to understand these beans easily—and, we hope, build many of your own.

PART 3

Applications Of Java Beans

Part III of this book is dedicated to developing Java Beans applications based on the fundamentals of Java Beans presented in Part II. Chapter 13 provides a multicast bean suite and Chapter 14 presents an auto-update bean suite. These beans are developed to solve specific problems; they are by no means third-party beans.

Chapter 15 is devoted to discussing the ActiveX bridge. We will develop a bean that pings a site URL and measures its average time delay. We'll then convert this bean into an ActiveX control, and use the control to develop a Visual Basic application.

Examining the materials and code listings of Part III should help you develop many Java Beans applications.

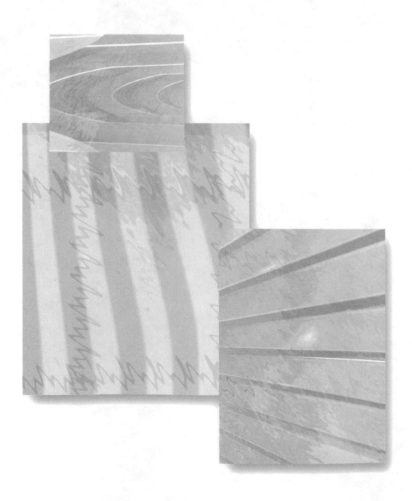

Chapter 13

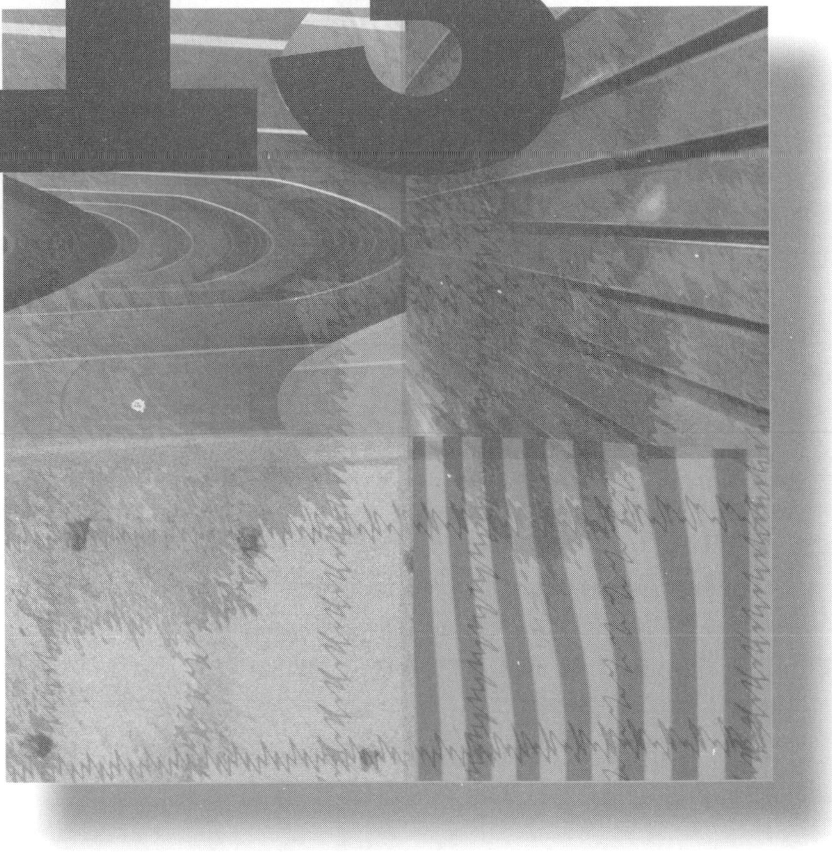

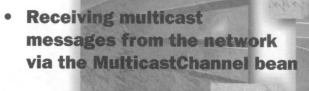

- **Receiving multicast messages from the network via the MulticastChannel bean**

- **Forwarding multicast messages to appropriate recipients**

- **Using TextChannel and AudioChannel to display multicast data**

- **Wiring the multicast beans in the BeanBox framework**

- **Multicasting messages in the network using McastSend**

- **Fundamentals of multicasting**

Chapter 13

Multicast Beans

by Jalil Feghhi

This chapter presents a suite of multicast beans—Multicast-Channel, TextChannel, and AudioChannel—that can be used to build real-world applications based on the Java Beans technology. The **McastSend** class, which sends multicast messages, is demonstrated as well. The beans communicate with each other through **MulticastEvent** and **MulticastListener** objects.

You create a multicast bean application by assembling a MulticastChannel bean that is connected to a TextChannel bean within a framework. You specify the multicast IP address and port number of the MulticastChannel bean by modifying its properties, and you instruct it to start listening. To test the application, you can execute the **McastSend** program and multicast a message on the IP address and port number that you just specified; if all goes well, the MulticastChannel bean will receive the message and dispatch it to the TextChannel.

The **McastSend** program can be anywhere in the network, and it can transmit messages to any number of MulticastChannel beans residing on different hosts. A MulticastChannel itself can have any number of listeners. This application can disseminate information from a source to many recipients in a network while minimizing the use of the network bandwidth. Alternatively, you can build an application with the AudioChannel bean that receives voice data from multicast sources.

In this chapter, we will provide a short overview of multicasting, followed by a step-by-step guide for assembling the multicast beans into applications. Each of the the beans mentioned above will be discussed at great length.

 *In order to run the MulticastChannel bean, your computer hardware must support multicasting. Otherwise, you will get a socket exception when you attempt to start this bean.*

Fundamentals Of Multicasting

A multicast group has an IP multicast group address. The IP multicast address space consists of addresses from 224.0.0.0 to 239.255.255.255 (although the range between 224.0.0.0 to 224.0.0.255 is reserved for multicast routing).

In order to listen to multicast messages, an application also needs a port similar to a TCP or UDP port, except that many applications can listen to multicast messages sent on the same port. The kernel uses this port to route messages to the applications.

When an application joins a multicast group, it only uses the IP multicast address. This means all multicast messages sent to that IP multicast group are received by the computer where the application is running, regardless of the port numbers. In effect, the IP multicast groups map to the addresses of the computers, and the ports map to the applications running on those computers. (Note that the multicast messages are based on UDP packets.)

A time-to-live (TTL) parameter is also used when sending multicast messages. As its value increases, multicast-enabled routers forward a multicast message over an expanded number of network hops or thresholds. The thresholds shown in Table 13.1 are enforced by multicast-enabled routers.

Table 13.1   Thresholds enforced by multicast-enabled routers.

Value	Result
0	same host
1	same subnet
32	same site
64	same region
128	same continent
255	no restriction

You don't need to join a multicast group to send multicast messages, but you must join in order to receive them. You can send multicast messages whose TTL value is 1 on any subnet that supports multicasting, such as Ethernet. For values greater than 1, the router connecting the subnet to the outside should be multicast-enabled and should also allow the passing through of multicast messages.

Multicast-enabled routers can be configured for the scope of multicast forwarding. For example, a router might be configured to allow only same-site multicasts. Such a router blocks multicast messages with a value of TTL greater than 32 on the interfaces that are not connected to the regional network.

Assembling The Multicast Beans Into Applications

In this section, we will discuss how to build sample applications using the multicast beans. We'll provide detailed instructions on how to load the multicast beans, receive multicast messages from the network, dispatch the messages to interested recipients, and send multicast messages.

Loading The Multicast Beans

Java Beans frameworks provide different methods for adding new beans into their palettes. With the BeanBox framework, you can simply use the File|LoadJar menu to load the Multicast.jar file from the jars directory on the CD-ROM. Figure 13.1 displays BeanBox after this loading is complete; note the addition of the three multicast beans to the ToolBox.

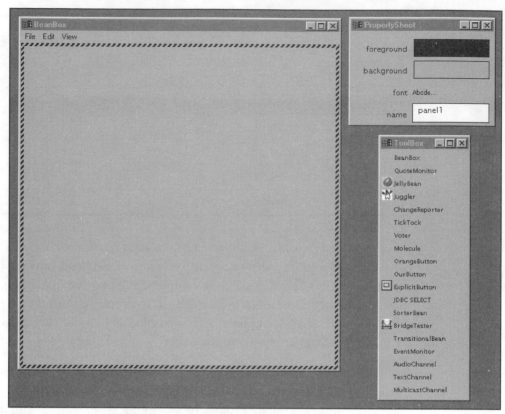

Figure 13.1 BeanBox after loading the Multicast.jar file.

Receiving Multicast Messages From The Network

To receive multicast transmissions, you must instantiate the Multicast-Channel bean in the BeanBox container and then configure it as follows. As shown in Figure 13.2, MulticastChannel exports three properties: **multicastAddress**, **packetSize**, and **port**.

The **multicastAddress** and **port** properties together uniquely identify a network multicast transmission. You can specify any value for **multicastAddress** as long as it falls within the legal multicast address range, as described earlier. Similarly, you can use any available port number for **port** (note that some platforms may have reserved the lower part of the available range). Finally, **packetSize** determines the size of the packets used in the UDP transmission; the default value provides an acceptable value for this property.

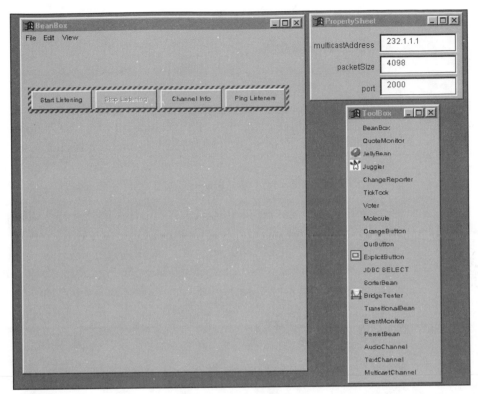

Figure 13.2 An instantiated and configured MulticastChannel bean.

*Some hardware platforms, most notably PCs, may drop UDP packets if **packetSize** is greater than 4,000 bytes.*

Now you are ready to receive multicast transmissions. To do this, simply press on the "Start Listening" button of MulticastChannel; the bean should disable the "Start Listening" button and enable the "Stop Listening" button. The MulticastChannel bean is now receiving multicast messages, and it is ready to forward them to interested recipients.

If you cannot start listening with the MulticastChannel bean, look into the window in which you started the BeanBox session. If MulticastChannel is reporting "java.net.SocketException: multicast join failed," you may not have the required hardware to support multicast transmissions.

Dispatching Multicast Messages To Recipients

MulticastChannel fires an event of **multicastMessage** type. Any target bean interested in receiving multicast transmissions can provide a method that takes one **multicastMessage** argument and thereby register itself with MulticastChannel. TextChannel illustrates a sample bean capable of connecting itself to MulticastChannel for this purpose. This bean assumes the transmission contains textual data; the data is displayed in the bean upon arrival.

Instantiate one or more TextChannel beans (see Figure 13.3) and proceed to connect them to MulticastChannel. Select the MulticastChannel bean, execute Edit|Events|Event|multicastMessage, and choose one of the TextChannel beans as the target (as shown in Figure 13.4). BeanBox will pop up a dialog box (see Figure 13.5); select the "multicastMessage"

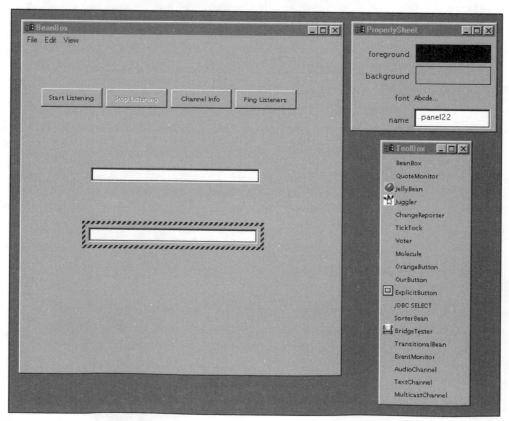

Figure 13.3 Two TextChannel beans.

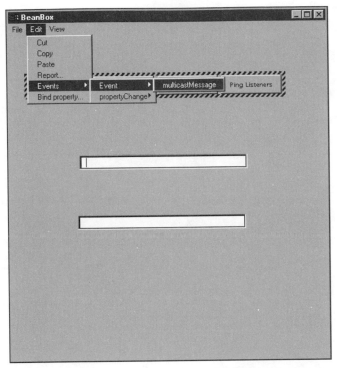

Figure 13.4 MulticastChannel generates a **multicastMessage** event.

entry and press on the "Ok" button. Repeat this procedure for each of the TextChannel beans.

The application is now complete. To test the wiring between the beans, click on the "Ping Listeners" button of MulticastChannel—the "Hello! Are you listening?" message should appear in all of the TextChannel beans (as shown in Figure 13.6). Alternatively, you can use the "Channel Info"

Figure 13.5 TextChannel handles **multicastMessage** events.

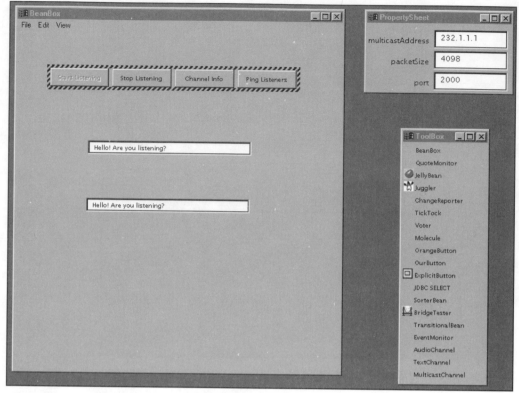

Figure 13.6   Pinging the **TextChannel** beans.

button, which prints statistical information about MulticastChannel in the start-up window of BeanBox.

 The "Ping Listeners" operation works only with the TextChannel bean; it cannot be used on AudioChannel.

Sending Multicast Messages In The Network

To test the application as a whole, start **McastSend** (a standalone Java program located in the multicast directory under mybeans in the CD-ROM) and multicast messages in the network. Be sure to specify the same values for the multicast IP address and port as those shown for MulticastChannel in the previous section (see Figure 13.7). You can use a value of 1 for the time-to-live field, directing **McastSend** to multicast to the local area network (LAN). The value of the packet size

Multicast Send	□|□|X
Muticast IP Address	232.1.1.1
Multicast Port	2000
Time-To-Live	1
Packet Size (bytes)	4098
File to send	
Text to send	Specify a file or a message to s
Multicast	Exit

Figure 13.7 Configuring the **McastSend** program.

field is used by the UDP transmission, which should be the same size as the one expected by the MulticastChannel.

To specify the multicast message, put the message in a file and select the file name, or simply type the message in the "Text to send" field. Figure 13.8 shows the TextChannel beans after **McastSend** multicasts the "Specify a file or a message to send" message.

As noted earlier, McastSend can reside anywhere in the network, and any number of MulticastChannel beans—each potentially on a different machine—can be tuned to pick up multicast messages.

Sending And Receiving Voice Data

Multicast transmissions may contain textual, voice, and video data, among other types. TextChannel, for example, is a bean that handles textual data.

In this section, we will demonstrate AudioChannel, a bean capable of receiving voice data. This bean (shown in Figure 13.9) exposes two properties: **audioSize** and **bufSize**. The **bufSize** property determines the number of bytes that must be received before AudioChannel starts to play.

When you send a voice file to AudioChannel, the last part of the file is usually not played because AudioChannel is still waiting to receive exactly **bufSize** bytes of data before it starts to play. To handle this problem, you can use **audioSize** to specify the total number of bytes expected to be received. AudioChannel can use this information to play the last segment of a voice file even if it has not yet received all of the data indicated for **bufSize**.

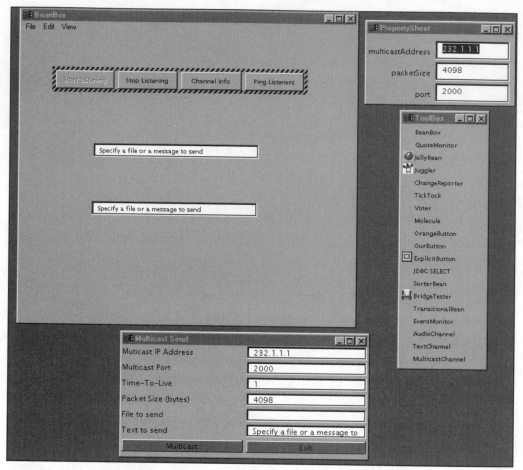

Figure 13.8 Multicast messages delivered to the TextChannel beans.

Select the instantiated MulticastChannel bean and wire it to the "audioMessage" method of AudioChannel, as shown in Figure 13.10. Multicast the lm.au voice file using **McastSend** (make sure the size of this file is entered as the value in the **audioSize** field of AudioChannel). The AudioChannel bean should receive and play the lm.au file.

MulticastEvent

MulticastEvent is used by MulticastChannel to forward the multicast data received from the network to all registered recipients. This event, shown in Listing 13.1, contains the source of the triggered event (the MulticastChannel bean), the multicast data, and the number of bytes in the data.

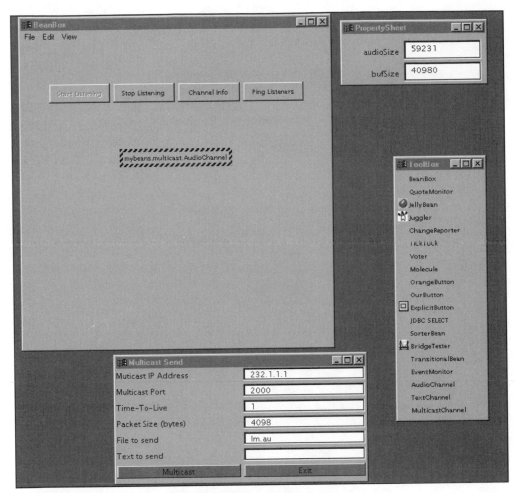

Figure 13.9 The AudioChannel bean.

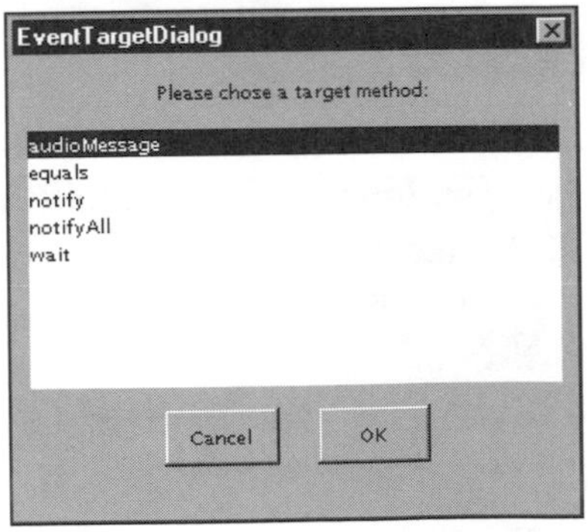

Figure 13.10 AudioChannel handles **multicastMessage** events.

Listing 13.1   The MulticastEvent event.

```
package mybeans.multicast;

// This interface describes the method that gets
// fired by the MulticastChannel bean.

public class MulticastEvent
extends java.util.EventObject {

  public MulticastEvent (Object src, byte[] buf,
                         int len){
    super(src);
    m_msg = buf;
    m_len = len;
  }

  // Called when the caller knows the data is string.
  public String getMessage (){
    return new String (m_msg, 0 , m_len);
  }

  public byte[] getData(){
    return m_msg;
  }

  public int getLength (){
    return m_len;
  }

  byte[] m_msg;
  int m_len;
}
```

MulticastListener

MulticastListener defines the interface between MulticastChannel and any target bean wishing to receive multicast messages. As shown in Listing 13.2, this listener identifies one method, **multicastMessage()**, which takes exactly one argument of **MulticastEvent** type.

Listing 13.2   The MulticastListener implementation.

```
package mybeans.multicast;
```

```
// This interface describes the method that should be
// implemented by classes that want to receive the
// MulticastEvent from MulticastChannel.

public interface MulticastListener
extends java.util.EventListener {
  void multicastMessage (MulticastEvent evt);
}
```

MulticastChannel

The MulticastChannel bean listens on a specified multicast IP address and port, receives multicast transmissions, and forwards them to all of the interested listener targets via **MulticastEvent** objects. It provides registration/deregistration methods for adding/removing listeners, and it exports its properties through three pairs of getter/setter methods. The source code for MulticastChannel is shown in Listing 13.3.

MulticastChannel implements the **ActionListener** interface in order to receive **ActionEvent** events from **Button** objects used in its GUI. This approach has resulted in a series of **if else** statements in the **actionPerformed**() method. Even though this approach is satisfactory due to the small number the buttons, a cleaner strategy would be to implement a number of listeners, each dedicated to one of the buttons. Note that the **startChannel**() method utilizes the **Channel** class to handle the details of opening multicast connections; this class will be discussed in the next section.

Listing 13.3   The MulticastChannel source code.

```
/**
 * This is the multicast channel bean. It listens on
 * the given IP/port and sends the received
 * messages to other beans that are interested.
 *
 */

package mybeans.multicast;

import java.awt.*;
import java.net.*;
import java.beans.*;
import java.awt.event.*;
```

```java
// MulticastChannel: A demo bean to listen on
// multicast messages. It uses a separate thread to
// listen on the multicast address/port specified.
// Here we assume the designer knows the type of data
// and will connect this bean to other beans that can
// display or play the data, like AudioChannel or
// TextChannel in this package.
//
public class MulticastChannel extends Panel
implements ActionListener {

    public MulticastChannel() {

    setLayout(new GridLayout(1,0,5,5));
    m_startButton = new Button("Start Listening");
    m_startButton.addActionListener(this);
    add(m_startButton);

    m_stopButton = new Button("Stop Listening");
    m_stopButton.addActionListener(this);
    add(m_stopButton);
    m_stopButton.setEnabled(false);

    m_infoButton = new Button("Channel Info");
    m_infoButton.addActionListener(this);
    add(m_infoButton);

    m_pingButton = new Button("Ping Listeners");
    m_pingButton.addActionListener(this);
    add(m_pingButton);

    }

  public java.awt.Dimension preferredSize() {
    return new java.awt.Dimension(400, 30);
  }

  public void setPacketSize (int newValue){
    int oldValue = m_packetSize;
    m_packetSize = newValue;
    changes.firePropertyChange("packetSize",
      new Integer(oldValue), new Integer(newValue));
  }

  public int getPacketSize() {
    return m_packetSize;
  }
```

```java
public void setMulticastAddress (String newValue){
  String oldValue = m_mcastAddr;
  m_mcastAddr = newValue;
  changes.firePropertyChange("multicastAddress",
    oldValue, newValue);
}

public String getMulticastAddress() {
  return m_mcastAddr;
}

public void setPort (int newValue){
  int oldValue = m_port;
  m_port = newValue;
  changes.firePropertyChange("port",
    new Integer(oldValue), new Integer(newValue));
}

public int getPort() {
  return m_port;
}

// Method to add property change listeners
public void
addPropertyChangeListener(PropertyChangeListener l){
  changes.addPropertyChangeListener(l);
}

public void
removePropertyChangeListener(
  PropertyChangeListener l) {
  changes.removePropertyChangeListener(l);
}


// Method to add MulticastEvent Listeners
public synchronized void
addMulticastListener(MulticastListener l) {
  listeners.addElement(l);
}

public synchronized void
removeMulticastListener(MulticastListener l) {
  listeners.removeElement(l);
}
```

```java
// Our internal method to fire events.
// It is called by Channel class when
// it receives a multicast message.
protected void fireEvent(byte[] buf, int len) {
  java.util.Vector listenerObjects;

  synchronized (this) {
    listenerObjects = (java.util.Vector)
      listeners.clone();
  }

  for (int i=0; i<listenerObjects.size();i++) {
    MulticastListener l = (MulticastListener)
      listenerObjects.elementAt(i);
    l.multicastMessage(
      new MulticastEvent (this, buf , len));
  }
}

// ActionListener implementation
public void actionPerformed(ActionEvent e) {

  Object source = e.getSource();

  try {
    if (source == m_startButton) {
      startChannel();
      return;
    }
    if (source == m_stopButton) {
      m_stopButton.setEnabled(false);
      m_startButton.setEnabled(true);
      m_channel.stopChannel();
      return;
    }
    if (source == m_infoButton) {
      // we don't have a channel
      if (m_startButton.isEnabled()){
        System.out.println (
          "Channel not started yet!");
        return;
      }
      else {
        System.out.println ("Channel Information:" +
          "\n\tStatus:\t" + "Active" +
          "\n\tIP:\t" + m_mcastAddr +
          "\n\tPort:\t" + m_port +
          "\n\tPacket Size:\t" + m_packetSize +
```

```
                    "\n\tNumber of listeners:\t" +
                    ((java.util.Vector) listeners).size());
                return;
            }
        }
        if (source == m_pingButton) {
            // Use this button only on TextChannels.
            // With audio, it may create
            // unpleasant sounds! It is for testing
            // purposes only and should be
            // removed from the final bean.
            String msg = "Hello! Are you listening?";
            byte[] buf = msg.getBytes ();

            DatagramPacket himsg =
             new DatagramPacket(buf, buf.length,
                m_group, m_port);

            // We really don't need a multicastSocket to
            // send this packet. A
            // DatagramSocket will do as well.
            DatagramSocket socket = new DatagramSocket();
            socket.send (himsg);
        }
    }
    catch (Exception ex) {
        System.out.println (
            "Got error while proccessing the action: " +
            ex);
    }

    return;
}

protected void startChannel(){
    try {
        m_group = InetAddress.getByName (m_mcastAddr);
        m_channel = new Channel (this , m_group ,
                            m_port, m_packetSize);
        m_channel.startChannel();
        m_startButton.setEnabled(false);
        m_stopButton.setEnabled(true);
    }
    catch (Exception e) {
        System.out.println (
            "Got exception while starting the channel: "
            + e);
    }
}
```

```
                // Default multicast packet size.
                private int m_packetSize=4098;
                private Channel m_channel;
                private int m_port;
                private InetAddress m_group;
                private String m_mcastAddr;
                private Button m_startButton;
                private Button m_stopButton;
                private Button m_infoButton;
                private Button m_pingButton;

                private PropertyChangeSupport changes =
                   new PropertyChangeSupport(this);
                private java.util.Vector listeners =
                   new java.util.Vector();
             }
```

Channel

The **Channel** class extends **java.lang.Thread** in order to maintain a con-
tinuous network connection. The **initChannel()** method opens up a multicast
port and joins it with a multicast IP address. The **run()** method creates
a **DatagramPacket** object, fills it with multicast data, and then delivers its
contents to the MulticastChannel bean via the **fireEvent()** callback.

Listing 13.4   The Channel class.

```
package mybeans.multicast;

import java.lang.Thread;
import java.net.*;
import java.io.*;

/**
 * Channel: a class used by our package to do the
 * listening.
 */
class Channel extends Thread implements Serializable
{
  Channel (MulticastChannel chl , InetAddress grp,
    int port)
  throws IOException {
    m_caller = chl;
    m_group = grp;
    m_port = port;
    initChannel ();
  }
```

```java
// Call this constructor if our multicast messages
// are bigger than the default size.
Channel (MulticastChannel chl , InetAddress grp,
  int port, int dblk)
throws IOException {

  m_caller = chl;
  m_group = grp;
  m_port = port;
  m_dblk = dblk;
  initChannel ();
}

// We really should make this method private because
// our startChannel method is meant to be used from
// outside but Java doesn't allow making methods
// more private than what is in the superclass.
public void run(){
  try {
    byte[] buf = new byte[m_dblk];

    while (true) {
      DatagramPacket dgrm = new
        DatagramPacket(buf, buf.length);

      // Receive blocks till it gets something.
      m_socket.receive(dgrm);
      m_caller.fireEvent (dgrm.getData(),
        dgrm.getLength());
    }
  }
  catch (Exception e) {
    System.out.println (
      "Got exception while receiving: " + e);
  }
}

protected void startChannel(){
  start();
}

protected void stopChannel() throws IOException {
  m_socket.leaveGroup(m_group);
  m_socket.close();
  stop();
}
```

```
private void initChannel() throws IOException {
  // Create the multicast socket on the specified
  // port and join the group.
  m_socket = new MulticastSocket(m_port);
  m_socket.joinGroup(m_group);
}


private int m_port;

// Default size of multicast packets
private int m_dblk = 4098;
private InetAddress m_group;
private MulticastSocket m_socket;
private MulticastChannel m_caller;
}
```

TextChannel

As shown in Listing 13.5, TextChannel provides a simple **TextField** to display textual data. In addition, it defines a method that takes exactly one argument of **MulticastEvent** type in order to receive multicast events.

Listing 13.5 The TextChannel bean.

```
package mybeans.multicast;

import java.awt.*;
import java.beans.*;
import java.awt.event.*;
import java.io.*;

public class TextChannel extends Panel
implements MulticastListener, Serializable
{
  public TextChannel (){
    msgField = new TextField(40);
    add(msgField);
  }

  public void multicastMessage (MulticastEvent evt){
    String msg = evt.getMessage();
    msgField.setText("");
    msgField.setText (msg);
  }

  TextField msgField;
}
```

AudioChannel

The AudioChannel bean is slightly more complicated than TextChannel. This bean exports two properties (**bufSize** and **audioSize**) and the **audioMessage()** method, which takes a **MulticastEvent** object as an argument. If the **bufSize** is specified, AudioChannel plays audio every time it receives **bufSize** amount of voice data. As noted earlier, though, in this case it can never determine the end of the voice transmission. If **audioSize** is also specified, AudioChannel knows the exact size of the voice data and can play the entire transmission.

The AudioChannel bean is shown in Listing 13.6.

Listing 13.6   The AudioChannel bean.

```
package mybeans.multicast;

import sun.audio.*;
import java.beans.*;
import java.io.*;

/**
 *
 * AudioChannel. A class that plays UDP multicast
 * audio.
 * In this class we are assuming there is no packet
 * loss in a multicast session.
 * This is obviously not true in real life, where
 * higher-level protocols like RTP
 * need to be used to get more information about the
 * data.
 */
public class AudioChannel implements Serializable
{

  public AudioChannel(){
    m_audio = new byte[m_bufSize];
  }

  // BufSize property: the size of our audio buffer
  public void setBufSize(int newValue){
    int oldValue = m_bufSize;
    m_bufSize = newValue;

    // For simplicity, we play the audio before
    // resetting the size of the buffer.
    // We don't expect this to happen while playing.
```

```java
      if (m_len > 0){
        playAudio();
      }
      m_audio = new byte[m_bufSize];
      changes.firePropertyChange("bufSize",
        new Integer(oldValue), new Integer(newValue));
  }

  public int getBufSize() {
    return m_bufSize;
  }

  // AudioSize property: the size of our audio file.
  // If zero, it is continuous.
  public void setAudioSize(int newValue){
    int oldValue = m_bufSize;
    m_audioSize = newValue;
    changes.firePropertyChange("audioSize",
      new Integer(oldValue), new Integer(newValue));
  }

  public int getAudioSize() {
    return m_audioSize;
  }

  // Methods for property listeners.
  public void addPropertyChangeListener(
    PropertyChangeListener l) {
    changes.addPropertyChangeListener(l);
  }

  public void removePropertyChangeListener(
    PropertyChangeListener l) {
    changes.removePropertyChangeListener(l);
  }

  // This method can be used as a hook by an
  // Event Adapter that wants to
  // implement the MulticastListener interface.
  public void audioMessage (MulticastEvent evt){
    byte[] data = evt.getData();
    int dlen = evt.getLength();
    int i;

    m_total += dlen;
```

```
      // Copy the audio data if we have space in our
      // buffer.
      if (m_len + dlen <= m_bufSize){
        for (i = 0; i < dlen ; i++){
          m_audio[m_len++] = data[i];
        }
      }
      else {
        // Start playing now to empty the buffer.
        playAudio();
        // Copy now that the buffer is empty.
        for (i = 0; i < dlen ; i++){
          m_audio[m_len++] = data[i];
        }
      }

      // Play if this was the last part of the audio
      // data. This is only good if we don't have
      // packet loss.
      // If m_audioSize is not set, audio is continuous
      // and we don't need to do this.
      if (m_total == m_audioSize){
        playAudio();
        m_total = 0;
      }
    }

    private synchronized void playAudio(){
      if (m_len == 0){ // nothing to play
        return;
      }
      try {
        m_clip = new AudioData (m_audio);
        AudioPlayer.player.start (
          new AudioDataStream (m_clip));
        m_len = 0;
      }
      catch (Exception e) {
        System.out.println(
          "Error Playing Sound - " + e);
      }
    }


    private byte[] m_audio;
    private AudioData m_clip;
```

```
// 40K  default buffer size
private int m_bufSize = 40980;
private int m_len;
private int m_audioSize;
private int m_total;
private PropertyChangeSupport changes =
  new PropertyChangeSupport(this);
}
```

McastSend

The **McastSend** program, presented in Listing 13.7, is very useful if your network does not receive any multicast data. In this case, you must multicast messages yourself in order to test the **MulticastChannel** bean.

Listing 13.7   The McastSend program.

```
package mybeans.multicast;

// A very simple application to send multicast
// messages. You can either send text using a text field
// or send a file containing binary data.
//

import java.awt.*;
import java.io.*;
import java.net.*;
import java.awt.event.*;

public class McastSend extends Frame
implements ActionListener {

  public McastSend() {
    super("Multicast Send");
    setBackground (Color.lightGray);

    setLayout(new GridLayout(0,2,5,5));

    add(new Label("Multicast IP Address", Label.LEFT));
    m_mcastGrpText = new TextField(15);
    add(m_mcastGrpText);

    add(new Label("Multicast Port", Label.LEFT));
    m_portText = new TextField(9);
    add(m_portText);
```

```java
add(new Label("Time-To-Live", Label.LEFT));
m_ttlText =
  new TextField(String.valueOf(m_ttl), 3);
add(m_ttlText);

add(new Label("Packet Size (bytes)", Label.LEFT));
m_sizeText =
  new TextField (String.valueOf(m_packetSize), 3);
add(m_sizeText);


add(new Label("File to send", Label.LEFT));
m_fileText = new TextField(20);
add(m_fileText);

add(new Label ("Text to send" , Label.LEFT));
    m_msgText = new TextField(
      "Specify a file or a message to send" , 60);
add(m_msgText);

m_mcastButton = new Button("Multicast");
m_mcastButton.setBackground(Color.gray);
m_mcastButton.addActionListener(this);
add(m_mcastButton);

m_exitButton = new Button("Exit");
m_exitButton.setBackground (Color.gray);
m_exitButton.addActionListener (this);
add(m_exitButton);

try {
  m_msocket = new MulticastSocket();
}
catch (IOException e) {
  logMessage ("Cannot initialize a Multicast " +
    "Socket. Exiting! - " + e);
  System.exit (-1);
}
}

public java.awt.Dimension preferredSize() {
  return new java.awt.Dimension(400,200);
}

private static void logMessage (String msg){
  //We just write to console.
  System.out.println (msg);
}
```

```java
private void
sendMsg (String msg, InetAddress gaddr, int port)
throws Exception{

  byte[] buf = msg.getBytes();

  DatagramPacket pack = new
    DatagramPacket (buf, buf.length, gaddr, port);
  m_msocket.send (pack , (byte) m_ttl);
}

private void
sendMsg (File file, InetAddress gaddr, int port)
throws IOException
{
  FileInputStream in = new FileInputStream (file);

  int off = 0;
  long len = file.length();
  byte[] data = new byte[m_packetSize];
  int nread;

  // Note that the receiver should use a packet size
  // at least equal to what we use here in order
  // not to lose data.
  while (
    (nread = in.read (data, 0, data.length)) != -1){
    len -= nread;

    // Send what we read so far.
    DatagramPacket pack = new
      DatagramPacket (data, nread, gaddr, port);
    m_msocket.send (pack , (byte) m_ttl);

    if (len == 0) {
      // read everything
      break;
    }
  }

  in.close();
}

// ActionListener implementation
public void actionPerformed(ActionEvent e) {

  Cursor oldCursor = getCursor();
  setCursor (new Cursor(Cursor.WAIT_CURSOR));
```

```
      Object source = e.getSource();
      if (source == m_exitButton) {
        dispose();
        System.exit(0);
      }
      else if (source == m_mcastButton) {
        multicast();
      }

      setCursor (oldCursor);
      return;
    }

    public void multicast() {
      String msg = m_msgText.getText();
      String  portStr = m_portText.getText();
      String  group = m_mcastGrpText.getText();
      String  ttlStr = m_ttlText.getText();
      String  sizeStr = m_sizeText.getText();
      String  fileStr = m_fileText.getText();

      InetAddress gaddr;
      int portno;
      int ttl,dblk;

      try {
        gaddr = InetAddress.getByName (group);
      }catch (Exception e) {
        logMessage ("Error - Bad multicast addr:" + e);
        return;
      }

      try {
        portno = Integer.parseInt (portStr);
      } catch (Exception e) {
        logMessage ("Error - Bad port number:" + e);
        return;
      }

      try {
        m_ttl = Integer.parseInt (ttlStr);
      } catch (Exception e) {
        logMessage ("Error - Bad ttl number: " +
          ttlStr + " - " + e);
        return;
      }
```

```
      try {
        m_packetSize = Integer.parseInt (sizeStr);
      } catch (Exception e) {
        logMessage ("Error - Bad packet size:" +
          sizeStr + " - " + e);
        return;
      }


      // If a file is specified, send the file
      // and not the message.
      try {
        if (fileStr.length() > 0) {
          File file = new File (fileStr);
          if (file.exists() && file.canRead()){
            sendMsg (file, gaddr, portno);

            // Clear the old text to send, if any.
            m_msgText.setText("");
            logMessage ("File \"" + fileStr +
              "\" sent to: " + group + " on port: " +
              portno );

          }
          else {
            logMessage ("Error - File: '" + fileStr +
              "' does not exist or not readable.");
          }
        }

        else {
          sendMsg (msg, gaddr, portno);
          logMessage ("\"" + msg + "\" sent to: " +
            group + " on port: " + portno);
        }
      }
      catch (Exception e){
        logMessage ("Error - Could not send message: "
          + e);
      }
    }

    static public void main (String[] args){
      Frame f = new McastSend();
      f.pack();
      f.show();
    }
```

```
    // Default maximum packet size to send
    int m_packetSize = 4098;
    int m_ttl = 1; // default time to live
    MulticastSocket m_msocket;
    Button     m_mcastButton;
    TextField m_msgText;
    Button     m_exitButton;
    TextField m_mcastGrpText;
    TextField m_portText;
    TextField m_ttlText;
    TextField m_sizeText;
    TextField m_fileText;
}
```

MulticastChannelBeanInfo

The **MulticastChannelBeanInfo** class, shown in Listing 13.8, provides explicit information about the properties and events of MulticastChannel.

Listing 13.8   The MulticastChannelBeanInfo class.

```
package mybeans.multicast;

import java.beans.*;


public class MulticastChannelBeanInfo
extends SimpleBeanInfo
{
  public PropertyDescriptor[] getPropertyDescriptors() {
    try {
      PropertyDescriptor packetSize = new
        PropertyDescriptor("packetSize",
          MulticastChannel.class);

      packetSize.setConstrained(false);
      packetSize.setBound(true);

      PropertyDescriptor multicastAddress = new
        PropertyDescriptor("multicastAddress",
          MulticastChannel.class);

      multicastAddress.setConstrained(false);
      multicastAddress.setBound(true);

      PropertyDescriptor port = new
        PropertyDescriptor("port",
          MulticastChannel.class);
```

```
      port.setConstrained(false);
      port.setBound(true);

      PropertyDescriptor pd[] = {packetSize,
      multicastAddress, port};
      return pd;
    }
    catch (IntrospectionException e) {
      // We throw an error here.
      throw new Error(e.toString());
    }
  }

  public EventSetDescriptor[]
  getEventSetDescriptors() {
    String[] listenerMethods = {"multicastMessage"};
    EventSetDescriptor event, changes;

    try {
      event = new EventSetDescriptor(
        MulticastChannel.class,
        "Event", MulticastListener.class,
        listenerMethods, "addMulticastListener",
        "removeMulticastListener");

      changes = new EventSetDescriptor(
        MulticastChannel.class,
        "propertyChange",
        java.beans.PropertyChangeListener.class,
        "propertyChange");


      EventSetDescriptor[] events = {event, changes};
      return events;
    }
    catch (IntrospectionException e) {
      throw new Error(e.toString());
    }
  }
}
```

Packaging

All the multicast beans, as well as the McastSend.class and the lm.au
sample audio file, are packaged together into one jar file. Listing 13.9
presents the makefile used for building the source files and packaging

all of the required .class files and the data file. Note in particular that the jar facility can easily manage the inclusion of more than one bean into a single package.

Listing 13.9   The multicast.mk makefile.

```
CODEBASE=mybeans\multicast
JARBASE=jars

DATAFILES = \
    $(CODEBASE)\lm.au

CLASSFILES= \
    $(CODEBASE)\MulticastEvent.class \
    $(CODEBASE)\MulticastListener.class \
    $(CODEBASE)\TextChannel.class \
    $(CODEBASE)\Channel.class \
    $(CODEBASE)\AudioChannel.class \
    $(CODEBASE)\McastSend.class \
    $(CODEBASE)\MulticastChannel.class \
    $(CODEBASE)\MulticastChannelBeanInfo.class

JARFILE= $(JARBASE)\Multicast.jar


all: $(JARFILE)


# Create a JAR file with a suitable manifest.

$(JARFILE): $(CLASSFILES) $(DATAFILES)
    jar cfm $(JARFILE) <<manifest.tmp $(CODEBASE)\*.
      class $(DATAFILES)
Name: mybeans/multicast/MulticastChannel.class
Java-Bean: True

Name: mybeans/multicast/TextChannel.class
Java-Bean: True

Name: mybeans/multicast/AudioChannel.class
Java-Bean: True

<<


.SUFFIXES: .java .class

{$(CODEBASE)}.java{$(CODEBASE)}.class :
    set CLASSPATH=.
    javac -deprecation $<
```

```
clean:
    -del $(CODEBASE)\*.class
    -del $(JARFILE)
```

Conclusion

This chapter presented our first real-world demonstration of the Java Beans technology. The MulticastChannel bean can be used in building much more sophisticated applications, and the AudioChannel and TextChannel beans may be enhanced to include more features. The **McastSend** program can be converted into a bean.

Multicasting messages in a network optimizes the use of the network bandwidth. A multicast message is sent to a local area network only once, regardless of the number of intended destinations on the network. (In contrast, unicasting sends a message once for each destination.)

The next chapter demonstrates another set of beans for building applications that manage the automatic update of software components. These applications use the multicast beans discussed in this chapter.

Chapter 14

- **Sending automatic software update notification messages**

- **Publishing software products to a repository**

- **Subscribing to software products**

- **Using the auto-update bean suite**

14

Automatic Software Update

by Jalil Feghhi

This chapter presents a suite of auto-update beans—Publisher, SoftwareBase, and EventRelay—that can be used to notify interested subscribers about the availability of new software releases. These beans communicate with each other through **PublishListener**, **SubscribeListener**, and **UpdateListener** listeners.

To create this auto-update bean application, assemble a Publisher bean in combination with a SoftwareBase bean within a framework; Publisher is used to publish software products into SoftwareBase. Then instantiate a Subscriber bean, connect it to the SoftwareBase, and inform the base about the products you are interested in. When a new version of a software product is published, the Subscriber bean receives an update notification message if it has expressed interest in that software.

The Subscriber bean can reside anywhere in the network. To multicast update messages in the network, use the EventRelay bean in conjunction with the MulticastChannel bean described in Chapter 13. A remote Subscriber can then receive update messages originating anywhere in the network.

In this chapter, we will provide instructions on how to assemble the auto-update beans into applications. We also discuss each of the beans in the auto-update suite at great length.

In order to run the MulticastChannel bean, your computer hardware must support multicasting. Otherwise, you will get a socket exception when you attempt to start this bean.

Assembling The Auto-Update Beans Into Applications

In this section, we will discuss how to assemble sample applications using the auto-update beans. Detailed instructions follow on how to load the auto-update beans, publish software, subscribe to software products, multicast software updates to the network, and receive multicast messages from the network.

Loading The Auto-Update Beans

Use the BeanBox File|LoadJar menu to load the swUpdate.jar file from the CD-ROM enclosed with this book. BeanBox will add the four auto-update beans to the ToolBox.

You must load the multicast beans before you attempt to load the auto-update beans. The current 1.0 implementation of BeanBox does not use the CLASSPATH variable to locate the multicast .class files, which are required by the auto-update beans.

Publishing Software Products

Instantiate the Publisher bean in the BeanBox container. As Figure 14.1 illustrates, this bean provides three input fields: Software, Version, and Location. The Software field captures the name of the software (for example, "Mortal Combat"), whereas Version stands for the version of the software (such as "1.0"). The Location input field captures the location of the software in the network (for instance, "Pegasus:/products/software," where "Pegasus" is the name of the machine and "/products/software" is the fully qualified pathname to the software).

Publisher does not enforce any constraints on the format of the above fields.

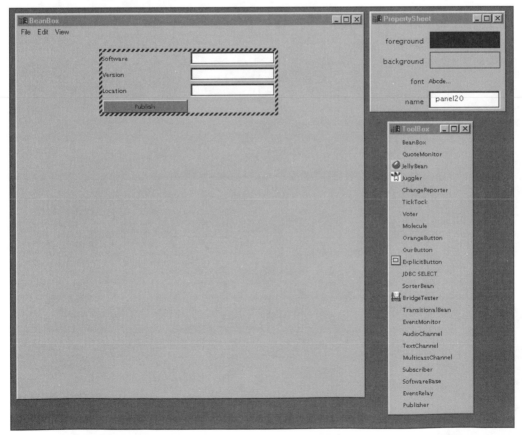

Figure 14.1   The **Publisher** bean.

Create an instance of SoftwareBase and connect the **publishMessage** event callback of Publisher to its **publishMessage()** method, as shown in Figure 14.2 and Figure 14.3. As illustrated in Figure 14.4, you can now use Publisher to publish new software releases into SoftwareBase.

Subscribing To Software Products

You are now ready to receive software update messages. Instantiate the Subscriber bean and hook up its **subscribeMessage** event callback to the **subscribeMessage()** method of the SoftwareBase bean (see Figure 14.5). To subscribe to the software product that you had published into SoftwareBase, simply fill out the Subscriber bean's Software field and press on "Subscribe". When you publish a new version of the software, the Subscriber bean will receive a notification message about the availability of the new version (see Figure 14.6).

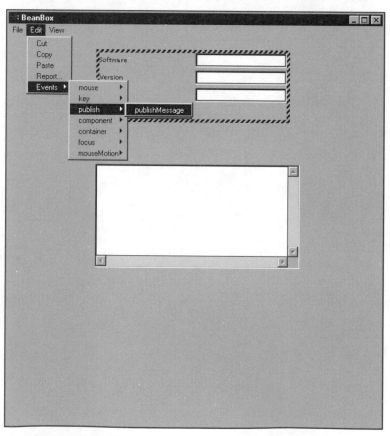

Figure 14.2   Connecting Publisher to SoftwareBase.

Figure 14.3 SoftwareBase target events.

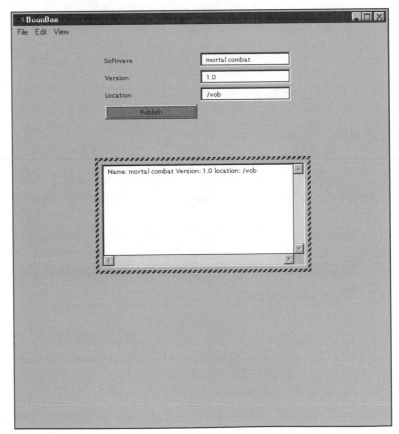

Figure 14.4 Publishing new software.

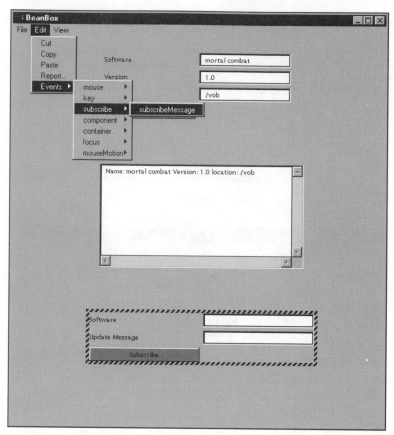

Figure 14.5 Connecting SoftwareBase to Subscriber.

Multicasting Software Updates To The Network

The subscriber to a software product almost never resides on the same machine as the publisher. The subscriber might be anywhere in the network, and it should be able to subscribe remotely to software products and receive update messages. To publish the software products to the network, create an instance of EventRelay in the container, select the SoftwareBase bean, and wire the **updateMessage** event callback of the base to EventRelay's **relayEvent()** method. Refer to Figure 14.7 and 14.8 for detailed illustrations.

Now configure the EventRelay bean by selecting it and using the PropertySheet editor to enter values for the **multicastAddress** and **port**

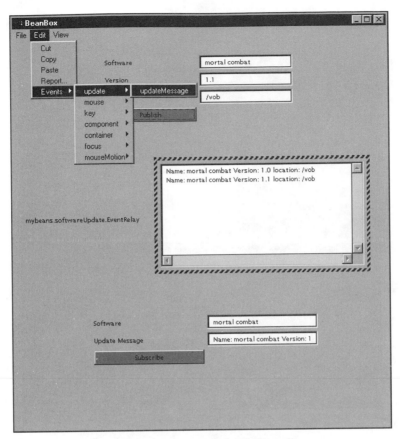

Figure 14.6 Receiving update messages in Subscriber.

properties, as shown in Figure 14.9. Refer to Chapter 13 for more information on these two properties.

Receiving Multicast Updates

Now you need to build another application to receive multicast software update messages. Start up a new session of BeanBox, either on the same machine where you just built the (local) application or on a different host. (To avoid confusion, we use the term "remote" to distinguish the second application from the local application.)

Instantiate a MulticastChannel bean in the remote container and configure it to receive multicast messages from the EventRelay bean of the local application, as shown in Figure 14.10. Click on "Start Listening" to start the channel.

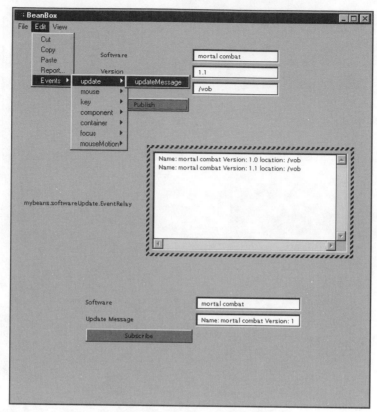

Figure 14.7 Connecting SoftwareBase to EventRelay.

Figure 14.8 EventRelay target methods.

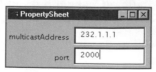

Figure 14.9 EventRelay properties.

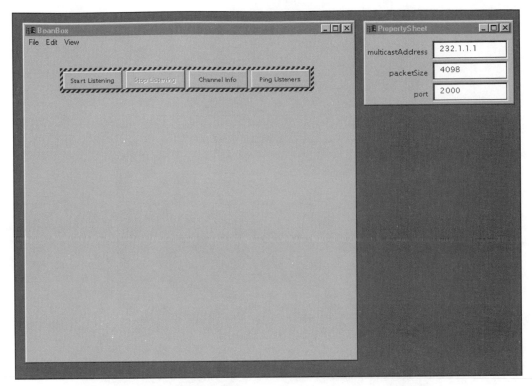

Figure 14.10   The remote MulticastChannel bean.

Your computer must have hardware to support multicasting. Otherwise, the MulticastChannel bean will not start.

As shown in Figure 14.11, assemble EventRelay and SoftwareBase beans into the remote container. Select the MulticastChannel bean and wire its **multicastMessage** event callback to the **multicastMessage()** method of EventRelay. Now select EventRelay and connect its **updateMessage** event callback to the **updateMessage()** method of SoftwareBase. Test the wiring by switching over to the local BeanBox and publishing a new version of your software (see Figure 14.12). As Figure 14.13 shows, the SoftwareBase bean in the remote application must receive an entry for the new software.

You are now ready to complete the remote application. Create a new instance of the Subscriber bean, wire it to the SoftwareBase bean, and subscribe to your software. Switch back to the local application and publish another version of the software. The Subscriber bean in the remote application should receive an update message, as shown in Figure 14.14.

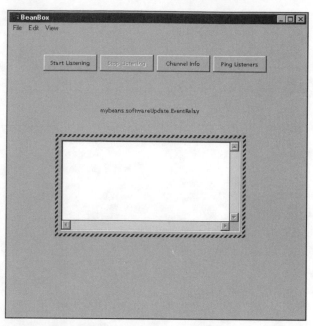

Figure 14.11 The remote SoftwareBase bean.

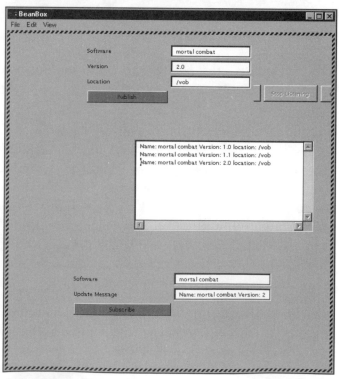

Figure 14.12 Publishing new software.

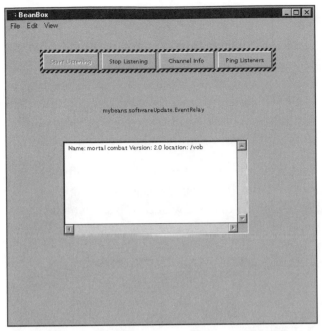

Figure 14.13   Receiving an update message in the remote SoftwareBase.

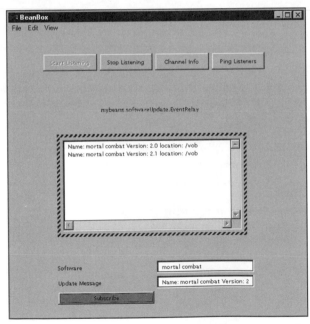

Figure 14.14   Receiving an update message in the remote Subscriber.

Publisher

The Publisher bean captures the name of the software, the release number, and the location of the software in the repository. Clicking on the Publish button causes Publisher to fire a **PublishEvent**, which is sent to all the interested listeners through the **publishMessage()** callback. The **PublishEvent** event contains a **Software** object, which contains all of the necessary information about the software being published.

This bean acts as the front end to the SoftwareBase bean. When you assemble the auto-update beans into an application, you should connect Publisher to a SoftwareBase bean, which keeps a repository of all published software. Listing 14.1 presents the Publisher source code.

Listing 14.1   The Publisher bean.

```
package mybeans.softwareUpdate;

import java.io.*;
import java.awt.*;
import java.net.*;
import java.beans.*;
import java.util.*;
import java.awt.event.*;

/**
 * Publisher is a bean to publish software. Normally,
 * a Publisher should talk to a SoftwareBase bean.
 */

public class Publisher extends Panel
implements ActionListener {

  public Publisher (){

    setBackground (Color.lightGray);

    setLayout(new GridLayout(0,2,5,5));

    add(new Label("Software", Label.LEFT));
    m_swText =new TextField(15);
    add(m_swText);

    add(new Label("Version", Label.LEFT));
    m_verText=new TextField(9);
    add(m_verText);
```

```
    add(new Label("Location", Label.LEFT));
    m_locText=new TextField(20);
    add(m_locText);


    m_pubButton=new Button("Publish");
    m_pubButton.setBackground (Color.gray);
    m_pubButton.addActionListener (this);
    add(m_pubButton);
}

public synchronized void
addPublishListener(PublishListener l) {
  publishListeners.addElement(l);
}

public synchronized void
removePublishListener(PublishListener l) {
  publishListeners.removeElement(l);
}

protected void firePublishEvent(Software sw) {
  Vector publ;

  synchronized (this) {
    publ = (Vector) publishListeners.clone();
  }

  for (int i=0; i< publ.size(); i++) {
    PublishListener l =
      (PublishListener) publ.elementAt(i);
    l.publishMessage (new PublishEvent (this, sw));
  }
}

public void addSoftware (Software sw){
  firePublishEvent (sw);
}


// ActionListener implementation
public void actionPerformed(ActionEvent e) {

  Object source = e.getSource();
  if (source == m_pubButton) {
    Software sw = new Software (m_swText.getText(),
        m_verText.getText(),
        new Location (m_locText.getText()));
```

```
        addSoftware (sw);
      }
      return;
    }

    Button     m_pubButton;
    TextField m_swText;
    TextField m_verText;
    TextField m_locText;

    private Vector  publishListeners = new Vector();
}
```

PublishListener

PublishListener, shown in Listing 14.2, extends **EventListener** to define **publishMessage()**. This method takes a **PublishEvent** argument, which contains information about the newly published software.

Listing 14.2   The PublishListener definition.

```
package mybeans.softwareUpdate;

import java.util.*;

/**
 * PublishListener
 */
public interface PublishListener extends EventListener
{
    public void publishMessage (PublishEvent evt);
}
```

PublishEvent

PublishEvent is designed to extend **SoftwareEvent** in order to inherit its **m_software** argument, which is required to embed information about a new software product. Listing 14.3 shows the class definition of **PublishEvent**.

Listing 14.3   The PublishEvent class.

```
package mybeans.softwareUpdate;

import java.io.*;
import java.awt.*;
```

```
import java.net.*;
import java.beans.*;
import java.awt.event.*;


/**
 * PublishEvent
 */
public class PublishEvent extends SoftwareEvent
{
  public PublishEvent (Object source, Software sw){
    super (source, sw);
  }
}
```

SoftwareEvent

The **SoftwareEvent** class, shown in Listing 14.4, keeps track of the published software and its publisher. It provides the **getSoftware()** getter method to extract the published software. **SoftwareEvent** does not supply the **setSoftware()** method, however, because events generally are considered to be immutable.

Listing 14.4   The SoftwareEvent class.

```
package mybeans.softwareUpdate;

import java.io.*;
import java.awt.*;
import java.net.*;
import java.beans.*;
import java.util.*;
import java.awt.event.*;


/**
 * SoftwareEvent
 */

public class SoftwareEvent extends EventObject
implements Serializable
{
  public SoftwareEvent (Object source, Software sw){
    super (source);
    m_source = source;
    m_software = sw;
  }
```

```
    public Software getSoftware (){
      return m_software;
    }

    private Object     m_source;
    private Software   m_software;
}
```

Software

As shown in Listing 14.5, the **Software** class defines three properties
for a software product: **name**, **version**, and **location**. The **name** and
version properties together uniquely identify a software product from
other products, while **location** determines the fully qualified pathname
to the software. **Software** defines the **version** property with the bound
semantics; as a result, changing the version of a software product causes
notification messages to be sent to all registered listeners.

The other two properties could also have been defined as bound, allowing
notifications to be sent out when the name or the location of a software
product changes. Note also that the **Software** class does not keep track
of the actual software binary: Upon being notified about a new software
release, a software subscriber is expected to use a file transfer mechanism
to automatically download the software specified in the **location** property.

Listing 14.5   The Software class.

```
package mybeans.softwareUpdate;

import java.io.*;
import java.awt.*;
import java.net.*;
import java.beans.*;
import java.util.*;
import java.awt.event.*;

/**
 * The Software Bean is an abstraction of the software.
 * For simplicity, we assume one component per
 * software product here.
 */
public class Software implements Serializable
{
  public Software (String name, String version,
                   Location location){
```

```java
    m_name = name;
    m_version = version;
    m_location = location;
  }

  public Software (String name ){
    m_name = name;
    m_version = null;
    m_location = null;
  }

  public void setVersion (String newValue){
    String oldValue = m_version;
    m_version = newValue;
    changes.firePropertyChange("version",
                        oldValue, newValue);
  }

  public String getVersion() {
    return m_version;
  }

  public void setName (String newValue){
    m_name = newValue;
  }

  public String getName() {
    return m_name;
  }

  public void setLocation (Location newValue){
    m_location = newValue;
  }

  public Location getLocation() {
    return m_location;
  }

  // Method to add version change listeners.
  public void
  addVersionListener (PropertyChangeListener l) {
    changes.addPropertyChangeListener(l);
  }

  public void
  removeVersionListener (PropertyChangeListener l) {
    changes.removePropertyChangeListener(l);
  }
```

```
      public String toString (){
        return new String ("Name: " + m_name +
           " Version: " + m_version + " " +
           m_location.toString());
      }

      private String     m_name;
      private String     m_version;
      private Location    m_location;

      private PropertyChangeSupport changes =
        new PropertyChangeSupport(this);
    }
```

Location

The **Location** class, shown in Listing 14.6, simply keeps track of the location of a software product in the network. This class can be enhanced to define and enforce a valid format for specifying the values passed as the location.

Listing 14.6   The Location class.

```
package mybeans.softwareUpdate;

import java.io.*;

/**
 * Location is a class to abstract the
 * location of the software. It can be enhanced
 * to include more useful methods for software
 * retrieval and installation.
 */
public class Location implements Serializable
{
  public Location (String loc){
    m_location = loc;
  }

  public String toString (){
    return new String ("location: " + m_location);
  }

  private String  m_location;
}
```

SoftwareBase

The SoftwareBase bean is perhaps the most complex bean in the auto-update suite. This bean must be able to connect to Publisher in order to receive publish messages, to Subscriber in order to get subscription information, and to EventRelay in order to send software update events into the network. Listing 14.7 presents the source code for SoftwareBase.

When a subscriber connects to it through the **subscribeMessage (SubscribeEvent)** method, the SoftwareBase bean registers the subscriber with the **Software** class via the **addVersionListener()** registration method. A new version of a software product published to SoftwareBase calls the **publishMessage (PublishEvent)** method, which in turn calls **setVersion()** to change the value of the **version** property for the software. As noted earlier, because this property is bound, changing its value causes notification messages to be sent to all registered subscriber listeners.

Listing 14.7   The SoftwareBase Bean.

```
package mybeans.softwareUpdate;

import java.io.*;
import java.awt.*;
import java.net.*;
import java.beans.*;
import java.util.*;
import java.awt.event.*;


/**
 * SoftwareBase. A bean where all information about
 * the published software is kept.
 */
public class SoftwareBase extends Panel
{
  public SoftwareBase (){
    m_dataBase = new Hashtable();
    m_swText =new TextArea ("", 10, 50,
      TextArea.SCROLLBARS_BOTH);
    add(m_swText);
  }
```

```java
public synchronized void
addUpdateListener(UpdateListener l) {
   updateListeners.addElement(l);
}

public synchronized void
removeUpdateListener(UpdateListener l) {
   updateListeners.removeElement(l);
}

public void updateMessage (UpdateEvent evt){
  updateSoftware (evt.getSource() , evt.getSoftware());
}


public void publishMessage (PublishEvent evt){
  updateSoftware (evt.getSource(),
    evt.getSoftware());
}

public void
updateSoftware (Object src, Software nsw){
  // Add the software to the display window.
  m_swText.append (nsw.toString());
  m_swText.append ("\n");

  // Add the software to the database.
  String nswname = nsw.getName();

  // Check if we have this software already.
  Software osw = (Software)m_dataBase.get (nswname);
  if (osw == null){
    System.out.println ("New software");
    try {
      m_dataBase.put (nswname , nsw);
    }
    catch (NullPointerException e){
    System.out.println (
      "SoftwareBase - " + e.toString());
    }
  }
  else {
    System.out.println ("Old software");

    // Software already exists. Just change the
    // version and location info.
    // Version property change event will fire
    // automatically.
    osw.setLocation (nsw.getLocation());
```

```java
        osw.setVersion (nsw.getVersion());
      }
      fireUpdateEvent (nsw);
    }

    public void subscribeMessage (SubscribeEvent evt){
      // We only accept subscription to the software
      // we already have.
      Software sw = evt.getSoftware();

      String swname = sw.getName();
      // Check if we have this software.
      Software csw = (Software)m_dataBase.get(swname);
      if (csw != null){
        System.out.println ("Sub accepted");
        csw.addVersionListener (
          (PropertyChangeListener) evt.getSource());

        // Register the subscriber for
        // the version property change event.
      }
    }

    protected void fireUpdateEvent (Software sw) {
     Vector upl;

     synchronized (this) {
        upl = (Vector) updateListeners.clone();
     }

     for (int i=0; i < upl.size() ; i++) {
        UpdateListener l =
          (UpdateListener) upl.elementAt(i);
        l.updateMessage (new UpdateEvent (this, sw));
     }
    }

  private TextArea     m_swText;
  private Hashtable    m_dataBase;
  private Vector     updateListeners = new Vector();
}
```

UpdateListener

UpdateListener, shown in Listing 14.8, provides the listener interface
to allow the EventRelay bean to receive callback messages when a new
version of a software product is released.

Listing 14.8   The UpdateListener class.

```
package mybeans.softwareUpdate;

import java.util.*;
/**
 * UpdateListener
 */
public interface UpdateListener extends EventListener
{
    public void updateMessage (UpdateEvent evt);
}
```

UpdateEvent

As shown in Listing 14.9, this event contains information about a new software product. It is used in conjunction with **UpdateListener** to provide a communication path with the EventRelay bean.

Listing 14.9   The UpdateEvent class.

```
package mybeans.softwareUpdate;

/**
 * UpdateEvent
 */
public class UpdateEvent extends SoftwareEvent
{
  public UpdateEvent (Object source, Software sw){
    super (source, sw);
  }
}
```

Subscriber

The Subscriber bean, shown in Listing 14.10, implements the **PropertyChangeListener** interface in order to receive **Property-ChangeEvent** objects when a new release of a software product becomes available. Note that the **addSubscribeListener** method has the unicast semantics, which means that the Subscriber bean can be attached to only one SoftwareBase.

Listing 14.10   The Subscriber bean.

```java
package mybeans.softwareUpdate;

import java.io.*;
import java.awt.*;
import java.net.*;
import java.beans.*;
import java.util.*;
import java.awt.event.*;


/**
 * Subscriber. A bean via which we can subscribe
 * to software. Normally, this bean gets connected
 * to a SoftwareBase and gets subscribed to one or
 * more software products already available there.

 */
public class Subscriber extends Panel
implements ActionListener, PropertyChangeListener {

  public Subscriber (){
    setBackground (Color.lightGray);

    setLayout(new GridLayout(0,2,5,5));

    add(new Label("Software", Label.LEFT));
    m_swText =new TextField(15);
    add(m_swText);

    add(new Label("Update Message", Label.LEFT));
    m_updateText =new TextField(25);
    add(m_updateText);

    m_subButton=new Button("Subscribe");
    m_subButton.setBackground (Color.gray);
    m_subButton.addActionListener (this);
    add(m_subButton);
  }

  public synchronized void
  addSubscribeListener(SubscribeListener l)
  throws  TooManyListenersException {
    if (listener != null) {
      throw new TooManyListenersException();
    }
```

```
      else {
        listener = l;
      }
    }

    public synchronized void
    removeSubscribeListener(SubscribeListener l){
      if (listener == l){
        listener = null;
      }
    }

    public void subscribe (Software sw){
      if (listener != null){
        listener.subscribeMessage
          (new SubscribeEvent (this, sw));
      }
    }

    public void updateMessage (UpdateEvent evt){
      System.out.println("klkdj\n");
    }

    public void actionPerformed(ActionEvent e) {
      Object source = e.getSource();
      if (source == m_subButton) {
        // Contact the subscribe listener and
        // subscribe.
        Software sw = new Software (m_swText.getText());
        subscribe (sw);
      }
      return;
    }

    // This method is called by SoftwareBase
    // when the software we are subscribed to
    // changes its version.
    public void
    propertyChange (PropertyChangeEvent evt){
      Software sw = (Software) evt.getSource();

      m_updateText.setText (sw.toString());
    }

    private Button     m_subButton;
    private TextField m_swText;
    private TextField m_updateText;
    private SubscribeListener  listener = null;
}
```

SubscribeListener

As shown in Listing 14.11, this interface identifies the **subscribeMessage()** method, which is called when Subscriber needs to subscribe to a new software product.

Listing 14.11   The SubscribeListener interface.

```
package mybeans.softwareUpdate;


import java.util.*;

/**
 ^ SubscribeListener
 */
public interface SubscribeListener
extends EventListener
{
  public void subscribeMessage (SubscribeEvent evt);
}
```

SubscribeEvent

SubscribeEvent communicates information about a desired software product from a Subscriber bean to a SoftwareBase. This event is shown in Listing 14.12.

Listing 14.12   The SubscribeEvent class.

```
package mybeans.softwareUpdate;

import java.io.*;
import java.awt.*;
import java.net.*;
import java.beans.*;
import java.awt.event.*;


/**
 * SubscribeEvent
 */
public class SubscribeEvent extends SoftwareEvent
{
  public SubscribeEvent (Object source, Software sw){
    super (source, sw);
  }
}
```

EventRelay

The EventRelay bean is used to multicast information about the availability of new software in the network. The MulticastChannel bean, described in Chapter 13, can be used on the other side of the network to receive the multicast information. EventRelay is presented in Listing 14.13.

This bean provides a good example of using Object Serialization to ship objects around the network. The **marshalEvent()** method uses the **ObjectOutputStream** class to serialize objects with the **writeObject()** method. The **multicastMessage()** method reverses the serialization process through the use of **ObjectInputStream** and **readObject()**.

Listing 14.13   The EventRelay bean.

```
package mybeans.softwareUpdate;

import java.io.*;
import java.awt.*;
import java.net.*;
import java.beans.*;
import java.util.*;
import java.awt.event.*;
import mybeans.multicast.*;

/**
 * EventRelay. An invisible bean capable of sending
 * and receiving SoftwareEvents to multicast groups.
 * It can be used to send software update messages
 * over the network.
 */
public class EventRelay
{
  public EventRelay () throws IOException {
    m_byteOutS = new ByteArrayOutputStream();
  }

  public void setMulticastAddress (String newValue){
    String oldValue = m_mcastAddr;
    m_mcastAddr = newValue;
  }

  public String getMulticastAddress() {
    return m_mcastAddr;
  }
```

```java
public void setPort (int newValue){
  int oldValue = m_port;
  m_port = newValue;
}

public int getPort() {
  return m_port;
}

public void relayEvent (SoftwareEvent evt){
  try{
    m_group = InetAddress.getByName (m_mcastAddr);
    byte[] buf = marshalEvent (evt);
    DatagramPacket swpkt = new DatagramPacket
              (buf, buf.length, m_group, m_port);
    MulticastSocket socket = new MulticastSocket();
    socket.send (swpkt ,(byte) 1);
  }
  catch (Exception e){
    System.out.println ("Relay failed - " + e);
  }
}

// Since the BinBox adaptor class will not catch
// Exception, we catch it here.
private byte[] marshalEvent (SoftwareEvent evt)
throws IOException {
  m_byteOutS.reset();
  m_objOutS = new ObjectOutputStream(m_byteOutS);

  // EventObject is not serializable.
  // Send the software.
  m_objOutS.writeObject (evt.getSoftware());
  return m_byteOutS.toByteArray();
}

public synchronized void
addUpdateListener(UpdateListener l) {
  updateListeners.addElement(l);
}

public synchronized void
removeUpdateListener(UpdateListener l) {
  updateListeners.removeElement(l);
}

public void publishMessage (PublishEvent evt){
  fireUpdateEvent (evt.getSoftware());
}
```

```
protected void fireUpdateEvent (Software sw) {
  Vector upl;

  synchronized (this) {
    upl = (Vector) updateListeners.clone();
  }

  for (int i=0; i < upl.size() ; i++) {
    UpdateListener l =
      (UpdateListener) upl.elementAt(i);
    l.updateMessage (new UpdateEvent (this, sw));
  }
}

public void multicastMessage (MulticastEvent evt){
  try {
    byte[] buf = evt.getData();

    m_byteInS = new ByteArrayInputStream(buf);
    m_objInS = new ObjectInputStream(m_byteInS);
    Software sw = (Software) m_objInS.readObject();
    fireUpdateEvent (sw);
  }
  catch (Exception e){
    System.out.println (e.toString());
  }
}

private Vector    updateListeners = new Vector();

private int       m_port;
private String    m_mcastAddr;
private InetAddress m_group;
private ByteArrayOutputStream   m_byteOutS;
private ObjectOutputStream      m_objOutS;
private ByteArrayInputStream    m_byteInS;
private ObjectInputStream       m_objInS;
}
```

Packaging

The auto-update beans are compiled and packaged using the makefile shown in Listing 14.14.

Listing 14.14   The swupdate.mk file.

```
CODEBASE=mybeans\softwareUpdate
JARBASE=jars
```

```
DATAFILES = \
  swupdate.mk

CLASSFILES= \
$(CODEBASE)\Software.class \
$(CODEBASE)\EventRelay.class \
$(CODEBASE)\Publisher.class \
$(CODEBASE)\PublishEvent.class \
$(CODEBASE)\SoftwareEvent.class \
$(CODEBASE)\PublishListener.class \
$(CODEBASE)\Subscriber.class \
$(CODEBASE)\SubscribeEvent.class \
$(CODEBASE)\SubscribeListener.class \
$(CODEBASE)\Location.class \
$(CODEBASE)\UpdateEvent.class \
$(CODEBASE)\UpdateListener.class \
$(CODEBASE)\SoftwareBase.class

JARFILE= $(JARBASE)\swUpdate.jar

all: $(JARFILE)

# Create a JAR file with a suitable manifest.

$(JARFILE): $(CLASSFILES) $(DATAFILES)
jar cfm $(JARFILE) <<manifest.tmp $(CODEBASE)\*.class
$(DATAFILES)

Name: mybeans/softwareUpdate/Subscriber.class
Java-Bean: True

Name: mybeans/softwareUpdate/Publisher.class
Java-Bean: True

Name: mybeans/softwareUpdate/SoftwareBase.class
Java-Bean: True

Name: mybeans/softwareUpdate/EventRelay.class
Java-Bean: True


<<


.SUFFIXES: .java .class

{$(CODEBASE)}.java{$(CODEBASE)}.class :
set CLASSPATH=.
javac -deprecation $<
```

```
clean:
-del $(CODEBASE)\*.class
-del $(JARFILE)
```

Conclusion

In this chapter we demonstrated a suite of beans that can be used to send automatic update messages about the availability of new software products. Although these beans are designed to manage new releases of software products, the techniques presented are general and can be employed for any product.

The auto-update beans are not commercial-grade third-party bean components. You should, however, be able to use our ideas to convert these beans into more complex third-party beans. For example, you can enhance these beans so that a Subscriber bean automatically downloads the new version of the released software when it receives an update message.

Chapter 15

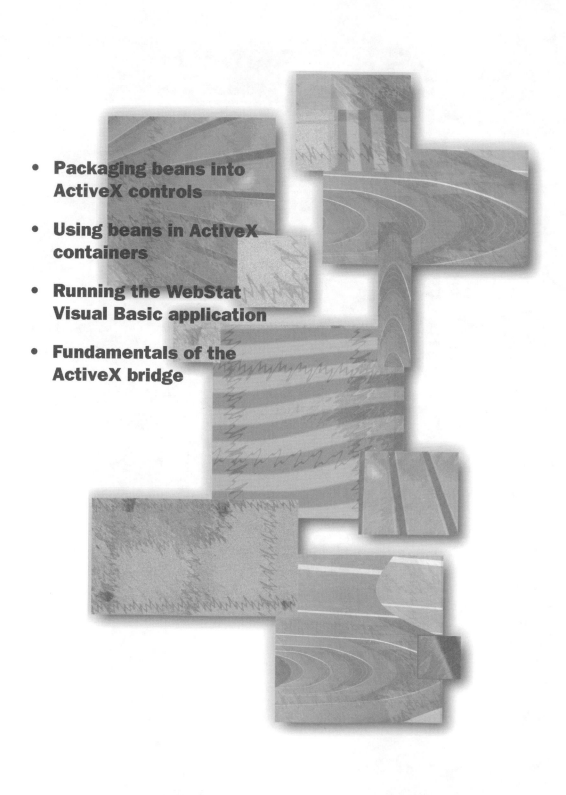

- **Packaging beans into ActiveX controls**

- **Using beans in ActiveX containers**

- **Running the WebStat Visual Basic application**

- **Fundamentals of the ActiveX bridge**

Chapter 15

The ActiveX Bridge

by Jalil Feghhi

The Java Beans technology provides a mechanism to convert a bean into an ActiveX control. The control can then be embedded in any container that supports ActiveX controls, such as Visual Basic, Internet Explorer, or Microsoft Office.

In this chapter, we'll create a bean, bridge (convert) it into an ActiveX control, and then use it as a custom control to build a Visual Basic application. The application, called WebStat, provides an input form to capture the Uniform Resource Locator (URL) of a site, the number of times to ping the site, and the interval between two successive pings. It then pings the specified site and reports the average time delay in contacting the site.

The WebStat application leverages the underlying bean first by setting the properties of the bean to the values captured in its input form. Then it invokes a corresponding method of the bean, which uses the information passed by the application to ping the site and measure its average response time. The bean communicates the result back to the WebStat application by invoking a listener callback method and passing the method an event as an argument, which contains the result. The Java callback method invocation results in a call to a corresponding Visual Basic routine of WebStat; the Java event argument is converted into a corresponding OLE object and delivered to this routine as an OLE object. Finally, WebStat uses the getter method of the Java event to retrieve the result from the OLE object.

In this chapter, we'll show you how to run the WebStat application. We'll then discuss the WebStatus bean, and provide step-by-step instructions on how to bridge this bean into an ActiveX control. We'll then proceed to examine the Visual Basic source code of WebStat.

You must install the ActiveX bridge to convert the WebStatus bean into an ActiveX control. You can download the bridge from the same site that you obtained the bean development toolkit (BDK). You also need to have Visual Basic.

Running The WebStat Visual Basic Application

In this section, we show you how to use the WebStat Visual Basic application. To run the application, simply double-click on WebStat.exe, as shown in Figure 15.1. WebStat pops up its main graphical user interface, shown in Figure 15.2, which consists of the Click To Configure and the WebPing buttons.

Click on the Click To Configure button to configure the WebStat application. As Figure 15.3 illustrates, you configure the application by specifying the URL for the site (**URL**), the number of times to ping the site (**Count**), and the interval between two successive pings (**Interval**). WebStat uses these values to gather statistical information about the site; this information, currently, consists of the average time delay to ping the site. The average is calculated by pinging the site **URL**, getting a response, and then obtaining the time delay. This procedure is repeated **Count** number of times, and all the time delays are averaged to yield the final result.

If the average time delay is below the value specified in the **Warning** field, WebStat paints its main window, as shown in Figure 15.2, in

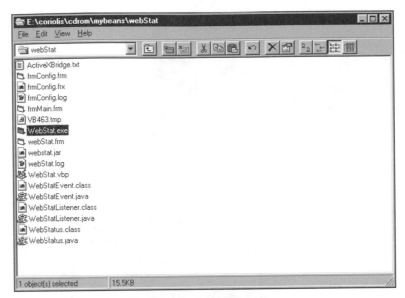

Figure 15.1 Running the WebStat application.

Figure 15.2 The WebStat main window.

green. It this value falls between **Warning** and **Critical**, the window's color is changed to yellow. Otherwise, if the average time delay exceeds **Critical**, the color is changed to red.

Apply the changes made to the dialog box in Figure 15.3 and then click on the WebPing button. After a short delay, the color of the WebStat window changes to reflect the response time of the specified site. Figure 15.4 shows the WebStat's main window after pinging the Coriolis Web site at **www.coriolis.com**.

The WebStat Package

The WebStat package consists of three classes: **WebStatus**, **WebStatListener**, and **WebStatEvent**. This section discusses these classes and presents their source files.

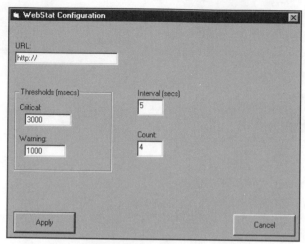

Figure 15.3   The WebStat configuration dialog box.

Figure 15.4   The WebStat main window after pinging **www.coriolis.com**.

WebStatus

The **WebStatus** class, which is the only bean in the WebStat package, exports three properties: **URL**, **Interval**, and **Count**. The **Interval** property defaults to 5, whereas **Count** has a default value of 4. **WebStatus** generates one event, **WebStat**, which has a pair of corresponding **addWebStatListener()** and **removeWebStatListener()** methods. Listing 15.1 presents the source code of this class.

WebStatus pings a specified site by attempting to open up a socket connection to it in the **collectStat()** method. This method uses **currentTimeMillis()** to obtain the system times prior to opening the socket connection and after the connection has been established. The difference between these two times is the time delay, which is then averaged by repeating this procedure **Count** number of times.

After the average time delay is calculated, **WebStatus** calls **fireWebStatEvent()** to inform all of its registered listeners about the time delay.

It is a requirement that a Java bean implement either the **Serializable** *or* **Externalizable** *interface in order to success-*
fully be bridged to ActiveX.

Listing 15.1   The WebStatus class.

```java
package mybeans.webStat;


import java.io.*;
import java.net.*;
import java.beans.*;
import java.util.*;
import java.awt.event.*;


/*
 *
 * WebStat.
 *
 */
public class WebStatus implements Serializable
{
  public WebStatus (){
    m_count = 4;
    m_interval = 5; // secs
  }


  public void setURL (String newValue) {
    m_url = newValue;
  }

  public String getURL() {
    return m_url;
  }

  public void setInterval (int newValue){
    m_interval = newValue;
  }

  public int getInterval() {
    return m_interval;
  }

  public void setCount (int newValue){
    m_count = newValue;
  }
```

```java
      public int getCount() {
        return m_count;
      }

      public synchronized void addWebStatListener
                                (WebStatListener l) {
        wstatListeners.addElement(l);
      }

      public synchronized void removeWebStatListener
                                (WebStatListener l) {
        wstatListeners.removeElement(l);
      }

      protected void fireWebStatEvent (int avg){

        Vector upl;

        synchronized (this) {
          upl = (Vector) wstatListeners.clone();
        }
        System.out.println ("Firing stat event: " +
          avg);

        for (int i=0; i < upl.size() ; i++) {
          WebStatListener l = (WebStatListener)
                                 upl.elementAt(i);
          WebStatEvent evt = new WebStatEvent (this);
          evt.setAverage (avg);
          l.webStatMessage (evt);
        }
      }

      public void collectStat()
      throws MalformedURLException {
        URL url = new URL (m_url);

        System.out.println ("WebStating: " +
          url.toString());

        long bf,af,total;
        String host = url.getHost();
        int port  = url.getPort();
        Socket skt;

        if (port == -1){
          port = 80;
        }
```

```
    try{
      total = 0;
      InetAddress addr = InetAddress.getByName (host);
      for (int i = 0; i < m_count; i++){
        bf =  System.currentTimeMillis();
        skt = new Socket (addr, port);
        af =  System.currentTimeMillis();
        skt.close();
        System.out.println ("connect time: "
                              + (af - bf));
        total += (af - bf);
        try {
          Thread.sleep (m_interval * 1000);
        } catch (InterruptedException e){}
      }

      System.out.println ("\nAverage connect: " +
      total / m_count);
      long val = total / m_count;
      fireWebStatEvent ((int) val);

    }catch (IOException e){
      System.out.println (e.toString());
    }
  }

  public static void main(String args[]){
    try {
      WebStatus wp = new WebStatus();
      wp.setURL (args[0]);
      wp.collectStat();
    }
    catch (MalformedURLException e){
      System.out.println (e.toString());
    }
  }

  private Vector wstatListeners = new Vector();
  private int      m_interval;
  private int    m_count;
  private String  m_url;
}
```

WebStatListener

As presented in Listing 15.2, **WebStatListener** identifies the **webStatMessage()** method as the callback method between the **WebStatus** event source and any target event listener object.

Listing 15.2 The WebStatListener class.

```
package mybeans.webStat;

import java.util.*;
/*
 *
 * WebStatListener
 *
 */
public interface WebStatListener extends EventListener
{
   public void webStatMessage (WebStatEvent evt);
}
```

WebStatEvent

This event class, shown in Listing 15.3, is used to pass the average time through the **webStatMessage()** method to all the interested listeners.

 You should provide getter accessor methods for the data members of an event in order to later retrieve them in an ActiveX container. This requirement can be relaxed if events are cracked before they are delivered to the ActiveX container. Cracked and uncracked events are explained when we discuss the ActiveX packager.

Listing 15.3 The WebStatEvent class.

```
package mybeans.webStat;

import java.net.*;
import java.util.*;
import java.awt.event.*;

/*
 *
 * WebStatEvent.
 *
 * To be able to see the properties when this event
 * is fired in VB, we need to make properties from
 * the fields
 *
 */
public class WebStatEvent extends EventObject
{
```

```
public WebStatEvent (Object source ){
  super (source);
  m_average = 0;
}

public void  setAverage (int newValue){
  m_average = newValue;
}

public int getAverage(){
  return m_average;
}

public int    m_average;
}
```

Packaging WebStatus As An ActiveX Control

The ActiveX packager generates a registry file, a type library, and Java stub files (both .java and .class) for a bridged bean. The source .java files are deleted after the completion of the packaging step; the .class files are added to the original jar file, which contained the bean.

In the rest of this section, we provide step-by-step instructions on how to convert a Java bean into a corresponding ActiveX control. We use the WebStatus bean as an example.

Specify The Jar File

To start the process of packaging your beans as ActiveX controls, run the packager from the CD-ROM enclosed with this book.

The packager pops up the dialog box shown in Figure 15.5. Enter the full pathname to the jar file containing the bean and click on the Next button.

Select The Bean

The packager examines the contents of the specified jar file and lists all of its beans in a dialog box, as shown in Figure 15.6. Select the WebStatus bean, which is the only bean in the jar file. Note that you cannot select more than one bean—you have to go through these steps for each of the beans in the jar file.

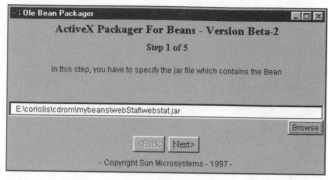

Figure 15.5 Step 1 of the packaging process.

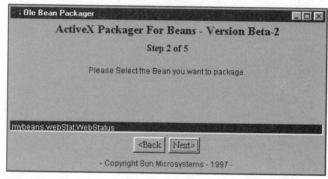

Figure 15.6 Step 2 of the packaging process.

Specify The ActiveX Control Name

In this step, you need to provide a name for the output ActiveX control, as shown in Figure 15.7. Note that you can use the same name for the ActiveX control as the Java bean. You will use this name later to refer to the ActiveX control.

Specify The Output Directory

The packager generates two output files: a registry and a type library. The registry contains an object ID, the path to the executable ActiveX control, the path to the type library, and some more bridging information. Refer to Chapter 3 to learn more about type libraries and registration files.

These output files are placed in the output directory that you specify in this step. Note that the registration file contains the location of the type library; you must manually update the registration file if you move the type library. It is also assumed that the beans.ocx file is located in this

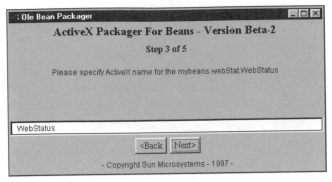

Figure 15.7   Step 3 of the packaging process.

directory. Provide the name of the output directory as illustrated in Figure 15.8 and click on the Next button.

Start The Generation

There are two ways to deliver events to the callback methods of an **EventListener** object in ActiveX containers: *cracked* and *uncracked*. In the cracked approach, all the properties exported by a Java event are extracted and the signature of the corresponding OLE callback method contains all the event properties. In contrast, the uncracked approach maps the Java event to a corresponding OLE object, which is passed to the OLE callback method. Note that the uncracked approach follows the Java Bean event model, in which an **EventObject** encapsulates all the information about an event.

The WebStat Visual Basic application is written using the second approach. To complete the packaging process, you need to instruct the packager to not crack the events, as shown in Figure 15.9. You can now

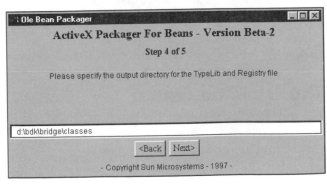

Figure 15.8   Step 4 of the packaging process.

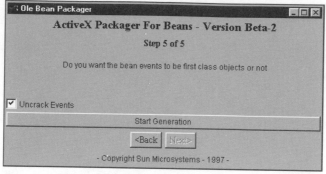

Figure 15.9 Step 5 of the packaging process.

proceed to generate the WebStatus ActiveX control by clicking on the Start Generation button.

Examining The WebStat Application

In this section, we'll discuss the WebStat Visual Basic application. You may want to use the WebStatus ActiveX control, which you created in the previous section, to re-create the WebStat application.

To import the WebStatus ActiveX control into Visual Basic, use the Tools|Custom Controls menu. This menu brings up a dialog box containing all the available controls; select WebStatus from the list and click on OK to add the bridged bean to the Visual Basic palette.

Start The Visual Basic

As shown in Figure 15.10, select the WebStat.vbp file from the CD-ROM and double-click on it to view the WebStat application. Visual Basic brings up the WebStat application and displays its two frames, as seen in Figure 15.11.

The frmMain Frame

The frmMain frame view and its associated code are presented in Figure 15.12 and Figure 15.13, respectively. Note the **cmdPing_Click()** routine, which calls the **ping()** routine of the frmConfig frame.

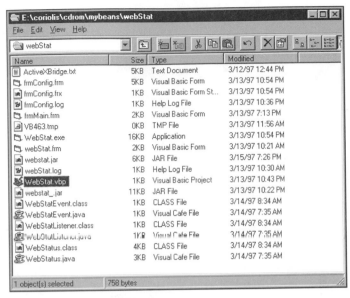

Figure 15.10   Invoking Visual Basic.

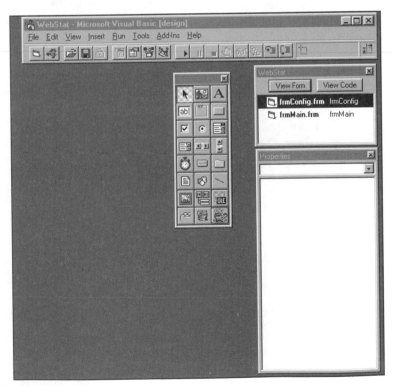

Figure 15.11   WebStat frames.

Figure 15.12   The frmMain frame view.

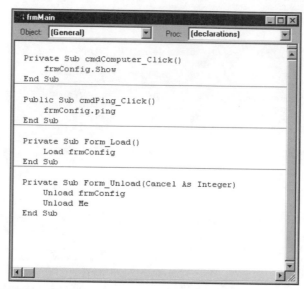

Figure 15.13   The frmMain frame code.

The frmConfig Frame

The frmConfig frame consists of a few Visual Basic custom controls and the WebStatus ActiveX control, as shown in Figure 15.14. Even though the WebStatus control is invisible, you may be able to see its trace in the upper-right hand corner.

The source code of frmConfig is presented in Figure 15.15. The **ping()** routine sets the **URL**, **Interval**, and **Count** properties of the WebStatus bridged bean and then calls its **collectStat()** method. We should emphasize that all three ot the properties and the method have been defined in the WebStatus bean, and, through the ActiveX bridge, are accessible in the Visual Basic container.

The **collectStat()** method is defined in the WebStatus Java bean. As noted earlier, this method measures the average time delay between

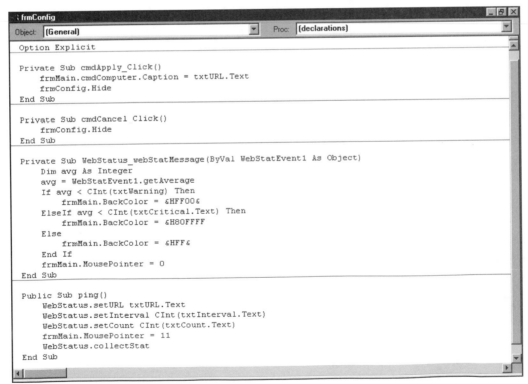

Figure 15.14 The frmConfig frame view.

pings to the specified site and calls **fireWebStatEvent()**, which invokes the **webStatMessage(WebStatEvent)**. The ActiveX bridge packager maps this callback to **WebStatus_webStatMessage()**, which was shown

```
frmConfig                                                                    _ 8 X
Object: (General)                          ▼    Proc: (declarations)                ▼
Option Explicit

Private Sub cmdApply_Click()
     frmMain.cmdComputer.Caption = txtURL.Text
     frmConfig.Hide
End Sub

Private Sub cmdCancel_Click()
     frmConfig.Hide
End Sub

Private Sub WebStatus_webStatMessage(ByVal WebStatEvent1 As Object)
     Dim avg As Integer
     avg = WebStatEvent1.getAverage
     If avg < CInt(txtWarning) Then
        frmMain.BackColor = &HFF00&
     ElseIf avg < CInt(txtCritical.Text) Then
        frmMain.BackColor = &H80FFFF
     Else
        frmMain.BackColor = &HFF&
     End If
     frmMain.MousePointer = 0
End Sub

Public Sub ping()
     WebStatus.setURL txtURL.Text
     WebStatus.setInterval CInt(txtInterval.Text)
     WebStatus.setCount CInt(txtCount.Text)
     frmMain.MousePointer = 11
     WebStatus.collectStat
End Sub
```

Figure 15.15 The frmConfig frame code.

The ActiveX Bridge **385**

in Figure 15.15. The argument to this method is **WebStatEvent1**, which is an uncracked event. The **WebStatus_webStatMessage()** method, therefore, needs to call the **getAverage()** method of **WebStatEvent** to retrieve the value of the **average** property. If we had enabled the event cracking, the **average** property would have been delivered to **WebStatus_webStatMessage()** as the argument instead of **WebStatEvent1**.

Conclusion

Having reached the end of this book, you should have a good understanding of software component infrastructures (SCI), most notably, ActiveX, Java Beans, and OpenDoc. You should also be familiar with the fundamentals of Java Beans technology: properties, methods, events, customization, introspection, and packaging. You have seen our multicast and auto-update bean suites. Finally, you can now convert your beans into ActiveX controls and use them in ActiveX containers.

We sincerely hope that we have provided you with the right foundation and understanding of the reusable software component technology. We also hope that you would apply the concepts and techniques that you have learned here to your everyday work.

References

Andert, Glenn. "Object Frameworks in the Taligent OS." Proceedings of the IEEE COMPCON, Spring 94.

The Common Object Request Broker Architecture and Specification; Revision 2.0, Object Management Group, 1995.

Cotter, Sean with Mike Potel. *Inside Taligent Technology*, Addison-Wesley, 1995.

Mowbray, et al. *The Essential CORBA*, Object Management Group, 1995.

Shebanow, Andrew. *The Power of Frameworks*, Addison-Wesley, 1995.

Siegel, Jon. *CORBA Fundamentals and Programming*, Object Management Group, 1996.

Strategic Focus January, 1995.

Index

methods, 272–74
properties, 266–69
Exported properties, 266–69
Extended AWT components.
See AWT components.
Externalizable interface, 222–23

F

Failure Command Module (FCM), 148, 154, 161, 183
FailureEvent, 154
FailureListener, 161, 162
FeatureDescriptor methods, 268
fgcolor, 135, 138
Field, 235, 241–44
fireEvent(), 322
firePropertyChange(), 129
fireVetoableChange(), 138
fireWebStatEvent(), 387
FocusListener, 198
Framework
    compound documents, 15–18
    horizontal, 15
    introduction, 11–15
    vertical, 18–19
frmConfig frame, 386
frmMain, 384, 386

G

General Inter-ORB Protocol (GIOP), 70
get(), 241, 251
get/set, 28
getAsText(), 281
getBeanDescriptor(), 274
getConstructors(), 240
getDeclaredField(), 241
getDeclaredFields(), 241
getDeclaredMethod(), 244
getDeclaredMethods(), 244
getDeclaringClass(), 241
getEventQueue(), 200
getEventSetDescriptors(), 270
getExceptionTypes(), 245
getField(), 241

getFields(), 240–41
getIcon(), 265
getLabel(), 100, 110
getMethod(), 244
getMethods(), 244
getModifiers(), 241
getName(), 206, 241
getNewValue(), 128
getNextEvent(), 200
getOldValue(), 128
getParameterTypes(), 245
getPropertyDescriptors(), 266
getPropertyName(), 128
getReturnType(), 245
getType(), 241
Global vs. specific listeners, 142–43
GUI, 99, 147–48
    builder, 91
    code, keeping separate, 175
    DirectBean, 256–58
    representation, 79
GUID (globally unique identifier), 49

H

handleEvent(), 148, 188
Handling exceptions, 173
Heavyweight applications, 234
HelloDisplay bean
    introduction, 105
    listing, 105–6
HelloWorld
    applet, 107, 110
    example, 209–11
    HTML file, 109
    source code, 210
HelloWorld bean application
    coding standards, 93
    frameworks, 90-93
    HelloWorld beans, 93-106
    introduction, 89
    programmatic assembly, 106-10
    visual assembly, 109–12
    Web resources, 113–18
Higher-level events, 156
Horizontal CORBA facilities, 35
Horizontal frameworks, 15

I

IBM Corporation, 91, 92
ICallback, 158–59
Icons, 264–66
IDL, 27–30, 33, 70
if else statements, 315
if statement, 190
ignore(), 262
IID (interface identifiers), 49
IIOP (Internet Inter-ORB Protocol), 23, 69–70
IllegalAccessException access violations, 251
Immutable, 49
Implementation details, 49
Indexed properties, 122–25
Indexed property, 117
Inheritance operator ":", 48
initChannel(), 322
In-place activation, 18
In-process server, 53
Inside-out activation policy, 62
Inspector, 235–39
Integrated design environments (IDEs), 90
Interface
   COM, 47–51
   identification, 49
   interface, 28
Interface definition language (IDL), 27–30, 33, 70
Interface description (MIDL), 48, 63
Interface implementation, 50
Interface Repository, 32
Internationalization, 79–80
Introspection, 81
Introspector, 275
Invariant partition, 14
Invisible beans, 79
Invoke(), 245
IP multicast group address, 306
IPC (interprocess communication), 54, 58
IUnknown, 51–52, 60

J

Java
   interfaces, 93

JAR directory, 110
JAR file, 83–84, 90, 103–4, 381
Java Beans
   address space, 78–79
   application developer's view, 72–78
   bean implementer's view, 71–72
   Developer's Kit (BDK), 73–74, 92–94, 104, 114
   end user's view, 78
   events, 80
   frameworks, 90–93
   IIOP, 69–70
   internationalization, 79–80
   introduction, 67–69
   invisible beans, 79
   JDBC (Java Database Connectivity), 69–71
   methods, 80
   multi-threading, 79
   properties, 80
   RMI, 69
   security, 80–82
   uniform data transfer (UDT), 82
Java Core Reflection API, 234–35
Java Security model, 250–52
Java Virtual Machine (JVM), 78, 182, 212
Java Workshop, 91, 113
java.util.EventListener, 127, 135, 161
java.util.EventObject, 128, 151, 164
JBuilder, 90, 112
JDBC, 69–71
JDK event model
   adapters, 178–82
   delivery, 168–75
   event-related objects, 150–52
   introduction, 147–50
   listeners, 157–64
   observers, 175
   registration, 165–68
   security, 182
   state objects, 152–57
   Web site address, 114
Juggler animation, 74
Just-in-time (JIT) compilers, 91
JVM, 78, 182, 212